FROM HEGEL TO MARX

From Hegel to Marx

Studies in the Intellectual Development of Karl Marx

BY SIDNEY HOOK

New Introduction

Ann Arbor Paperbacks
for the Study of Communism and Marxism

THE UNIVERSITY OF MICHIGAN PRESS

Fourth printing 1971
First edition as an Ann Arbor Paperback 1962
Copyright © by Sidney Hook 1950
New Introduction copyright © by The University of Michigan 1962
ISBN 0-472-06066-x
All rights reserved
Published in the United States of America by
The University of Michigan Press and simultaneously
in Don Mills, Canada, by Longman Canada Limited
Manufactured in the United States of America

To
ANN

CONTENTS

CONTENTS

CONTENTS

CONTENTS

Translated by Sidney Hook

NEW INTRODUCTION

I HAVE CONSENTED with some reluctance to the republication of my book, *From Hegel to Marx*, because with the years I have become increasingly aware of the many ways in which it could have been improved. Originally, I had hoped to complete these studies in the intellectual development of Karl Marx with supplementary investigations of his relationships to the French Utopian socialists and the English economists. With the years, however, the center of my interests shifted to more strictly philosophical themes, particularly to the philosophy of experimental naturalism which I regard as a continuation of what is soundest and most fruitful in Marx's philosophical outlook upon the world. Nonetheless the increasing interest in the thought of Marx in Anglo-American culture, and the sharpening of the conflict between totalitarian Communism and the imperfectly democratic welfare economies of the world, justifies its republication.

For reasons indicated in the Introduction to the original edition Marx is not an easy writer to understand. He wrote with greater passion than precision, almost always in the context of criticism or polemics, and often in an idiom foreign to the thoughtways of the empirically oriented cultures of England and America. No man can completely emancipate himself from the past, even when he revolts against it. Some of Marx's writings are drenched with references to the Hegelian philosophical traditions in which he was nurtured. Even when the specific expressions are lacking, the overtones are there. It is not only Hegel with whom Karl Marx wrestled in coming to critical maturity but also with the Young Hegelians— David Strauss, Bruno Bauer, Arnold Ruge, Moses Hess, Max Stirner, Ludwig Feuerbach, to mention only the most notable. Marx's relation to Hegel has been the subject of considerable publication but comparatively little inquiry has been undertaken of his even more interesting relations with the Young Hegelians. With respect to this theme I believe my studies in Marx's intellectual development have a continuing usefulness. Some of the more common misconceptions of Marxism, particularly the interpretation of historical materialism as a form of egoistic hedonism, and the notion that he was a Judaic-Christian heretic whose social ideal was love—to be expressed in the arts of loving!—can hardly survive a study of his criticisms of Stirner and Feuerbach, of Hess, Grün, and Heinzen. It is, however, the conception of Marx's social philosophy which emerges from these studies that seems to me to be one of the chief justifications of their republication. For they confirm a view I propounded more than a quarter century ago that what Marx understood by Communism was profoundly different from the system of political despotism and terror, of *gleichgeschalte* culture and economy, which prevails in the Soviet Union. Marx was a democratic socialist, a secular humanist, and a fighter for human freedom. His words and actions breathe a commitment to a way of life and a critical independence completely at odds with the absolute rule of the one party dictatorship of the Soviet Union. During his lifetime, Marx at various times called himself a Communist in order to distinguish his position from other contemporary socialists. His differences with them were over the means and conditions necessary to establish a rationally planned economy in which there would be no opportunity for human beings to exploit other human beings. Were he alive today, confronted by the grotesque and terrible caricature of his social ideals in countries which call themselves "people's democracies" and "communist" societies, he would undoubtedly have characterized himself differently. He would have done this not only in protest against the semantic outrage but to draw the most emphatic line of differentiation between his own ideals of a socialist society, in which the free development of each is the condition for the free development of all, and current Communist practices in which the individual, especially the critical individual with a sense of the value of human dignity, is ruthlessly destroyed.

Nonetheless an objective analysis must recognize that as removed as Communist cultures are from Marx's own conception of socialist society, their very existence poses a very fundamental challenge to the validity of his theory of historical materialism. For his theory failed to predict, or even to allow for the very possibility of, a variety of industrial serfdoms, even further removed from socialist society than from capitalist society—the only alternatives Marx envisaged on the agenda of history. It may be argued with some show of plausibility that according to Marxian theories of historical causation, broadly interpreted, it is impossible to achieve socialism in a culturally backward and economically underdeveloped country in which democratic political traditions had taken no firm root; and further that the attempt to introduce it was bound to fail. Leon Trotsky on occasions offered this explanation of the failure of the Bolshevik Revolution to develop the promise of socialism even as conceived by the early Communist leaders. Even so, this does not gainsay the fact that neither the attempt to achieve the impossible, nor the new and powerful social system which resulted from this attempt, are explicable in traditional Marxian categories.

As democratic socialists of the free world behold the face of the Communist Leviathan, many of them in revulsion are prepared to abandon Marx to the Soviet Byzantinism which has made a religious cult of the founder of scientific socialism. Instead they seek to develop their social philosophy on the basis of contemporary ethical values and available scientific knowledge. To the extent that Marx's genuine contributions to our understanding of history and society have entered into the scientific tradition, nothing is lost by such reorientation. There is no more reason for calling oneself a Marxist in pursuing social sciences than in calling oneself a Newtonian or Einsteinian in pursuing the physical sciences—*but* there are obvious and weighty reasons grounded primarily in fidelity to truth, and secondarily in political considerations, why Marx and his legacy should not be surrendered to the enemies of human freedom.

With respect to key questions of belief and commitment, the meaning of Marx must be construed primarily from his major writings published while he was alive and for which he took full responsibility. The chapters in this book that trace in part Marx's intellectual development were written to throw light on Marx's intent, language, and some of his presuppositions. Like all human beings Marx took many things for granted which had been settled in his own mind but not in the minds of many of his readers. These chapters were not written to suggest that the early philosophy of Marx is *toto caelo* different from the position he subsequently developed but only as aids to understanding it.

It has become all the more necessary to emphasize this because of some recent attempts to erect a new shining image of Marx on the basis of some of his earliest unpublished writings, to find not only glints but a new golden vein of ethical thought in them. The Marx of the mature years is being made over to fit a model of a man

and thinker approved by some fashionable schools of psycho-
therapy. There have not been wanting claims that Marx was a forerunner of Dr. Erich Fromm if not of Dr. Norman Vincent Peale.
Perhaps the ultimate in absurdity is the contention of the former
that the thinking of Marx "is closely related to the thinking of
Zen-Buddhism."*

There is, of course, some continuity between Marx's early and
later thought but there is also considerably more discontinuity.
An adequate study of Marx's intellectual development should do
justice to both. To seek what was distinctive and characteristic
about Marx in a period when he was still in Hegelian swaddling-
clothes, or when he was still more or less of a Feuerbachian, before
he had fought his way clear of every variety of seductive idealism
and reductive materialism, is to violate accepted and tested canons
of historical scholarship. A period of intellectual maturation,
surveyed and evaluated from the perspective at which a thinker
has subsequently arrived, is significant more for the doctrines and
attitudes which have been *abandoned* than for those which have
been retained. Otherwise there is no explanation of the process of
development and we should have to conclude that Marx was born
a Marxist.

The following chapters will show that it is the criticisms Marx
made of his predecessors and contemporaries, rather than his temporary agreements with them, which are more significant for an
adequate understanding of his thought. They should also safe-
guard Marx, the thinker, from being taxed with holding theoretical
positions he had abandoned in the course of his development. Because of the emotive associations his name evokes, which are exacer-
bated by his deification in the Communist empires of the world, this
is rather unlikely. But perhaps it is not too much to hope that at
least in academic quarters of the Western world, in time he will not
be dismissed as a simple economic monist or as an egoistic hedonist.
These misunderstandings are to be deplored. They cannot be corrected by giving Marx the benefit of the dubious insights of his
latter day existentialist admirers.

This is particularly true of Marx's theory of human "alienation"
about which an extraordinary amount of nonsense is being written
these days. The abiding sense in which Marx believed that human
beings were "self-alienated" is expressed in the section on "the

*Marx's Concept of Man, by Erich Fromm, New York 1961, p. 33

fetishism of commodities" in the first volume of *Capital*. This is prefigured in his early writings but it is also accompanied there by a number of Hegelian and young-Hegelian notions which Marx later ridiculed and explicity repudiated. His criticisms of Moses Hess and Karl Heinzen show clearly that he abandoned his early moralism. In the *Communist Manifesto* he pokes fun at those socialists who make great play with the obscure term "alienation" to conceal their borrowing of the commonplaces of French socialist thought.

Aside from the specific sociological doctrine of "the fetishism of commodities"—which explores with brilliant suggestiveness the ramifications of the fact that men as social creatures are ruled not by intelligence or reason but by forces generated by their own handiwork in a commodity producing society—the central notion of "self-alienation" is foreign to the historical, naturalistic humanism of Marx. For it is a concept which is originally and primarily religious in nature, and derivatively, metaphysical. The basic "existential predicament" of man is given by his Fall from Divine Grace in the Hebraic-Christian tradition and from Ideal Perfection or the One in the Greek philosophical tradition. The human soul is alienated from God; salvation is the process by which this self-alienation is overcome. In Plotinus, the concept derives from the myth of the soul descending into the world or matter because of a Narcissus-like infatuation with its image, and then making the flight back again to the ineffable totality. In Hegel the term has several meanings; one of them is applied in a primitive and exaggerated way to the process of work. But the root notion is still religious. Marx regarded the entire Hegelian philosophy as a transliteration into obscure prose of the underlying ideas of Western Christianity and therefore shot through, despite itself and the dialectical method, with dualism. God and Self are regarded as implicitly one. The end of man is logically predetermined—union with the Absolute or God. The process of self-alienation is a process of self-development in which the limits of one's self are progressively overcome, in which what is implicit becomes explicit. Man's historical development is really a spiritual pilgrimage in quest for fulfillment—union with God or the Absolute. Man finds himself not in the sense that he recovers something he once had and lost but in the sense that he acquires a self-justifying awareness of his unity in the Totality of things.

Marx's scientific naturalism or materialism banishes these beautifully colored soap bubbles to the realm of poetic fantasy and literary psychology.

It is easy to show that the notion of human alienation—except for the sociological meaning it has in *Capital*—is actually foreign to Marx's conception of man. First of all, ·what does it mean to say that the nature of man is alienated from itself? The nature of anything, including man, is not found in a fixed essence which is separate from, or even distinguished from, its manifestations. To speak of a particular expression of a man's nature as distorted or alienated or at odds with itself makes sense only when we already assume (1) either that there is an already agreed upon *ideal* or *norm* of what man's nature *should* be in contradistinction to the variety of possible manifestations of his nature, or (2) that there *already* exists some ideal or norm, determined statistically or on the basis of some classificatory system, which is identical with the *natural* essence of man, and from which the forms of human behavior dubbed alienated, are aberrant. Most discussions of "alienation" confuse when they do not ignore this distinction. When the first assumption is made, discussion of self-alienation cannot be intelligible until we reach agreement on what kind of self it is desirable to aim at or educate for. The ethical question must be decided, to be sure, on the basis of psychological and biological knowledge; but it cannot be logically deduced from the latter. When the second assumption is made, it expresses precisely that conception of human nature as a constant or fixed character in history, departures from which are perpetually lamented as forms of self-alienation, which the letter and above all the spirit of Marx's philosophy of history and society rejects.

Secondly, if the essence of man's nature is considered as a constellation of traits whose character alters with changes in the fundamental organization of society, then whatever man becomes in history—call it alienated or not—is just as much an expression of his essence as the state out of which he developed. The nature of man is for Marx historically conditioned—so much so that he suggests that even man's biological nature is affected significantly by historical and cultural determinants. Like John Dewey, Karl Marx seemed to believe that human behavior required for its proper study the biological and social psychological approach, and that the field of individual psychology considered in independence of biological and social coordinates was a vestigial survival of medieval rational psychology which predicated the existence of man's soul. Marx, however, seems to go further than Dewey because, as a result of a hangover from early exposure to the romantic Hegelian *Naturphilosophie*, he held that man's biological drives could be transformed by culture. From this point of view, to speak literally of human alienation requires that one assert in Aristotelian fashion that the fulfillment of one's natural set of potentialities represents an authentic mode of life and all others inauthentic. This would transform Marx into a believer in the metaphysical doctrine of natural law which would entail the acceptance of a natural law morality. It may seem anti-climactic to read ontology into Marx's social philosophy after he has been hailed as a Zen-Buddhist. But it is just as much a piece of obscurantist legerdemain.

Thirdly, to the extent that man, as Marx insists, changes his own nature by acting upon the world of nature and history, he can and must, when he is free to make his history rationally, *choose* among different values, different paths of development. In class societies in which economic production is in private hands, men can initiate social and historical actions but cannot control their consequences. In the future, presumably, he will be limited in his foresight and power only by natural limitations. But his nature within these limits will be a function of his choice, and of the changes his choice sets up in the behavior of things and institutions. Here again, we must ask, how can man alienate himself from himself unless some standard of an unalienated self, of a desirable or to be preferred self were operating, in relation to which all the possible ways in which a man could act were evaluated? Human needs and wants and lacks, to be sure, will always be among the points of reference in determining our judgment that some forms of behavior show human nature to be self-alienated. But which needs and wants will be taken as central? And once we decide, even when we define them objectively, will they not vary from place to place and time to time? In the end the view that man makes himself or creates his own nature even in part renders untenable most notions of human self-alienation.

For these, and many other reasons of detail which need not be elaborated here, the contention that socialism spells the abolition of human self-alienation is either a risky prophecy, when it is taken as an empirical prediction that a new relation will be established between the worker and the object of his labors, or a metaphysical extravaganza when it is taken, as one interpreter takes it, as "the return of man as a real human being"—as if man had an original nature to which he is returning under socialism.

To Marx, the empirical and historical sociologist, human alienation under capitalism signified that men are not free to create or redetermine their own natures, that they are compelled to labor for subsistence and not as means of self-fulfillment, that where the market is king and Mammon is God human beings are degraded, reduced to passive subjects, progressively deprived of the powers of uncoerced choice. Even under capitalism this account was exaggerated if taken as a literal account of the life of labor in all historical periods rather than as a description of an ideal type. Even in the interstices of the capitalist economy there existed unalienated men. The unalienated man is the creative man, any man engaged in significant or meaningful work voluntarily assumed as a means toward self-realization. Yet it is undeniable that even under the most highly developed welfare economies of the West, in which because of monopoly, administered prices, government regulation, and the divorce between ownership and control of industry capitalism has been profoundly modified, there are very few unalienated human beings, very few for whom, in John Dewey's phrase, "earning one's living" is at the same time "living one's life."

Does the abolition of a market economy guarantee the abolition of human self-alienation? The spectacle of Communist countries in operation suggests that man, especially the working man, may be more alienated in a highly planned socialized economy in which political democracy is absent than in a relatively unplanned, mixed economy in which political democracy is present. Certainly in terms of Marx's own categories any economy in which free trade unions are lacking, the legal right to opposition non-existent, and the right to strike taboo is an economy of *forced labor*, the very essence of human self-alienation. From this empirical point of view, without relying on the dubieties of existential metaphysics or psychoanalysis, it is obvious that the Communist countries of the world, in which there are no rights except for those who agree with the dictatorial rule of a minority political party, are much farther removed from the Marxian ideal of a society of unalienated men and women than the imperfectly democratic welfare economies of the West.

If the foregoing analysis is valid, then in the very interests of the socialist society which Karl Marx anticipated, and, more important, in the interests of the truth, we must conclude that at the present juncture of world history, it is not the mode of economic production but the mode of political decision which is of decisive importance. So long as political freedom and democracy as a way of political life exists, the economy may be humanized and brought into consonance with reflective moral ideals. Where political freedom and democracy are lost, the economy becomes another means of ushering in "the dark night of the soul."

INTRODUCTION

THE PURPOSE of these studies in the intellectual development of Marx is threefold. The first is to present material hitherto unavailable in English on a relatively neglected but important phase of Marx's life. Marx was evidently not born a Marxist. He reached his position only after the most serious wrestling with alternative social, economic and philosophical views. His criticism of his early contemporaries and fellow travellers has only in recent years been made completely available. Old manuscripts have been published and new ones have come to light. The most impressive feature of Marx's intellectual development, aside from its intrinsic historical interest, is its relevance to the clash and conflict of doctrines in contemporary England and America. It would be no exaggeration to say that the phases through which Marx's thought developed recapitulates the difficulties faced by critical minds to-day when confronted with the Marxian position. There is hardly a doctrine urged against it, from the latest variety of ethical idealism to the newest twist in psychological self-interest theories, which does not have its precursory expression during the years when Marx fought his way to the philosophy of dialectical materialism. I do not here claim that Marx's criticisms of these views constitute adequate replies to the doctrines arrayed against him. This is not the task I have set myself. But I do claim to have established that Marx's ideas, true or false, were not dogmatically arrived at by arbitrary choice. Important manuscripts lie behind every one of the major positions he took.

The second purpose of these studies is to furnish some corroborative evidence in behalf of an hypothesis concerning Marx's meaning presented in my *Towards the Understanding of Karl Marx* (New York and London, 1933). I argued there that the apparent contradictions in Marx's thought, for example between his social determinism and class teleology, his theoretical analyses and his revolutionary activism, could be interpreted as relative emphases arising in the course of criticism of opponents whose positions were antithetical to each other. When the specific context of his writings is overlooked as well as the polar character of the doctrines of the men he opposed, it is easy to make out a case of flagrant self-contradiction against Marx. The evidence presented here, however, is only partial, since it is restricted to an account of Marx's *Auseinandersetzungen* with the post-Hegelian German philosophers from Hegel to, and including, Feuerbach. Further studies must be undertaken on the development of Marx's thought in relation to French and English economic and political doctrine.

The third purpose of this book is to provide readers of Marx's early writings with the necessary information about the social and intellectual climate of his times, its doctrinal issues and technical idioms, without a knowledge of which not even Marx's *language* can be understood.

Current interpretations of Marxism make it necessary to say a word in behalf of the mode of exposition adopted in the following pages. According to some conceptions of historical materialism, the last thing in the world relevant to an understanding of a theory is the reasons advanced for holding it. Ideas and principles are held to be the instruments by which power is won or defended, and *only* that. They must be exposed as rationalisations and not answered as arguments. But however it may be with a great many of the alleged disciples of Marx, Marx himself was very sensitive to the logic of his opponents' positions and always attempted to assess the validity of their arguments before probing into their social motivation. To dismiss questions of logic, evidence, and truth as outside the purview of the historic-materialistic approach is obviously self-defeating. It would mean that the theory of historical materialism itself would have to be adjudged a socially and class conditioned attitude without any possibility of establishing its superior methodological adequacy over other theories which are likewise socially and class conditioned. And so I have felt it incumbent upon me to make clear the *grounds* on which Marx rejected alternative theories as well as those that originally commanded his allegiance. The grounds are not always strictly logical particularly where a normative point of view, that is, the affirmation of a value judgment, is concerned. But where a definite theory is propounded which sets up a claim to be true, Marx's rejection of it is primarily based upon his contention that it is false, not upon its social origin or import.

The social and political analysis of the German cultural *milieu* of the first half of the nineteenth century, of which the hectic philosophical development treated below is a part, is given by Marx and Engels in their early writings, and reproduced in their appropriate context below. But it must be borne in mind that even if we desire to understand *why* Marx believed what he did, as distinct from the truth of his beliefs, knowledge of the social conditions of Germany of the '40s is not sufficient although it may be necessary. For at the same time and in the face of the same social conditions, different ideologies flourished. Nor can the differences between these ideologies be simply correlated with differences in class interests, for, as we shall see, Marx repudiated a great many ideologies defended by his comrades-in-arms. This indicates that at least two other factors besides the common and pervasive social conditions of the time must be considered. They are Marx's purposes and his method of analysis.

Some explanations are in order bearing on the form of these studies. The disproportionate amount of direct quotation I believe to be justified in view of the fact that hardly any of the thinkers discussed are familiar to English readers and that little of their work is available in English translation. Extensive quotations from Marx are given only where *Die heilige Familie* and *Die deutsche Ideologie* are the sources, for it does not seem likely that these books will be translated into English for many years to come. In any case the citations will enable the reader to control to some extent my interpretations. The difficulty of finding the same bibliographical sources available in places like Berlin, Munich, Vienna, Moscow and New York accounts for occasional references to different editions of the work of the thinkers considered. I have tried to make these references as uniform as possible particularly in relation to Marx, but since some of the volumes of the Marx-Engels *Gesamtausgabe* appeared after several of these studies had been completed, I have let the reference to earlier sources stand.

In my very first essay I have chosen to present the mature philosophy of Marx in opposition to, and continuity with, the philosophy of Hegel so that the reader can form some idea of Marx's *terminus a quo* as well as his *terminus ad quem* before examining the phases in the development from Hegel. In the other studies, as distinct from the first, there is no important reference to any work of Marx written after 1848.

The first essay " Hegel and Marx " originally appeared in the *Columbia University Studies in the History of Ideas*, Vol. III. Some of the material in the other essays has been published in the *New International* and the *Modern Quarterly*. I am obliged to several librarians in Berlin and Munich for aid in tracking down some important references. For obvious reasons I cannot mention them by name without exposing them to reprisals by Nazi officials. To D. Riazanov, former director of the Marx-Engels Institute, Moscow, whose recent death in a Russian concentration camp was a heavy blow to Marxian scholarship, I am indebted for an invitation to make what turned out to be a fruitful summer's visit to the Institute.

SIDNEY HOOK

January 1, 1936.

CHAPTER I

HEGEL AND MARX

" Hegel's dialectic is the fundamental principle of all dialectic only after its mystical form has been sloughed off. And that is precisely what distinguishes my method."—MARX *to* KUGELMANN.

No TWO NAMES are at once so suggestive of both agreement and opposition as are the names Hegel and Marx. To conjoin them is not so much to express a relationship as to raise a problem— one of the most challenging problems in the history of thought. How did there develop from what was ostensibly the most conservative system of philosophy in western-European tradition, the revolutionary ideology of the greatest mass movement since Christianity? This is a theme of more than theoretical significance. Professional historians of philosophy—when they have not ignored it—have been puzzled by it. They can see an historical sequence between Hegel and Marx but not a logical connection.[1] Some have even gone so far as to deny any actual influence of Hegel upon Marx save a *psychological* one.[2] On this view, the Hegelian terminology with which all of the classic Marxian literature is shot through is regarded as a curious verbal fixation. Even some of Marx's disciples have discreetly sought to suppress the traces of his Hegelian origin, for fear that they might suggest speculative excesses.

These interpretations, however, cannot explain the *persistence* not merely of Hegelian terminology but of basic Hegelian categories in the Marxian philosophy. This combined with the common opposition of Hegel and Marx to all varieties of Kantianism on the one hand, and atomistic positivism on the other, suggests more than an extrinsic connection. And when we add the acrimonious and almost unanimous rejection of the dialectic

[1] For example, the last edition of Ueberweg's *Grundriss der Geschichte der Philosophie* (1923), reputed to be the standard of philosophical objectivity, in its brief notice of Marx mentions the fact that Hegel influenced him. But it then goes on to add, " In opposition to idealism Marx possessed an extraordinarily keen eye for the lower instincts of man. In fact, they were the only ones that existed for him " (IV, 227).

[2] Cf. Croce, B., *Historical Materialism and the Economics of Karl Marx*, English trans., New York, 1914, p. 82.

method by all critics of the Marxian philosophy,[1] we have reason
to believe that the Hegelian elements in Marx are integral to his
system. Nor could it have been merely philosophical piety
which led men like Lenin to turn aside from the exigencies of
revolutionary civil war and advise fellow Marxists to constitute
themselves into a "society of materialistic friends of the
Hegelian dialectic."[2]

No one can plausibly call into question the historical influence
of Hegel upon the formation of Marx's thought. That has been
amply documented by Marx himself in published and unpublished writings. The difficulty has been to evaluate that influence; especially since Marx subjected the Hegelian philosophy
itself to keen criticism in his analysis of the left-Hegelianism of
B. Bauer and the pseudo-Hegelianism of Proudhon. Here we
shall consider the direct relationships which exist between
Hegel and Marx, reserving for other essays the analysis of
Marx's relation to his Young-Hegelian friends, the Bauers,
Ruge, Hess and Stirner, who to some extent were the
intermediate sources of Marx's early Hegelianism.

The influence of Hegel upon Marx was a twofold one—
methodological and doctrinal. The special, detailed views for
which Marx is indebted to Hegel (certain sociological and
economic *aperçus* contained in the latter's *Rechtsphilosophie*),
will not concern us here, for they belong to a discussion of the
cultural implications of Marx's criticism of political economy.
Our primary interest will be with the significance of the dialectical method in Hegel and Marx, its place and function in the
Marxian philosophy and its relation to a variety of philosophical
methods and doctrines which have been opposed to it. But in
order to understand the way in which Hegel's *method* became
the legacy of Marx and his followers, we must begin with the

[1] I except here the criticisms of Marx made by avowed Neo-Hegelians like
Plenge, Hammacher, Croce and others. All others are quite unceremonious in
their characterisation of the dialectic method. E.g., Masaryk, T., *Die philosophischen und soziologischen Grundlagen des Marxismus*, 1893, p. 45, confesses that
the Hegelian dialectic even in its materialistic form appears to him to be the
veriest hocus-pocus. Bernstein, it will be remembered, was particularly bitter
about *die Fallstricke* of the Hegelian dialectic method which "prevented all consistent analysis of things." *Die Voraussetzungen des Sozialismus*, . . . 3rd ed., 1923,
p. 59.

[2] *Unter dem Banner des Marxismus*, German ed., 1925, p. 7, translated from the
Russian edition of 1922.

Marxian criticism of the Hegelian *system*. For Hegel system and method are indissoluble. Indeed he sometimes says that they are one and the same.[1] How, then, was it possible for Marx to discard the Hegelian system of philosophy and yet adopt its method ?

I

HEGEL AND MARX IN OPPOSITION

1. *The Religious Motif in Hegel and the Activistic Atheism of Marx*

That the spirit of the Hegelian philosophy was primarily religious and its systematic logic a rational theology, Hegel was the first to admit. Does not he himself tell us that his logic is " the exposition of God as He is in His eternal essence before the creation of the world and man " ?[2] And if Hegel was the first to admit it, Marx was among the first to make the most of that admission.[3] All his differences from Hegel are consistently deduced from an opposition to the teleological spiritual idealism which received its profoundest expression in the Hegelian philosophy. The heart of the Hegelian philosophy Marx declares to be nothing but " the speculative expression of the Christian-Germanic dogma of the opposition between spirit and matter, God and the world."[4] True, Hegel had tried to transcend all dualisms between form and content, mind and matter, self and community, conscience and law by interpreting them as relatively objective aspects of a continuing process. If there was any creation in the Hegelian system, it was an *immanent* creation. At the danger of having his orthodoxy impugned, he had written, " Without the world, God is not God."[5] But Marx pointed out that the developmental process in Hegel was

[1] *Science of Logic*, English trans., 1929, I, 65, " Method is no-ways different from its object and content."

[2] Ibid., I, 60.

[3] After Feuerbach, of course. Marx was acquainted with Trendelenburg's criticisms of the Hegelian philosophy in the latter's *Logische Untersuchungen* but was not over impressed with it. In fact, he planned, at Bauer's instigation, an attack upon it.

[4] *Die heilige Familie*, p. 186. All references to this work in this essay are to Mehring's *Aus dem literarischen Nachlass Marx-Engels*, 1902, Vol. II.

[5] *Philosophy of Religion*, English trans., 1895, I, 200.

a very peculiar one. It purported to be a development of ideas in terms of a logical and timeless order of necessity, not in terms of the succession of temporal structures. The process is the method by which a cosmic subject attains self-consciousness. The sensuous object, the contingent and underivable, the material world in space and time—all dissolve into appearance. This is what Marx means when he speaks of Hegel's philosophy as the final expression of traditional religion. He is referring to Hegel's *idealism*, not to all aspects of his method.

The logical difficulties which led Marx to abandon absolute idealism for dialectical materialism we shall treat below. Those logical difficulties, however, were sensed from the point of view of an attitude definitely hostile to the doctrinal supernaturalism with which Marx identified objective idealism. In and behind the Hegelian system, Marx saw the God of Western Christendom. A red thread of Promethean atheology runs through all of Marx's philosophical writings. Already in his doctor's dissertation on the *Differenz der demokritischen und epikureischen Naturphilosophie* he uses as a motto the avowal of Æschylus' Promethus, " In one word—I hate all the Gods."[1] He was struck with the incompatibility between any revolutionary ethics and an objective idealism which sanctified the existing order with ambiguous formulæ about the identity of the real and the rational. The emphasis on *the* whole in Hegel, on man *as such* in Feuerbach, made it difficult to re-make, re-do, or re-form existence. The social whole develops by a principle of division and conflict. Not by automatic division but by the conscious *action* of men in pursuit of their aims. As a student Marx had already written in the spirit of Hegel's method, " Without parties no development, without division no progress."[2] His repudiation of the disguised social absolutism of Hegel, of the Feuerbachian religion of ethics and the *Liebesduselei* of the " true socialists " followed from the realisation that what must be done in behalf of all men in *theory* can be achieved only by proceeding against some men in *practice*. Marx saw no contradiction in believing that to preserve peace it may sometimes be necessary to fight for it. A class struggle, e.g., which gives victory to one group,

---

[1] *Gesamtausgabe*, ed. by Riazanov, 1927–Abt. I, Bd. 1, p. 10.
[2] Ibid., Abt. I, Bd. 1, p. 250.

under certain conditions will more readily abolish classes than will class collaboration which by negotiating class interests tends to perpetuate them.

We stress this activistic aspect of Marx's thought for several reasons. First, it calls attention to the extralogical *interest* of Marx's thought. It helps us to define the locus of Marx's problems not merely in the objective social and ideological *milieu* in which he found himself but in the relationship between that *milieu* and his revolutionary *purposes*. It affords insight into the kind of evaluating criteria Marx brought to bear upon the strife of philosophic systems. Secondly, it reveals a constitutional antipathy to any type of social quietism which makes almost pathetic the ingenious attempts on the part of Marx's critics to spell out another variety of economic fatalism from his doctrines.

2. *Political Accommodation in Hegel and Social Revolution in Marx*

As a corollary from the above we should expect to find a cognate political opposition between Hegel and Marx. And we are not disappointed. The political accommodation of Hegel[1] and the revolutionary activity of Marx are acts spread on the pages of history, not *Gedankenbilder* of historians. Here, however, the obvious facts are not so important as Marx's consciousness of the facts. As a Young-Hegelian, even before he had taken up the cause of social reform, Marx wrote in an unpublished criticism of Hegel's *Rechtsphilosophie* that both Hegel's philosophy of law and philosophical-religious pantheism were political *teleologies*. " Diese Metaphysik," he claims, " ist der metaphysische Ausdruck der Reaktion, der alten Welt als Wahrheit der neuen Weltanschauung."[2] Now it is true enough that the main features of Hegel's political philosophy are compatible with his underlying metaphysics. But that does not mean that they are therefore *deducible* from his metaphysics. It was the presence of a fundamental ambiguity in that metaphysics which

---

[1] Despite the attempts of many critics to rehabilitate Hegel's political objectivity, close study has convinced me that the situation stands even worse for Hegel than it was pictured by the most critical of his biographers (Haym, R., *Hegel und seine Zeit. Cf. Journal of Philosophy*, XXVI, 529).

[2] *Gesamtausgabe*, I, 1, lxxv.

facilitated the illegitimate conversion of the temporal institutions of the Prussian state into the awesome mansions of the spirit of reason. In Hegel's system " reason " (*Vernunft*) was identified with " reality " (*Wirklichkeit*). Consequently, when Hegel proclaimed his famous dictum, " Whatever is real is reasonable, and whatever is reasonable is real," he was expressing the barest tautology. For by definition everything finite, everything short of the absolute totality is neither perfectly real nor perfectly reasonable. In the popular mind, however, " real " if not synonymous with " existence " at least includes it in its meaning. From the tautology, " Whatever is *real* is reasonable," there seemed to follow the absurdity, " Whatever *exists* is reasonable." It was not until the third edition of the *Encyclopädie* (1830) that Hegel clearly and emphatically distinguished " reality " from " existence." All of Germany had understood the intent of the dictum (published in the introduction to the *Rechtsphilosophie* in 1819) as a justification of the *status quo.*[1] Hegel protested that the maxim was not a defence of political quietism, for not all existence was real. The truly real was the perfectly ideal, the logically complete, the norm. Phrases in popular parlance like " a real man " or " a real triangle " suggest its meaning. The existing state was reasonable only in so far as it was real. But how real was it ? And what was the criterion for distinguishing between the greater and lesser reality of any *finite* existence—such as the Prussian state under Frederick William III ? It was an easy wisdom to say that no state was completely real or completely unreal. That did not tell us whether a republican democracy was superior to a limited monarchy. Nor did it attempt to. But it did pretend to derive the historical character, for example, of constitutional monarchy from the purely formal concepts of sovereignty and will.

This last might serve as an illustration of Hegel's approach. He begins his discussion (*Rechtsphilosophie*, Sec. 279) by identifying sovereignty with unlimited self-determination. Nothing can

---

[1] Hegel had already sent his *Rechtsphilosophie* to the press when the revolutionary disturbances at Wartburg took place. He withdrew it in order to add his condemnation of Fries and the liberals. By 1830 his preface had become a public scandal and he hastened to make explanatory amends. But in 1831 he still registered his disapproval of the English Electoral Reform law and the July revolution in France (cf. *Schriften zur Politik und Rechtsphilosophie, passim*).

compel or determine the will of that which has the power of final decision. Consequently, sovereignty must be individualised. It cannot be shared, for that would imply the absence of a power of last resort which in turn would involve calling into question our *definition* of what it is to be a sovereign. But only a subject, i.e., what has mind, can be a true individual. And in this world that which is both a subject and an individual must be a " person." Not personality as such " *sondern ein Individuum, der Monarch.*" To which Marx properly retorts in the course of a detailed commentary upon Hegel's philosophy of law.

> " Hegel converts all the attributes of constitutional monarchy in contemporary Europe into the absolute self-determination of the *will.* He does not say ' with the will of the monarch lies the final decision ' but ' the final decision of will is—the monarch.' The first proposition is empirical; the second transforms the empirical fact into a metaphysical axiom " (*Gesamtausgabe,* I, 1, 428).

Hegel could no more deduce the existence of monarchy as a metaphysical truth than he could the virgin conception.

The difference between the empirical and the metaphysical approach to politics is best revealed in the opposing definitions Hegel and Marx give of the state, and in the contrary functions they assign to it in relation to society. For Hegel the state is the realisation of moral principles and concrete freedom (*Rechtsphilosophie,* Secs. 257 ff.). It is logically primary to society, the condition of all social life. For Marx the state is a product of social life, not its condition. It is an historic outgrowth of society. There are societies without states. The first must therefore be logically and historically prior to the second. Society is an organism in which the state functions as a principle of " organisation."[1] It arises, however, only when the organic nature of society threatens to be disrupted by social antagonisms. It functions as an instrumental agency in preserving those antagonisms and yet preventing social disruption. Fundamental social antagonisms ultimately express themselves in conflicting class interests and struggles. They grow out of the whole social

[1] Marx is the source of Tönnies' famous distinction between *Gemeinschaft* and *Gesellschaft.* See the preface of his *Gemeinschaft und Gesellschaft,* 1st ed., 1887.

process whose secret is to be sought in the relationships which those who produce goods bear to those who control production and distribution.[1] Not only is the state far from being the *Stellvertreter* of absolute reason in affairs political, it is not even an umpire in the class tug-of-war. It is one of the means by which that war is fought. It does not come to bring reconciliation between classes but to reconcile subject classes to their lot. In the *Communist Manifesto* Marx declares that " the modern state power is merely a committee which manages the common business of the bourgeoisie." The historic mission of every subject class is to seize power and establish its own state as an engine of social consolidation. States will exist so long as economic classes exist.

There is no way of softening or compromising this opposition between the Hegelian and the Marxian philosophies of state. For Hegel the state represents the principle of absolute reason and spiritual power which bestows upon man whatever value he has.[2] In some mysterious way it is to transcend the rational egoism of bourgeois society. For Marx the state is both the expression and the proof of the irreconcilability of class egoism. For one, the state has an independent character grounded in logical-ethical formulæ; for the other, the state is rooted in the class divisions of existing society. Since for Hegel the state is an institutional sublimation of all social difference he sees what men *theoretically* have in common by closing his eyes tight to what *practically* separates them. His political philosophy is therefore of a piece with his religious philosophy.

3. *Philosophy as Retrospective Evaluation : Philosophy as Contemporary Social Activity*

Poles apart in Hegel and Marx are their very conceptions of the nature and function of philosophy. For Hegel philosophy in its broadest sense is the *denkende Betrachtung der Gegenstände—* " the thinking view of things " (*Encyclopädie*, Sec. 2). Sometimes, even more simply, it is *Nachdenken*. It is self-enclosed and self-sufficient. It is an activity of thought; literally a *thinking-after*. A thinking, *after* things have been done. Its subject matter is that which *has* happened and its sole purpose

[1] *Das Kapital*, III, 2, 324.   [2] *Philosophie der Weltgeschichte*, Lasson ed., I, 90.

the clarification of the happening. To clarify an event is to explain it in terms of logical necessity. It must be fitted into some developing whole. We must see that it can be no other than what it is. In this way its *meaning* is revealed. All things have a meaning both distributively and collectively. The task of the philosopher is to discover that meaning, progressively correcting his conceptions *after* more and more of the web of cosmic structure has been disclosed to him. The meaning of things is God and the quest for meaning is divine office. " Die Philosophie," Hegel says, " ist in der Tat Gottesdienst " (*Werke*, Bd. XI, p. 4). There is no call, then, for philosophy " to do " anything. It neither sows nor reaps. Like a virgin consecrated to God, it bears no fruit. It does not come to reform but to understand. In that understanding the world comes to self-consciousness and man rests in God. Hegel reminds his readers in the preface to his *Rechtsphilosophie* that they are not to look for any hints in his work as to how the world is to be changed.

" Philosophy comes too late to teach the world what it should be. . . . When it paints its grey upon grey, a form of life has already become old: and in grey and grey it can no longer be made young again but only understood. The owl of Minerva begins its flight when the shades of twilight have already fallen " (Lasson Ausgabe, p. 17).

From this professedly impractical philosophy, however, there flowed consequences of a very practical sort. To understand the nature of the world and at the same time to regard the good, the true and the beautiful as *objective* aspects of that world is to make the task of philosophy the rationalisation of the existent. It was no accident that Hegel was accused, on the one hand, of sucking the world from his finger tips by a process of logical deduction, and on the other, of writing apologies for the brute given. Nor is there anything contradictory in these criticisms. For within a system of teleological metaphysics, where things have immanent purposes and ends which serve as objective criteria of evaluation, all explanation *is* justification, all history *is* theodicy. Evil is interpreted as the necessary counterpoint in a metaphysical harmony. The social order, together with the ethical values and vision generated within it, is part of the systematic interconnection of things. There is a rhythm and pattern in the whole such that no aspect could be affirmed good without affirming the relative necessity of evil. And the philosopher beholding the totality of the world and its works, must declare after Genesis, " And lo ! it is good." Once more in keeping with philosophical tradition, a temporary and local ethics is transformed into an absolute metaphysics. The gaping seams in this arbitrary metaphysical construction were apparent even to Hegel. His distinctions between " reality " and " existence " and his belief in the objectivity of chance indicate that. They were doctrines developed to meet three types of difficulties raised by those among his contemporaries who stood under the influence of the French enlightenment and the philosophy of Kant: (a) that the world in some respect could have been different from what it was; (b) that not all lost causes were necessarily unworthy causes; and (c) that irrespective of what the world *has* been, in certain respects it can be made different from what it *now* is.

Marx's conception of philosophy breathes a strikingly different spirit. Practice is the life of theory; theory the guide to practice. The subject matter of philosophy is not " the whole universe indivisible " but specific problems of man, history and culture. An answer to these problems may be recognised as genuine only in so far as it gives us a leverage in something concrete: it may be recognised as true in so far as it enables us to settle the concrete difficulties out of which those problems have arisen. Hegel himself had already proclaimed that all truth is concrete. But for Hegel the most concrete of all things was an ideal logical system which coherently organised all experience. Thought could discover the truth about this system by thinking itself, i.e. by pure logical analysis, for there was nothing intelligible outside of the system. For Marx the concrete was an existential affair, accessible to thought but not constituted by it. Activity is an integral part of thinking.

" The question whether human thought can arrive at objective truth [he writes] is not a question of theory, but a practical question. In practice man must prove the truth, i.e. the reality, power and this-sidedness (*Diesseitigkeit*) of thought. The dispute as to the reality or unreality of thought which is separated from practice is a purely *scholastic* question."[1]

A characteristic emphasis on the unity of theory and practice runs through not only Marx's writings but all of his revolutionary activity as well. A social theory is to be judged by what it effects —and all social theories have practical effects—directly or indirectly. We cannot stop with enunciating what is merely possible. We must choose between actualising that possibility or accepting the actuality at hand. There is, so to speak, an ethics or politics of thinking which reminds us that merely to speculate about possibilities without inquiring whether they can be converted into actualities, is to countenance that particular possibility which already finds itself " accidentally " embodied in existing practices.[2] To theorise about the nature of the good society without trying to make the existing society good is in effect to accept the existing society. In this way, a theory proud of its impracticality is in reality viciously practical. Pretending to be indifferent to the effects of thought, it has very definite effects of its own. Contemplative philosophies are not removed from life. They represent a way of life and as such must be judged by their consequences. In this analysis of social and philosophical theories, Marx shows himself to be intensely alive to the social practices with which, no matter how reconditely, they are involved. The purpose of his own social theories was to provide that knowledge of social tendencies which would most effectively liberate revolutionary *action*. Philosophy is not retrospective insight into the past; it is prospective anticipation of the future. It explains why the present is what it is in order to make it different. So often an expression of social quietism, or a means of individual escape, philosophy must now function as an instrument of social liberation. The

---

[1] Marx's second gloss in Feuerbach, *Marx-Engels Gesamtausgabe*, Abt. I, Bd. 5, p. 534.

[2] Criticising his Young-Hegelian friends in the *Deutsche Ideologie*, Marx writes, " Their demand that our consciousness be changed reduced itself to the demand that the existent be differently interpreted, i.e. that it be accepted by means of another interpretation. Despite their use of ' world-shattering ' phrases, the Young-Hegelian ideologists are the greatest conservatives " (*Marx-Engels Gesamtausgabe*, Abt. I, Bd. 5, p. 9).

social world is not inherently reasonable as Hegel claimed. It must be made reasonable. In the words of his well-known gloss on Feuerbach, " Until now philosophers have only *interpreted* the world differently; the point is to change it."

There is even a more fundamental sense in which practice is involved in theory. That is the way in which it enters into the process of *thinking* as such. From a wider point of view, practice may or may not be the *goal* of thought, but it always enters as some form of *activity* into the very process of testing our ideas. But a discussion of the way in which Marx transcends the coherence and correspondence theories of truth belongs to a detailed treatment of Marx's logic rather than to his conception of philosophy. We shall elsewhere return to it.

Contemporary philosophers will find it difficult to understand Marx's conception of philosophy. It will become clearer when it is realised that despite the violent opposition between Marx and Hegel on the place and function of philosophy in social affairs there is one point upon which they are agreed. Philosophy is in some sense a *normative* inquiry. In Hegel this is disguised in the form of a rational theology; in Marx it is explicit. The modern conception of philosophy as an analysis of the fundamental categories of space, time, implication, etc., would have been regarded by Marx, at least, as no part of philosophy proper but as problems in the logic of science. Remove logic, mathematics and the natural sciences from the purview of philosophy and there is nothing left as its distinctive subject matter but the critical consideration of values. For Hegel, values were objectively grounded in the nature of things so that he could delude himself into believing that his philosophy was disinterested and free from any presuppositions. Marx, on the other hand, denied that any philosophy as normative inquiry could be disinterested and frankly avowed his own presuppositions and bias. When Marx speaks of philosophy he is referring to ethical, political or social philosophy and the metaphysical disguises in which they often masquerade. That is why he speaks of philosophical method as criticism.[1] It is a criticism which reveals the values and attitudes, the starting point and secret wishes of our thought. It

[1] Throughout his *Zur Kritik der hegelschen Rechtsphilosophie, Gesamtausgabe,* Abt. I, Bd. 1, p. 607.

is a sociology of values investigating the social roots and conditions of what human beings desire. It is not an axiology of values deducing what human beings *ought* to do from self-evident first principles. Philosophy, then, is a criticism of standpoints and methods in the light of the conditions under which they emerge and the purposes which they serve. Its criticism, Marx reminds us, " is no passion of the head, it is the head of passion." It is intelligent criticism, however, because it is passion or will *conscious* of itself.

Against those who would substitute direct criticism of conditions for a criticism of the philosophy which those conditions produce, Marx argues that philosophy in the form of value judgments and attitudes is really part of those conditions and plays a part in keeping them as they are (*Gesamtausgabe*, I, 1, 613); against those who would restrict criticism to a consideration of technical philosophy, Marx argues that since every philosophy has its material presuppositions, a truly radical criticism must involve changing the material conditions which are at their basis. The new philosophy will triumph, not merely because it represents objective truth in the Pickwickian sense in which truth is relevant to ultimate questions of value, but because it fulfils the *needs* of human beings and the social conditions which generate those needs. " Theory becomes realised in a people only in so far as it is the realisation of its needs " (Ibid., 616).

In any given society in which class divisions give rise to conflicting needs, values and ideals, each class sets itself up as a representative of the common interest of the community. Each class develops an ideology which it holds to be objectively true and around which it seeks to rally society at large. But according to Marx, only that class has a right to speak in the name of society which in emancipating itself removes the source of all further class conflicts. In bourgeois society, that class is the proletariat. The proletariat will not seek to found social freedom " upon the inhuman conditions which society itself creates, but will reorganise the conditions of human existence upon the basis of human freedom " (Ibid., 619). In attempting to do this, the proletariat finds in philosophy its intellectual weapons and philosophy finds in the proletariat its material weapons. " Philosophy cannot realise itself without abolishing the proletariat; the proletariat cannot abolish itself without realising philosophy." In a classless society there is no longer a philosophy of law, ethics and politics but a positive *science* of law, ethics and politics. For where fundamental needs and values are the same for all classes, their administration and control depend only upon intelligence. Only under such presuppositions can there exist such sciences. That is the kernel of Marx's conception of philosophy as opposed to that of Hegel. It expresses the insight that in a class society all social sciences are class sciences. In the classless society all social philosophy is transformed into social science; while even now, technical philosophy, which regards itself as the queen of sciences, disappears without remainder in the special sciences.

In discussing the nature of ethics in class societies, Engels underscores Marx's view that there can be no truly objective theory of value where fundamental antagonisms obtain in the relations of production and in the interests of classes defined in terms of the rôle they play in the economy:

> " We maintain that up to the present time all moral theory has been the product, in the last analysis, of the economic conditions prevailing within given societies. And since society has hitherto developed through class antagonisms, morality has always been a class morality. . . . We have not yet advanced beyond class morals. A really human morality which transcends class antagonisms and their memories will not be possible until a stage in human history has been reached in which class antagonisms have not only been overcome but forgotten in practical life."[1]

4. *Systematic Philosophical Idealism* versus *Scientific Materialism*

The philosophical opposition of Marx to Hegel was not confined to political and social philosophy. It extended to the wider domain of the relation between man and nature, thought and things—to the field of metaphysical and logical analysis. Marx's materialism, as we should expect, is not defended as a form of traditional philosophy or metaphysics at all. Like Feuerbach, he believes that critical materialism spells the end of

[1] *Herrn Eugen Dührings Umwälzung der Wissenschaft*, 12th ed., 1923, pp. 89–90.

traditional philosophy. Why ? Because he regards materialism as the clearest expression of the methodology of science. In fact, he often uses the two terms synonymously as when he says that a certain method is " the only materialistic, and therefore the only scientific one " (*Capital*, I, 406, English trans.). It was inevitable that he reject absolute idealism and embrace a thoroughgoing naturalism which, like science, took the world as it found it and limited itself to piecemeal description. Marx's naturalism, however, is only the beginning of his philosophy, not the end of it; for he was interested in taking the world as he found it in order to change it more effectively. It is, therefore, possible to share Marx's opposition to Hegelian idealism and use the same arguments against it without subscribing to Marx's social philosophy. And in the interests of historical accuracy, it should be noted that Marx's criticisms of Hegel are really an abbreviated restatement of Feuerbach's brilliant analyses in his *Zur Kritik der hegelschen Philosophie* (1839) and his *Vorlaüfige Thesen zur Reform der Philosophie* (1842). Marx himself was a Feuerbachian when he penned his criticisms, but a Feuerbachian, as we shall see, with a difference.[1]

Hegel had claimed that his philosophy was " the exposition of God as He is in His eternal essence before the creation of the world and man." The nub of Marx's criticism is that everything which makes that exposition intelligible is derived from the nature of the world and man as already exhibited in actual experience. Like all *a priori* philosophies purporting to express significant material truths about existence, the Hegelian philosophy succeeds only where it has sublimated and hypostasised those aspects of the world which have been revealed in the long course of human discovery. Secretly starting from " what is," it proceeds to a demonstration that " what is," is, because it " must be." This becomes possible only when the last fruits of what has developed in *time* are illegitimately converted into the first principles of what subsists in logic. The forms which experience has shown to be *conditioned* by nature and human activity, Hegel declares to be conditions of both nature and human activity. The consciousness of real subjects which appears in history as an effect of natural causes, Hegel

[1] The relation between Marx and Feuerbach will receive detailed treatment below.

has transformed into an " absolute subject " which is the cause
and ground of those natural causes. The interaction which
takes place between the human mind and its external environment, Hegel interprets as a continuous process of diremption
and progress on the part of logical categories.

"There are three elements in Hegel [wrote Marx], Spinozistic
substance, Fichtean self-consciousness and the Hegelian contradictory yet necessary unity of both—the absolute spirit.
The first element is metaphysically travestied nature in its
separation from man; the second is metaphysically travestied
spirit in its separation from nature; the third is the metaphysically travestied unity of both, real man."[1]

The result of Hegel's procedure is to make the familiar appear
to be a mysterious product of the ghostly conjugation of categories. Instead of starting with the familiar and working out
the logical categories involved in ordinary experience, he tries
to deduce the character of ordinary experience from presumably
simple and necessary logical truths. As it is, complains Marx,
" What should be a point of departure becomes a mystical
result and what should be a rational result becomes a mystical
point of departure."[2] The source of the mystery is that for Hegel
the process of thinking about things is a process of construction. Not content to say that we clarify our ideas by controlling and manipulating things which have an antecedent existence, Hegel maintains that the clarification of ideas is a method
of *deducing* the very existence of those things. He scorns abstractions because they give partial knowledge of only the aspects
of concrete things. A true idea is one which systematises all
abstractions into a patterned unity which *is* the concrete. There
is nothing intelligible in anything which is outside of that unity.
For Marx the existence of a thing is as intelligible as it is discovered to be. It is the subject of all possible attributes which
may be predicated of it but it is not therefore merely the systematic totality of such predicates. The more we know about the
attributes, the more we know about the thing. But the existence
of the thing does not depend upon the order in which we learn

[1] *Die heilige Familie, Nachlass*, 1902, II, 247–8.

[2] *Aus der Kritik der hegelschen Rechtsphilosophie*. A commentary on Sections
261–313 of Hegel's *Philosophy of Law, Gesamtausgabe* I, 1, 447.

of its attributes nor upon their subsistence in some non-temporal realm of being.

" The method of advancing from the abstract to the concrete [Marx argues], is but a way of thinking by which the concrete is grasped. It is by no means, however, the process which itself generates the concrete."[1]

What Marx is protesting against is Hegel's attempt to deduce the historical succession of things in time from the immanent development of ideas out of time. From logic we can never get to existence. Nor from existence to logic, some modern logicians would add. But this is just what Marx attempted to do. " In opposition to German philosophy which descends from heaven to earth, we rise from the earth to heaven."[2] Thought can discover logical relationships only because objects of thought possess them. The object of thought is always ultimately some aspect or dimension of existence. We can speak intelligibly of logic only as the logic of some existential subject matter. It is not itself a *separate* subject matter, although it can be considered in distinction from other subject matters.

The thinking that discovers this logic is utterly foreign to the romantic personifications of the self to be found in German idealism. It is the consciousness of human beings and is rooted on the one hand in the " life-process of the brain " and, on the other, in the social community from which man draws his language and culture. " Consciousness can be nothing else than conscious existence." The only conscious existence we know is man. As a close student of Hegel's *Phänomenologie des Geistes*, Marx was impressed with the emphasis upon the *activity* of mind in the knowing process. As distinct from the metaphysical materialism of the eighteenth century, he believed that the object of knowledge does not impress itself upon a passive consciousness. What is known is not something finally given but also something acted upon. It is the product or outcome of the inter-acting development of consciousness with things existing antecedently to consciousness. Hegel and Marx are agreed that consciousness plays an active rôle in knowing. They differ as

[1] *A Contribution to the Critique of Political Economy*, Introduction, English trans., 1904, p. 293.

[2] *Deutsche Ideologie, Marx-Engels Archiv*, 1926–7, I, 239.

to the nature of consciousness and the degree of its activity. For Marx all thought is human, not absolute; it transforms but does not create. Hegel's theory of mind is a mythological expression of empirical psychology. Criticising Hegel in *Die heilige Familie*, he writes:

" The *Phänomenologie*, consistently enough, ends by putting in place of all human existence ' absolute knowledge ': knowledge, because that is the only form in which self-consciousness exists and because self-consciousness is supposed to be the only proper form of human existence; absolute knowledge, because self-consciousness is concerned only with itself and is no longer embarrassed by an objective world. Instead of treating self-consciousness as the self-consciousness of real men, living in a real, objective world and conditioned by it, Hegel transforms man into an attribute of self-consciousness. He turns the world upside down " (*Nachlass*, II, 304).

Having done so his problem is to get all the furniture of heaven and earth out of the absolute unity of self-consciousness. In keeping with the Neo-Platonic tradition of German idealism, he is compelled to resort to the mystical and magical device of making " ideas," or the states of self-consciousness, the activating and creative forces of the real world.

" For Hegel the process of thinking, which under the name of the Idea, he even transforms into an independent subject, is the demiurgus of the real world, while the real world is only its external appearance. With me, on the contrary, the ideal is nothing else than the material world reflected by the human mind, and translated into forms of thought " (*Capital*, I, 25).

As a thoroughgoing naturalist Marx was particularly sensitive to the place and importance of *time*. Hegel's difficulties with time were notorious. He cannot grant its " reality " since there is a contradiction in supposing that the absolute self undergoes real change in time. He must, however, acknowledge its " existence " and he does so grudgingly by referring to it as the external and alienated form in which the absolute self appears. " Only the natural in so far as it is finite is subject to time; Truth, Idea and Spirit, however, are eternal."[1] This distinction

[1] *Encyclopædia of the Philosophical Sciences*, Sec. 258.

between time and eternity serves to justify the contention that the *logical* development of categories is outside the temporal process; only our knowledge of that development is temporal. But by Hegel's own method it can be shown that this distinction between time and eternity does not help matters. Time and eternity cannot be contrasted unless both are aspects of a concrete whole. They must be *relative distinctions* within *every* situation and not metaphysical absolutes. They are given together and have as variable a content as the distinction between matter and form. One is not prior or superior to the other. Every significant existence in time is part of the eternal and nothing is eternal which cannot be intelligibly predicated of what has temporal being. In Marx's eyes, to refer to the development of categories as ontologically independent of the development of existential subject matter, was metaphysical extravaganza. It could only be done by first dissociating development from time and then reducing development to a purely formal attribute of the absolute. But when the eternal contents of the absolute were examined, all that could be found was an inverted and skeletal transcript of what existence had previously been discovered to be. The very conflicts and polar antagonisms between the logical categories—which were supposed by Hegel to represent the " Life-history " of spirit—could only be concretely and harmoniously unified because there was already an implicit reference to the productive activity of temporal existence. The logical resolution of categorial conflicts followed, and did not precede, the actual forms of natural, temporal behaviour.

Marx's naturalism leads him logically enough to a critical historicism, especially in the field of social science and culture study. Critics have unjustifiably interpreted Marx's historicism as implying extreme relativism, as denying any element of objective truth, and as involving the radical failure to distinguish between the subject matter of development and the logical formula of that development. Marx does definitely say that

" ideas and categories are not more eternal than the relations which they express. *They are historical and transitory products.*" [1]

[1] *Poverty of Philosophy*, English trans., 1910, p. 119.

But here he is speaking of the *social relations* which are so expressed. It does not follow, because the social relations and categories have a history in time, that the physical and logical categories which enable us to express that history have themselves the same *kind* of historical careers. Everything cannot be historical, for then the word unhistorical would have no intelligible meaning. The term " historical " in Marx's writings is relative and is used to distinguish his standpoint from those who would reduce the life of men in society to the " natural." If we say that nature too has a history, we are distinguishing it from that which we call " logical." The logical must then be regarded as the limit of that which is always involved in existence.

This naturally poses the question as to the relation between logic and existence or the problem of universals. It cannot be too strongly emphasised that Marx is not a nominalist. His criticism of the concrete universal in Hegel amounts to a proof that if logical relations are to be regarded as states of absolute mind—an essentially anthropomorphic view—then ontological nominalism cannot be avoided.[1] Historically Marx recognised the philosophical kinship of nominalism with the crude materialistic metaphysics of Hobbes (*Nachlass*, II, 236) and the subjective idealism of Berkeley, positions from which he never hesitated to dissociate himself. Even Feuerbach was suspect at one period for suggesting that natural laws were interpretations of social experience and not objective reports of the inherent structure of things. It is clear that a philosophy which sought to formulate a programme of action on the basis of the objective tendencies of social development could not adopt the nominalistic position according to which those tendencies would be merely convenient names.

If any further proof of Marx's realism were needed, his objective theory of value and the whole methodology of abstraction in *Capital* would be sufficient to establish this position. The value of a commodity is not something we can see or smell or touch; it depends neither upon our desire nor will. But given social conditions of production, values are discovered to be

[1] Marx's criticism of the Hegelian concrete universal will be found in that brilliant section of *Die heilige Familie* entitled " The Secret of Speculative Construction " (cf. Appendix).

involved in the exchange of commodities without anyone's intending that it be so. "Although invisible, the value of iron, linen and corn has actual existence in these very articles " (*Capital*, I, 107). But it does not follow that because Marx rejects nominalism he must accept an extreme, objective, logical realism which converts the outcome of a process of natural discovery and classification into the ontological presuppositions of that process. Exchange values have no subsistence prior to the existence of commodities in space, time and society. In repudiating Hegel, Marx is also repudiating Plato and the whole Platonic tradition. Exchange value is not a concrete universal since its nature is not altered by the differently qualitied use-values which exemplify it. Neither is exchange value, nor any other category of political economy for Marx, an abstract universal such that it can be significantly applied to all possible historical economies. Marx left the investigation of what was invariant in all possible systems of ethics, law, economics, etc., to those whose ideal of scientific method forbade them to consider the specific determining categories of any historical phenomena and who were content with the help of formal logic to elaborate upon purely formal definitions. Anything which exists is an exemplification of some universal. That is why it can be understood. But there are no universals without exemplification. That is why universals have meanings which can be communicated. There are no incommunicable meanings.

In turning Hegel, to use Marx's own words, " right side up again," Marx was definitely returning to the position of one whom Hegel had turned " wrong side down "—Aristotle. If Marx's philosophical method was Hegelian, his fundamental metaphysical starting point, as Engels admits,[1] was Aristotelian —an Aristotelianism saturated with temporalism, freed from

[1] In a much neglected passage in his *Ludwig Feuerbach und der Ausgang der klassischen Philosophie* (Duncker ed., 1927, p. 28), Engels categorically states that the question of the relation of thought to existence is essentially the same as the questions: Which is primary, spirit or nature ? Did God create the world or does the world exist from eternity ? Depending upon whether we answer the first or second alternative of the disjunction affirmatively, we are idealists or materialists. He then adds: " Originally the expressions Idealism and Materialism signified nothing else than this, and we shall not use them in any other sense but this. Confusion results when we import any other sense into them." The connection with the methodology of science on the one hand and the naturalism of Aristotle on the other is obvious. Cf. also " Dialektik und Natur," *Marx-Engels Archiv*, Bd. 2, p. 15, where Engels links Hegel and Aristotle together.

the dogma of fixed substantial forms and the poetry of the Prime Mover. Dialectical materialism has its basis, but not its fulfilment in Aristotle's naturalism.

5. *History as the Autobiography of God: History as the Pursuit of Human Ends*

The fundamental systematic opposition between Hegel and Marx focuses itself most sharply in their respective philosophies of history. For Hegel history is the march of the spirit toward freedom. Freedom can be found only in self-consciousness. Absolute self-consciousness is God. History is the autobiography of God. The logic of the system demands not only that reason pervade the universe but that the rule of reason be established in the historical chronicle of human experience. There is an objective meaning in history. It is to be traced in " the development of the Idea of freedom." Not merely your conception of freedom or mine, for that is but a subjective moment in a process which includes it and infinitely more. That process can best be read (*after* the event, to be sure) in the " objective mind " of the community, in its traditions, laws, ethical use and wont. When we grasp the structure of this cultural pattern and realise the minor part our subjective will plays in it, then we shall correct the critical one-sidedness of trying to make the world reasonable according to our own petty conceptions. Instead of trying to reform or revolutionise things, we shall devote our lives to understanding them. And understanding, as we have seen, consists in catching the vision of the reasonable already embodied in the real.

But this is almost too much—the un-Hegelian reader is tempted to exclaim. The historically real is a depressing record of tragedy, stupidity and heartbreak. Its pages reek with the blood of the innocent. Its logic is the logic of force. Only by chance does anything reasonable emerge. But here Hegel rises to truly great speculative heights. All of this record of confusions is the work of *die List der Vernunft*—" the cunning of Reason." In its operation is to be found the mechanism of history. Everything is grist to its mill. It realises its own secret purposes through events which seem to man arbitrary and meaningless. The near-sighted passions of the mob, the flaming ideals of the hero, the coward's fear as well as the fool's blunder—all serve its ends. Revolution and reaction help. It dangles the bait of personal interest before men and thereby gets its own work done. Nothing is altogether meaningless nor without significance in world history. It must merely be properly construed. And if anyone fails to recognise in this teleological fatalism a belief in Divine Providence, Hegel himself confesses it.[1]

Marx's objection to the Hegelian philosophy of history is that as a *philosophy* it has nothing to do with history, the latter being added as an afterthought; and that as actual *history* it disproves his philosophy.

" An esoteric, speculative history preceded the exoteric empirical history. . . . The history of man is transformed into the history of an abstraction" (*Heilige Familie, Nachlass*, p. 186).

Discounting the apologetic element in Hegel's treatment, even his empirical interpretations were inadequate. Instead of taking as point of departure the activities of human beings in pursuit of their workaday aims and the conditions under which they are formulated, he begins with the ideas and thoughts which men offer as an explanation of those ends. It was inevitable, then, in accordance with Hegel's pernicious habit of turning a temporal existent into an ontological pre-existent, that these ideas be transcendentally capitalised into *Vernunft*. After that it was child's play to apply the logical scheme of the dialectical triad and " prove " that a certain highly selected series of temporal data " progressively realised " an end which had been set before history proper began.

Very often Hegel resorts to mere abstractions as directive principles of specific events. Speaking, for example, of the disappearance of slavery from western Europe, he writes:

[1] " Reason is as cunning as it is powerful. Cunning may be said to lie in the inter-mediative action, which, while it permits the objects to follow their own bent and act upon one another, till they waste away, and does not itself directly interfere in the process, is nevertheless only working out the execution of its aims. With this explanation, Divine Providence may be said to stand to the world and its process in the capacity of absolute cunning. God lets men direct their particular passions and interests as they please; but the result is the accomplishment of—not their plans, but His, and these differ decidedly from the ends primarily sought by those whom He employs " (*Encyclopädie*, Sec. 209, Zusatz, Wallace trans. Part of this passage is quoted by Marx in an interesting connection in *Capital*, I, 199 *n*).

" The question has been asked, Why has slavery vanished
from modern Europe ? One special circumstance after another
has been adduced in explanation of this phenomenon. But the
real ground why there are no more slaves in Christian Europe
is only to be found in the very principle of Christianity itself,
the religion of absolute freedom" (*Encyclopädie*, Sec. 163,
Zusatz, Wallace trans.).

Marx did not deny that there was an order to be found in
history. He denied that there was a teleological order. He did not
deny that there was determinism in history. He denied prede-
terminism or fatalism. He shares with Hegel the belief that the
order of historical events is more than a confused record of
chance occurrences. He does not claim that anything could have
happened in the past. Nor that there are unlimited degrees of
freedom in the present and the future. But he differs from Hegel
in refusing to believe that what did happen has any more meaning than what individual men can find in it.

History, Marx is never weary of repeating, is made by men. It
is not the product of the *automatic* operation of impersonal forces
whether they be spirit, nature, the mode of economic production or what not. Human effort is the mode by which the historically determined comes to pass. Nor does history make itself
in the form in which story tellers and idealists love to personify
it.

" History does nothing; it 'possesses no colossal riches'; it
' fights no fight.' It is rather man—real, living man—who
acts, possesses and fights in everything. It is by no means
' History ' which uses man as a means to carry out its ends
as if it were a person apart; rather History is nothing but the
activity of man in pursuit of his ends " (*Nachlass*, II, 179).

Now in places even Hegel admitted *malgré lui* that men make
their own history. He even has a keen eye for the conditioning
factor of geography. But in trying to explain any specific event,
he seeks for causal insight in the ideas men carry in their heads
and the slogans with which they march into battle. Marx, however, seeks a causal explanation of historical activity not in the
way people think, not in their abstract ideas, but in their concrete needs and in the conditions out of which those needs arose.

Human need is the driving force behind action and behind plausible reasons we advance to justify that action. Need gives man his problems and the strength to conquer them. Need—" the practical expression of necessity " as Marx calls it—brings human beings to consciousness, to class consciousness, to revolution. *History, then, can be explained rationally but it is not made by reason.*

It is true that man, generically, makes his own history. It is not true that any individual man makes his own history. Marx is not interested in what the individual man makes or does not make. He is primarily interested in the behaviour of groups or classes and in the individual only in so far as he is a member of a group or class (*Capital*, I, 15). Human history is social history. But society since primitive times is class society. History, therefore, is the record of the rise, fall and struggle of classes. The succession and struggle of classes—now rapid and violent, now slow and peaceful—centres ultimately around the possession of property and the power which that possession gives. Not that individuals *as such* are necessarily motivated by economic considerations, but that no matter what their motives as individuals are, the resultant effects of their common activity differ from the outcomes they had severally anticipated. In movements of large masses, extreme variations in the will or actions of individuals are compensated by other variations. The constant and pervasive pressure of needs arising from economic conditions makes itself felt in the ultimate upshot of the activity of the aggregate. The activity of a class and the consequences of that activity are therefore not *necessarily* deducible from the motives of individuals composing that class, nor vice versa. It follows that from the point of view of a history interested in *class* struggles, the activity of any particular individual is a chance event (not, however, from the point of view of a biologist or a psychologist). That chance events are important, the existence of great men at any time indicates. Yet they are not of determining importance in social history. They are limited by the objective class issues which exist independently of them. And they are even more significantly limited by the contemporary interests of the group or class without whose support they can accomplish nothing. It may be a chance event that a great man appears when and where he does, but the scientific historian cannot regard it as a chance event that a great man becomes a representative of a certain class. Classes do not make any individual " great." But they give him both the opportunities of greatness and the means to make that greatness effective.

If all history is the history of class struggles, how and why do these struggles occur ? Here instead of Hegel's *List der Vernunft* and the other unverifiable notions of eclectic historians (chance, unconscious, will, etc.), Marx offers an empirical principle of determination, viz. the development of the mode of economic production. Man is continually improving the quality of the tools he uses in earning his living. The possession of the new productive forces and the invention of new methods give a natural advantage over those who still live by the old. The class which has title to the new forces of production has economic power—a power, however, which is hampered by the legal and political property relationships which express the *earlier* forms of material production. When the opposition is acute, a social revolution takes place. Unless society is destroyed in such a conflict, victory comes to those who fight for a form of social organisation which corresponds to the changes in the mode of economic production thereby permitting the liberation and expansion of the productive forces. *Political* power is transferred to that organised class which has *economic* power. The development in the mode of economic production is continuous and irreversible. Consequently, with the passage of time, there is an ever-narrowing range of possibilities of social organisation. The development of human society shows a *direction*, by no means linear, but which is none the less empirically observable. It is a direction which points from a crude, primitive communism, through the various forms of private property in the instruments of production—slavery, feudalism and capitalism—to a complex industrial communism in which " the free development of all is the condition for the free development of each."

If for Hegel history is a progressive realisation of *freedom*, for Marx it is a progressive development toward the *socialisation* of the means of life. Without such socialisation, freedom is a fetish—an empty, formal right which cannot be exercised. As contrasted with Hegel, Marx's philosophy of history is at once realistic and dynamic, empirical yet hostile to the belief that "social facts" exist ready made *in rerum natura*. It fuses the logic of analysis with the poetry of passion. It is the philosophy of a class which does not merely desire to "understand" revolution but to make one.

II

HEGEL AND MARX IN CONTINUITY

We have emphasised the systematic contrasts between Hegel and Marx for two reasons. First to make more effective the exposition of what unites them in a common opposition to formal Kantian idealism on the one hand, and to sensationalistic empiricism on the other; and secondly, to close the door tight to attempts at "*Ergänzung*" Marx by Hegelianising him, which is commonly expressed in a rather patronising interpretation of Marxism as an erring and one-sided variety of Hegelianism.[1] The two philosophies are utterly opposed in substance and in spirit. But how, then, it may be asked, can they be linked together? What can they significantly have in common? The answer may be suggested by a double metaphor. Because they fought against the same opponents, they share certain positive *doctrines*. These receive, however, characteristic emphases in terms of their systematic standpoints. Because they fought against each other with the same weapons, they share a common method. The method, too, bears traces of their different metaphysical allegiances. In Hegel the method is derived from the system; in Marx the system—or whatever there is of one—from the method. In this section, we shall be concerned with the leading positive doctrines common to both philosophers; in the next, we shall examine their method.

1. *Opposition to Social Atomism*

The three fundamental propositions of the Hegelian philosophy are: reality is spiritual; reality is systematic; and reality is rational. The doctrine of the existence of a corporate social

[1] Plenge's *Hegel und Marx* (Tübingen, 1911) is the best illustration of this. Croce in Italy and, to some extent, Lindsay in England are also cases in point.

consciousness, whose meaning was to be found in the order of objective mind, was a logical consequence of these positions. And from it there followed as a corollary the denial of the different varieties of metaphysical and social atomism which flourished in France and England. Whether it was the theory of the " social contract " of natural man or the doctrine of the " well-understood interests " of utilitarian man, Hegel sensed in them a dissociation of the individual from the social whole without which individuality could have no meaning. He regarded the social whole as both logically and historically prior. Doctrines which tried to base a social philosophy upon the desires of the empirical self—a self which made its own bargains, selected its vocation, and ordered its life in independence of the lives of others—were viewed by Hegel as attempts to splinter the unity of social activity into innumerable, tiny fragments. Each fragment—partial, limited, and unconscious of its history and interrelations—regards itself as a cosmos in which the other fragments are mirrored as distorted reflections of itself. In multiplying these atomic absolutes the organising relations which bind them into a larger whole are dissolved. For example, take civic society which Hegel in the *Phänomenologie* calls a *geistiges Tierreich*, " society as a human herd." Here every atom regards himself as central and treats all other atoms as extrinsic means to the fulfilment of his personal, irrational ends. There can be no rational planning or purpose in this type of organisation, since rational willing for Hegel means willing informed by the structure of the whole.

For Hegel genuine individuality is an articulation of both the logic and the ethics of the whole. It is not the starting point of activity but the realisation of activity; not the presupposition of society, as in the abstract individualism of the contractualists, but the outcome. It must be noted that in the eyes of a naturalist this individuality is of a very peculiar sort. Since the truly individual is revealed in the systematic character into which things enter, Hegel claims that the higher the system the truer the individual. The family is more of an individual than its members, the community more of an individual than the family, etc. Obviously the only completely " real " individuality is the Absolute. In it the finite personality is realised (to the finite mind, however, destroyed). But even the naturalist must grant the Hegelian insight into the social basis of individuality. And it is in terms of this insight that we are to understand Hegel's opposition to the untrammelled individualism of the Enlightenment; his denunciation of all conscience philosophies whose " *ich* kann nich anders " was erected into a universal and categorical imperative for the world at large; and finally his rejection of all supernatural theories of duty and reward.

The social relation between individuals Hegel substantialises as the institutions, customs, and laws of the community. *Moralität* has its roots in *Sittlichkeit*—the ideals of social life in the practices of social life. Hegel's *Sittlichkeit* is a jealous God. It is the source, substance and repository of all that the individual creates. It owes little to him, he owes everything to it. It countenances no revolts especially when they fail. In his early years Hegel shows no hesitancy in attacking Christ and his disciples for their divisive and non-social morality. He scornfully contrasts their activities with the life of Socrates who, although opposed to the existing order, accepted the state and its laws to the very death (*Jugendschriften*, ed. Nohl, pp. 219 ff.).

The crux of Hegel's opposition to social atomism lies in his demand that human activity be organised not in terms of personal motives or interests but in terms of an objective *status* in a differentiated social whole. Rights are the natural expression of one's station and duties, not the result of a contract between independent individuals. Independence is conditional upon a myriad of prior dependencies which flow from one underlying social bond. The ideal community for Hegel is a *Schicksalsgemeinschaft* in which all would find a common, even if differentiated, fulfilment. It is the ocean floor which links together islanded and isolated selves. It does this by a continuous tradition which furnishes the individual with the goals of his activity and with ideals to judge his performance. Personal, exclusive interests cannot enter here at all. Whoever attempts to answer the question, " Whether and how one is to act," by an appeal to personal interest is guilty of a form of self-diremption (*Phänomenologie*, p. 262). He does not know his own real interest nor the nature of the self in whose presumable behalf he is acting. This is the position into which the tradition of classic German

idealism develops. Through Lasalle, who had absorbed everything in the Hegelian philosophy except its conservatism, and
through Marx, who eliminated its transcendental psychology
and makes class needs and interests central, the corporate or
collective ideal of social life profoundly influenced the ideology
of social democracy.

In Marx the analysis of the nature of social activity is conducted on an empirical plane. The unity of social consciousness
is an historical and sociological fact, not a metaphysical assumption. Marx does not ask as the idealists did, " How is social
consciousness possible ? " but " How does social consciousness
arise ? " And he answers this question not merely by a genetic
inquiry but by an investigation of the social conditions under
which consciousness is discovered. Before there is *a* man, there
are men.

> " Since he comes into the world neither with a looking-
> glass in his hand, nor as a Fichtean philosopher, to whom ' I
> am I ' is sufficient, man first sees and recognises himself in
> other men. Peter only establishes his own identity as a man
> by first comparing himself with Paul as being of like kind.
> And thereby Paul, just as he stands in his Pauline personality,
> becomes to Peter the type of the *genus homo* " (*Capital*,
> English trans., I, 61).

Not only is the nature of the bond between Peter and Paul non-
metaphysical, it is not even, in the first instance, psychological.
It is practical. Peter discovers Paul's body and Paul's acts before
he discovers Paul's mind. Men need one another in order to live
before they need one another in order to converse. In fact, says
Marx in a passage which sounds amazingly modern, man's
consciousness is his speech; and speech arises out of the concrete
needs of social exchange. Consciousness is social before it is
individual. Peter discovers the *us* before the *me*.

> " Man has consciousness . . . but it is not pure consciousness.
> ' Spirit ' is cursed with the burden of matter which here takes
> the form of sounds and currents of air in motion, in short,
> speech. Speech is as old as consciousness. Speech *is* practical,
> real consciousness, existing for other people and consequently

existing for me. Speech like consciousness arises from the need, from the necessities of social intercourse."[1]

Society is just as " real " as any or all of its members. The reality is not of a higher order but of a different dimension. Although it does not exist apart from the individuals who constitute it, it cannot be completely reduced to them. It is an order out of which individuals arise and acquire their very individuality. From it they receive an atmosphere for their short flight, and through the social memory funded in tradition, an opportunity for immortality.

The interdependence of human beings, Marx claims, is both logically and historically found in the division of labour—a principle which applies to every type of organised society within which men work. But when under certain historical conditions, a commodity system of production arises, the principle of division of labour links together the social status and opportunities of men in such a way that the latter can no longer intelligently regard themselves as independent. The organic unity of the mechanism of production makes it impossible to calculate the significance of an economic event in terms of personal intent or immediate consequence. The wealth of one class means the poverty of another; a bankruptcy here means distress there, and prosperity somewhere else. Yet the official theory of commodity-producing society with its *laissez-faire* economics and politics, without denying the facts of economic interdependence within society, denies the psychological, ethical and social consequences of that interdependence.

These consequences may be summed up in the proposition that the effects of *uncontrolled* interdependence produce different social status; produce different manners of living and thinking; in short, produce different men. The denial of this conclusion may be expressed in the proposition that different social status does not affect the essential equality and freedom of the human will. Say the *laissez-faire* philosophers, man is free to work or

[1] *Deutsche Ideologie, Marx-Engels Archiv*, 1926–7, I, 247. Marx's empirical analysis of social consciousness in this work seems to me to give the *coup de grâce* to the perversely ingenious attempts of Prof. Max Adler to derive the whole concept of " socialised man " in Marx from Kant's " transcendental unity of apperception " (cf. " Kausalität und Teleologie im Streite um die Wissenschaft," *Marx-Studien*, 1904, I, 195 ff. Also *Kant und der Marxismus*, 1925, pp. 135 ff.).

not to work. His contracts to sell or buy are the legal expression of that freedom. The open market is an avenue to an open career. Nominally and actually the man who comes to sell his labour-power is just as independent as he who comes to buy it. Their negotiation is a fair battle of wits, stamina and courage. Whoever gets the better of the bargain is the better man. It is no one's concern if society is the loser. Listening to these doctrines, especially as they bear upon the sale and purchase of labour-power, one would believe, Marx declares, that in this sphere we had a

" veritable Eden of the innate rights of men. There alone rule Freedom, Equality, Property and Bentham. Freedom because buyer and seller . . . of labour-power are constrained by their own free will. . . . Equality because each enters into relation with the other, as with a simple owner of commodities, and they exchange equivalent for equivalent. Property because each disposes only of what is his own. And Bentham because each looks only to himself. The only force that brings them together and puts them in relation with each other, is the selfishness, the gain and the private interests of each. Each looks to himself only, and no one troubles himself about the rest " (*Capital*, I, 195).

Bourgeois society is a society officially antisocial in theory. It treats its members as if they were atoms—as if they were almost as hard, elastic and impenetrable as the atoms in the kinetic theory of gases. But the nature of society makes it impossible to carry this policy out. Individuals are not atoms; none is self-sufficient. " The egoistic individual of bourgeois society may in his silly imagination and petrified abstraction puff himself up into a self-sufficient atom, that is to say, into an absolutely complete and blessed creature, independent and free from any need,"[1] but his daily experience and activity compels him to recognise his manifold interrelationships with others. There are social bonds that none may escape. But what he in effect does is to convert one kind of social bond into another. He can only live by making demands upon others. He therefore must tie them to himself by powerful cords of need. But in so doing

[1] *Die heilige Familie, Nachlass*, 1902, II, 227.

his very own qualities and characteristics become " needs " which others must fulfil. In these others, however, he can see only the instruments of satisfaction for his needs. Human beings therefore become means not ends. The whole social environment of persons and things now become objects of *interests*. To be is to be perceived in relation to some interest. These relations are objectified in numerical figures in cashbook and ledger. They potentially dominate and ultimately dissolve other relations which at first sight seem utterly foreign to lowly economic interests—family, school, church and culture. Pretending that individuals are free and equal before the law and in the market, the bourgeoisie has cynically torn away the countless social ties which make men members of one another's body and " left no other bond betwixt man and man but crude self-interest and unfeeling ' cash payment ' " (*Communist Manifesto*).

2. *Rejection of Abstract Ethical Idealism*

Opposition to the excesses of rabid individualism, however, comes not only from social realists but even more often from ethical idealists. Indeed it is in this latter form that it is most vocal and emphatic. What age has not heard a cry for justice in the name of Christ, Kant or some other ethical prophet? When has not someone's conscience, someone's devotion to things invisible led to conflict with the social order? And yet both Hegel and Marx regarded abstract ethical idealism, whether it have its roots in Christ, Rousseau or Kant, as Utopian and unreasonable—as even more dangerous than any philosophy of social atomism. It involved the same denial of the priority of the group over the individual; the same acceptance of the natural rights, or conscience, ethics which lies at the basis of philosophical anarchism. Because it endangered the stability of the state, Hegel stamped it as a revolutionary doctrine; because it hampered militant class activity, Marx condemned it as incipiently counter-revolutionary.

That Hegel's thought is marked by an intense antipathy to abstract ethical idealism, all of his published writings unmistakably show. The extra-philosophical motives and problems which drove him to that antipathy have been clearly revealed in his early manuscripts, published since his death.[1] Here, however, we merely wish to present the expression of that opposition at the very outset of his philosophical career. The corpus of manuscripts which have been edited by Nohl under the title *Theologische Jugendschriften* contains a critically hostile evaluation of Christianity both as a theoretical doctrine and as a social movement. Greek religion and morality fused into an organic political entity is held up as a model of what a people's religion should be. Social ties exist before ethical commands. The function of the latter is to enforce the former. From this point of view, Christ's injunction to his followers to love one another, as well as all the deliverances of Kant's categorical imperative, are declared to be vapid when not actually dangerous. " A love of man which is to extend to everyone even to those who are not known to us and with whom we stand in no relation is an empty notion " (p. 295). It is an artificially conceived ideal which has no roots in the rich loam of daily experience. Its impracticality is the reverse face of its sentimentality. It is something imagined, a product of thought. But " *ein Gedachtes kann kein Geliebtes sein.*" Social and political stability is the base from which ethical excursions are to be made. Rules of morality are not to be derived from alleged principles of absolute justice but from the social practices enshrined in tradition and the state. It is obviously political considerations which make Hegel say of Christ's injunctions that many of them

> " are opposed to the primary foundations of bourgeois society, to the fundamental principles of the law of property and of self-defence. . . . A state that made the attempt to live up to the commandments of Christ would go to pieces " (p. 41).

In a later manuscript—*Kritik der Verfassung Deutschlands* —Hegel makes short shrift of those who would seriously

---

[1] We may dogmatically state them here and document them at another time. They were (1) opposition to the slogans of personal liberty and political freedom which Hegel believed had prevented German national unity and prepared the way for the degradation experienced by Germany at the hands of Napoleon. Hegel bitterly characterises this view as being equivalent to, " Fiat justitia, pereat Germania "; (2) a desire to draw the teeth of French rationalism which believed that thought could legislate for society. Hegel connects the revolutionary excesses of the French revolution with this doctrine. (3) A profound absorption in and nostalgia for the classic Greek tradition which represented for Hegel the reconciliation of freedom and law. The influence of Hölderlin was significant here.

subordinate public law to private morality. Both individual law
and private morality have their ground, nature and limits in
the life of society and the state. How differently he speaks when
he is discussing the relationship between individuals in a state
which has *Wirklichkeit* and when he is describing their relationships in a state which merely has *Existenz* ! All rights are based
on interests[1] and all interests flow from social differentiations
within the state. The chief interest of the state is interest in its
self-preservation. *Moralisten* and *Menschenfreunde* are con-
temptuously spoken of as " men without country or interest."
In denouncing politics as an art in which expediency was the
only recognised principle, they were really undermining the basis
of whatever peace and order existed. If *every* right is based on
some interest, why should the state whose interest lies in self-
preservation be regarded as immoral in enforcing *its* right ?
There is no right so pure that we cannot discover the interest
out of which it grows. Conflicts of rights are conflicts of interests.
Only in so far as the latter permit of settlement, can the former
be adjudged or resolved. Conflicts of interest, however, are not
necessarily resolvable. That is why appeals to abstract ethical
rights—presumably universal and objective—are hollow. Where
there is a collision of rights then we must look to " war or whatever else it may be to decide not which of the rights maintained
by the conflicting parties is the valid one—for both are valid—
but to decide which right must give way to the other. War must
decide this because both contradictory rights are equally valid "
(p. 101).

In Hegel's published writings these Hobbesian tones are
skilfully blended in a metaphysics of history which seeks to
show that the actual outcome of war is already contained in
the logical notions of the real, the right and the reasonable. A
double motive which is productive of considerable ambiguity
runs through the discussion. This arises from the conflict between Hegel's natural *Realpolitik* and his supernatural metaphysics. The first position is advanced against adherents of the
natural-rights doctrine, who desire to achieve political power;

[1] *Schriften zur Rechtsphilosophie und Politik*, Lasson ed., 1913, p. 100. The
essays and manuscripts published here throw a significant light on the development of Hegel's philosophical views.

the second is offered to them as a consolation for not getting it. The general argument runs briefly somewhat along the following lines.

Any criticism of the world on the basis of what ought to be is easy enough. Everyone can give hints to the Creator as to how the world may be improved. But in view of the fact that no two people urge the same system of improvements, some objective standard of the " better " is necessary. Only that is really better which is continuous with some existing thing already recognised as good. We cannot start *de novo* as if the world had no history and as if the men to whom we appeal could change their nature merely by taking thought. All who come proclaiming new theories of what ought to be, Hegel greets with a " *Hic* Rhodus, *hic* saltus " (*Rechtsphilosophie*, Vorrede). Possibilities must be grounded in the nature of the actual. Then, his opponents retort, at least there *are* possibilities. Hegel cheerfully grants this in his rôle of political statesman analysing a situation *before* its history is made. The actual, although it never by itself tells us what the specific " ought to be," is, determines the *range* of what " ought to be." As a metaphysician, however, as one interested in understanding and justifying history *after* it has happened, Hegel tries to prove that what *did* happen is what ought to have happened. He then adds to this assertion the even more galling one to the effect that the conflicting conceptions of what should have happened were all necessary to ensure the victory of the better conception or of the one that did happen. And the better is known—after the fact—as that which actually happened. *Die Weltgeschichte ist das Weltgericht.* The only difficulty is that on the basis of his metaphysics, Hegel has no right to argue against those whose politics he despises, while in behalf of his immediate politics, he has no right to claim the support of his metaphysics.

All his life Marx like Hegel was compelled to take a stand against abstract ethical idealism, not only as a consequence of his social theories but as a necessity of revolutionary practice. In every country eloquent voices were preaching a new social evangelium in the name of justice, love and brotherhood. Weitling, Feuerbach and the *wahre Sozialisten* in Germany, St. Simonians and Proudhonians in France, Owenites and Pre-Raphaelites in England, Christian Socialists everywhere—were making impassioned pleas for social reform. All the saints and rebels in the calendar of history were invoked in appeals to such diverse things as conscience, reason, mercy, social consciousness and God. Even avowed revolutionists like Bakunin and Mazzini formulated their demands for social change with cries for liberty and self-determination. And most significant of all, Marx was compelled in 1875 to criticise the platform of his own political party for demanding " the full product of one's labour," " just distribution " and " equal rights." He characterised these expressions as meaningless and hollow phrases.

In combating the excesses of ineffective and sentimental " moralising " Marx leaned so far backward that, soon after his death, the myth became current that he had no place for any ethics in his philosophy of social activity. This is associated with a narrowly mechanical theory of social causation also usually attributed to him. Both interpretations are profoundly in error. For Marx no social life is possible without human consciousness. And there is no characteristically *human* consciousness without ethical ideals of some kind. But Marx went on to inquire what the source of these ideals is, when, why and where they change, and what provided relative justification of any ideal in the present. He does not deny the reality of ideals in seeking to explain their social basis. Nor does he deny their normative character in grounding them on human need. He differs from all whom he criticises as Utopian not in that he has no ethics but in that he has a *naturalistic* ethics. And he departs from the disguised Machiavellian ethics of Hegel and the Hobbesian morality of latter-day social Darwinists—which are both in essence naturalistic—in that he has a *revolutionary* ethics. Against the abstract morality of Kant and Christ, Marx held that ethics represents a series of demands, not a series of demonstrations or intuitions. His ethics is a class ethics. The ethics which were opposed to it were also, he maintained, class ethics. Peel their pseudological husk away and the kernel will be found to be a concrete class need. It is inevitable that each class consider its ethical demands as absolute: it is not inevitable that it pretend that these demands are impartial or universal. Behind class rights are class needs.

In *Capital* Marx speaks continually of the " exploitation " of the worker's surplus labour-power, i.e. that part of his working-day for which the worker receives no equivalent. He refers to it as booty, robbery and embezzlement.[1] And it is a justifiable characterisation—from the point of view of the worker. But the latter cannot *prove* his rights, he can only *enforce* them. He attempts to enforce them, however, against those who not only have a legal right to what the worker claims but, from the point of view of their class needs, a moral one as well. Tradition, religion, ethical use and wont stand behind them. There is no appeal to a " higher " ethical standpoint from which conflicting class claims can be settled. And that is all Marx meant when he proclaimed that he never appealed to justice or absolute morality. Class claim opposes class claim. One must give way.

" The capitalist maintains his rights as purchaser when he tries to make the working day as long as possible. The labourer maintains his right as seller when he wishes to reduce the working day to one of definite normal duration. There is here, therefore, an antinomy, right against right, both equally bearing the seal of the law of exchanges. Between equal rights force decides. Hence it is that in the history of capitalist production, the determination of what is a working day, presents itself as the result of a struggle, a struggle between collective capital, i.e. the class of capitalists, and collective labour, i.e. the working class " (*Capital*, I, 259).[2]

Morality, then, for Marx is natural. He therefore rules out any ethics based on divine revelation. Morality, he adds, is social. And all mystic and purely personal intuitions about the nature of " the good " and " the better " must go by the board. Morality is active. Marx is consistently bitter against the religion of suffering and the duty of forgiveness in all of its numerous Christian forms. Morality is based upon needs, upon what man as a social creature desires. These desires are determined as much by man's *class* relationships as by his original nature,

---

[1] *Capital, passim*, especially I, 259, 583, 653, 649, 670.
[2] For a rediscovery of the logic of the situation in a concrete way, *see* J. H. Tuft's experiences as chairman of a board of arbitration, related in *Contemporary American Philosophy*, New York, 1930, II, 342.

whatever that may be.[1] For Marx all ethical systems which pre-suppose a scale of objective values—of values that are above the battle of class and party—are direct or indirect disguises which mask the hidden interests of one of the contestants. Health, leisure, education, truth, beauty, etc., may appear to be objective values, since all classes seem to strive for them. But they have a different content and meaning for different classes. Once ask in any concrete situation of conflict, " *Whose* health is valuable, *what* kind of leisure and education is to be encouraged, *when* is truth-speaking a value," and in a class society the answers will reveal a class standpoint.

Class morality for Marx is rational when it is aware of its own irrational roots. It is evolutionary because those roots have a growth and a history. It defines its good in relation to class needs. The nature of class needs obviously depends upon the nature of the environing world. Since the latter is constantly changing, the concrete moral demands of the class change. Some-times it is a demand for greater freedom, sometimes for power: sometimes it shows tolerance, sometimes intolerance. There are no fixed needs or final values. The " ought-to-be " is never identical with " what-is." But yet it is a temporal function of " what-is." The ethics of Marx did not merely express a demand for social justice but a specific *kind* of justice dependent upon the objective possibilities created by capitalism. And since, to repeat, every ethics is basically a series of demands and not a series of demonstration, Marx's ethics was a *fighting* ethics. The only thing eternal about morality is man's desire for the better. But what the " better " is, time and circumstances re-determine from situation to situation. That is the moral of Marx's denial of the theory of natural rights.

" Communists do not preach morality [wrote Marx in his biting criticism of Stirner's petty-bourgeois anarchist heroics]. They make no moral demands upon people such as ' Love one another ' or ' Do not be egoistic.' They know very well that egoism as well as sacrifice under certain circumstances are necessary forms of individual assertion."[2]

[1] *Dokumente des Sozialismus*, III, 265.
[2] Ibid., 215.

3. *The Centrality of the Process in Hegel and Marx*

Hegel's system has been characterised as a philosophy of evolutionary idealism. It was not evolutionary in a biological sense. That was a doctrine which Hegel had decisively repudiated when it had first appeared as a suggestive intimation in the writings of his romantic contemporaries.[1] His philosophy was evolutionary in a historical sense—but historical, as we have seen, with time left out. The result was an abstract scheme of what had actually evolved in the course of natural and human history, translated into the language of logic and shifted to an ontological plane. In this logic nothing could be understood in its bare immediacy. Nothing was self-evident. Nothing was independent of anything else. A meaning could only be grasped in relation to some meaning (or system of meanings) which it implied and which implied it. In effect, if not in intent, what Hegel did was to dissolve all things into their relations, construe these relations as logical categories and present the interrelationships of the logical categories as a process. The order of the logical development of ideas in this realm of abstraction was the same as the order of the succession of events in history. To establish even a semblance of plausibility for his view, Hegel was compelled to introduce and work over into his system a tremendous amount of cultural material. Religion, art, politics, law, history, and the natural sciences had to illustrate his metaphysical principles. It was with good reason that Engels referred to him as the most encyclopædic mind of his day and that later generations are beginning to see him as *der grosse Geistesempiriker*.[2] In all of these fields Hegel strove to show that the process was more fundamental than the substance or body of subject matter at any definite moment. He tried to reveal how principles of construction and interpretation arose from the processes at work; how, as a consequence of the activity of these principles, the subject matter to which they were applied was gradually transformed; and how these principles

[1] *Encyclopædia*, Sec. 249. Although regarding nature as a system of levels, he holds that metamorphosis is a purely *logical* concept; and that to apply it to the actual development of plants and animals from lower forms is quite fanciful.

[2] *See* Engels' review of Marx's *Introduction to Critique of Political Economy*, reprinted as an appendix in the Duncker edition of Engels' *Feuerbach*, 1927, p. 119. The phrase, however, is Plenge's.

became embodied in a different subject matter out of which new principles—wider in connotation, richer in denotation, and truer in interpretation—evolved. All of this presented not in terms of empirical history but in the language of logical myth.

The recognition of the primary character of change, process and development on every plane of existence appears even more strongly in Marx's philosophy than in Hegel's. For Hegel, the process was cramped by his system. Change was the form in which an unchanging absolute exhibited itself. And since the Christian Germanic Empire was the closest embodiment of the absolute, history was arrested in Hegel's own time. Even as a Young-Hegelian, however, Marx would have none of the absolute. The system *was* the process. With Bruno Bauer he made the principle of *Negativität* central in Hegel's exposition. With Bauer he said, " The Absolute is not Substance but Subject." Activity and power are prior to matter and structure. All apparently self-included existence is a mode of logical activity. Logical activity is the all-including process. Later, when as a result of his attempt to understand the nature of the *historical* process Marx was compelled to abandon his idealism, he still retained his belief in the underivable character of activity. But it was now a *natural* activity, not a logical activity. It was the activity of matter, not of spirit. Every existing thing had a place in a material continuum of directed movement. The logic of Hegel received a naturalistic foundation. Nothing could exist outside of this continuum of directed movement. Nothing could be understood except in terms of the logical relations of this continuum. In different ways this holds on every level. That which appears to be immediately given to sense perception is revealed as a mediated product of the process of human sensory activity. The character of the historical present is shown to involve the past and to suggest the future. The " perfect " state of Hegel is viewed not only as the end term of a historic process but as the first term in a contemporary one which is certain to dissolve it. The independent object of theoretical political economy—the commodity—is shown to involve a definite dependence upon a whole complex of social, historical and ethical presuppositions. Everything which is *given*—be it the price of a commodity, a system of morals or a style of art—has at some time been *produced.* That is what in the first instance the dialectical method of Hegel meant for Marx. He says of it in *Capital* :

> " In its rational form it is a scandal and abomination to the bourgeoisie and its doctrinaire spokesmen because it includes in its positive understanding of the existing state of things at the same time an understanding of its negation, of its necessary disappearance; because it regards every historically developed social form as in a fluid movement, interpreting it from its transitional side; because it lets nothing impose on it and is in its essence critical and revolutionary " (*Capital,* I, 26, Aveling's trans., slightly revised).

This does not mean, as some critics imagine, that Marx was so much interested in the flow of existence that he neglected the analysis of the formal structure of what flowed. Indeed, that was what Marx conceived his life work to be—an analysis of contemporary bourgeois society whose anatomy he discovered in political economy.[1] He described the anatomical structure of civic society exhaustively enough, but his most distinctive contribution was to show that the very anatomy of society—i.e. political economy—was not a frame upon which and within which the body politic was built up, but that it was the gradual product of the social relations into which men entered, that it was modified by these relations and modified them in turn. It was Marx's merit to show that just as a good anatomist must know more than anatomy, so a good economist, in order to have real insight into the nature of the surface relationships which constitute the " science " of political economy, must know more than political economy.

4. *End in Hegel and Ends in Marx*

The attempt commonly made to read into Marx an economic fatalism necessitates some consideration of the nature and function of ends in his philosophy. Here again his relationship to Hegel has been misunderstood.

In Hegel the developmental process is of necessity teleological. For there is only one process, one systematic whole in which

[1] *Introduction to Critique of Political Economy,* English trans., p. 11.

everything moves and has its being. Just as the organism as a whole is involved in the functioning of any one of its parts, so the universe as an organic whole is involved in the structure and activity of every finite entity. And if the systematic structure of the whole be regarded as the realised *end* of the process, then any of its aspects may be regarded as the means by which it is realised. As a means it is not something extrinsic and external to the end, as when we say that the hammer is the means by which we drive the nail fast, but something intrinsic or internal, a part of the end, as when we say that the blood is the means by which the body is built. The end is in the means as much as the means in the end. For example, from the point of view of the state as an organic totality (on a relatively incomplete level), the individual citizen is a means to the whole. His nature, worth and status are evaluated in respect to the end, i.e. to the idea of the state. His personality is realised through the state, and as an ideal man (i.e. not as animal or angel) he can no more be separated from the state than a mathematical point from a line. The state, on the other hand, is also a means to the expression of the ideal personality of *all* its members. The same logic holds for the whole universe. Everything is both means and end to everything else. The universe is through and through purposive.

In Marx the developmental process is purposive only where the social categories of the material continuum are involved. Processes that are purely physical, like the movement of the waves or the heavenly bodies, are neither constituted nor explained by desire, want or purpose.[1] *Social* movement very definitely involves reference to volition. Volition depends upon two sets of relations: relations between nature and man; and relations between man and man.[2] In either case the point of departure is human need. It is human need expressed as purpose which splits the one Absolute Whole of Hegel into pieces. Not into a friable mass of atomic units as in sensationalistic empiricism, but into several well defined wholes. The earth, for example, is a whole for the geologist. It is a different whole— although related to the first—for a man in quest of nourishment.

---

[1] It is thoroughly consistent for Hegel, but not for a naturalist, to use *Bedürfnis* and *Trieb* as illustrations of *Zweck*; *Encyclopædia*, Sec. 204.

[2] *Deutsche Ideologie, Marx-Engels Archiv*, 1926–7, I, 254.

It is still a different whole for the economist seeking to discover
the laws of rent. The kind of whole we have depends upon the
kind of purpose we have. This is apparent even in the type of
objects human beings construct. The natural object (as distinct
from thing), the esthetic object, the ethical object, the economic
object are in a sense *objectifications* of human purpose. Purpose
is not creative, but rather selective, for we can always significantly examine purpose as created by other elements which are
not purposive in the same sense.

This supplies the key to Marx's conception of purpose. The
process of social development has no ends to realise which are
not the ends willed by men. But those ends are not realised
merely because they are willed by men. *What* is willed must
be continuous with a discovered situation which is not willed but
accepted. *When* it is willed must be determined by objective
possibilities in the situation. Only when these conditions are
fulfilled, can the ends willed by men be realised. Only, for
example, when the process of production has been sufficiently
developed to permit of mass manufacture can socialism, as an
end willed by the proletariat, be realised. And only when the
consequences of mass production under capitalism produce
widespread *need* is socialism effectively willed. Marx's theory of
social activity sees in the presence of need the explanation of
why socialism is willed at all; and in the presence of certain
objective conditions why what is willed, will probably be
realised.

> " Need gives man strength; he who must help himself will
> do so. The real situation of this world, the sharp opposition
> in modern society between Capital and Labour, Bourgeoisie
> and Proletariat, which stands out most clearly in industrial
> relations, serves as the other powerful generating source of
> the socialist outlook, of the desire for social reform. These
> circumstances cry out: ' Things cannot remain that way, they
> must become different and we ourselves, we human beings,
> must make them different.' "[1]

Needs develop as objective conditions develop. They are at
the base of those objective possibilities which human beings

[1] *Aus dem literarischen Nachlass*, II, 416.

strive by *action* to realise. The logic and pattern of social development is determined by a triadic, interacting relationship between objective environment, human need and class activity.

Like Hegel, Marx never dissociated man from his social environment. In speaking either of man or man's environment there is always an implied reference to the *other* term in the relation. Both make one interacting whole. Often, however, Marx refers synoptically to the development of this interacting whole without stopping to point out how these elements are specifically related, and how they operate. Man's ideas and purposes are immanent in the process. Their immanent character appears more clearly when we examine the rôle they have played in the past than when we try to understand our own ideas and purposes in the hectic flush of the present. Even religious ideas and theories which profess to hold up transcendental standards of the true and the good express some aspect of the immanent social process. Nor did Marx ever pretend that his own theories were more than the expression of an existing class struggle, that they were valid outside of the existing context in which they were generated. It is in this sense that we are to understand his oft-repeated assertion:

"We do not set ourselves up against the world in doctrinaire fashion with a new principle: Here is the truth ! Here you must kneel ! We develop new principles of the world out of the principles of the existing world. We do not proclaim to it: Cease from your struggles ! They are silly ! We will tell you what to fight for ! We only show the world what it is that it *must* acquire even against its will.[1]

The function of a social theory is to bring human beings to self-consciousness, not the mystical self-consciousness which for Hegel was the end of all history, but a class consciousness arising from concrete needs.

Social needs and purposes are not subjective. They are as genuine a part of the objective *milieu* as the classes themselves. The theories and ideals to which those needs give birth are *forms of response* to the existing scene. They must be brought to consciousness in order to function effectively. Here we have a

[1] *Gesamtausgabe*, I, 1, 575, Letter to Ruge.

critical social behaviourism which does not deny that human beings are influenced by beliefs but which seeks to make intelligible the *historical* impact of dominant social beliefs—their rise, acceptance and decline—by interpreting them as forms of class behaviour. For Marx all social theories including his own are not hypothetico-deductive systems seeking to formulate objective and eternal truths. They are social judgments of practice. They are methods of making history. Marx's method is " truer " than others because it is more effective. To counter by saying that it is more effective because it is truer is to utter a proposition that can never be tested without reference to further effectiveness. The theories of Marxists are projections of a class will enlightened by knowledge of the conditions and historical antagonisms which have produced class divisions. " They serve," declares the *Communist Manifesto*, " merely to express in general terms the concrete circumstances of an actually existing class struggle; of an historical movement which is going on under our very eyes."

With this emphasis on the rôle of class consciousness in the historical process, we reach that specifically dialectical aspect of Marx's thought which best shows what he owes to the Hegelian dialectic.[1] It is only by appreciating the dialectical nature of class consciousness, that we can understand the concluding sentence of Engel's *Feuerbach*: " The working-class movement is the heir of classical German philosophy."

III

THE DIALECTICAL METHOD IN HEGEL AND MARX

A witty Frenchman once said that Marxism like Christianity has its Bible, its councils, its schisms; its orthodoxies and heresies; its exegeses, profane and sacred. And like Christianity it has its mysteries of which the principal one is the dialectic ! It seems to me, however, that if Marx's dialectic has remained a mystery to his critics, the reason has been that they did not

---

[1] Compare in this connection Lukač's interesting book on *Dialektik und Klassenbewusstsein* (1923), which does justice to the dialectical aspect of Marx's thought at the expense, alas, of Marx's *naturalism*.

know where to look for its solution. They took his metaphors about turning Hegel's method right side up too literally. As if a method can be studied in the way we test a sow's rump ! The life of a method lies in its application. Only in application can its meaning be truly grasped. Too often, however, have critics stopped at passages, especially in *Capital*, to muse over the " deeper meaning " of an Hegelian terminology which Marx, by his own confession, had taken over in a spirit of coquetry. The influence of Hegel's dialectical method on Marx was indeed profound ; but it is not to be ferreted out of the formulas for the commodity or money cycle—C-M-C or M-C-M. It must be construed from his actual intellectual procedure, from his economic and historical analyses.

The least significant aspect of the dialectical method is its division into triadic phases. Although there is an historical tradition behind the idealistic dialectic which carries the " triad " at least as far back as Proclus, it is not logically essential to the method. Psychological and religious (Christian) motives have played a part in keeping it focal among idealists. It is not so much the number of phases a situation has which makes it dialectical but a *specific relation* of opposition between those phases which generates a succession of other phases. The necessary condition, then, of a dialectical situation is at least two phases, distinct but not separate. The sufficient condition of a dialectical situation is given when those two phases present a relation of *opposition* and *interaction* such that the result (1) exhibits something qualitatively new, (2) preserves some of the structural elements of the interacting phases, and (3) eliminates others.

1. *Defects of the Dialectical Method in Hegel*

In a letter to Dietzgen in 1876, Marx writes of Hegel what he had earlier written to Engels and to Kugelmann:

> " When I have shaken off the burden of my economic labours, I shall write a dialectic. The correct laws of the dialectic are already included in Hegel albeit in mystical form. It is necessary to strip it of this form."[1]

[1] Josef Dietzgen's *Sämtliche Schriften*, 3rd ed., 1922, I, 166.

What does Marx mean when he speaks of the dialectical method in Hegel as mystical ? On the basis of our earlier discussion, his position may be briefly summarised. (1) The dialectical method in Hegel is mystical because it seems to generate out of its own ghostly activity the very subject matter to which it is applied or in which it operates. It involves the familiar and inevitably futile attempt to deduce existence. " Hegel fell into the error of considering the real as the result of self-co-ordinating, self-absorbed, and spontaneously operating thought."[1] (2) Mystical again is the dialectical method in Hegel because it is used as an instrument to establish the logical structure of *one* all-inclusive whole. Strictly speaking this means that all of existence becomes relevant in considering the nature of any part of it. From which it follows that piecemeal knowledge is impossible; since if everything must be known before anything can be known, nothing can be *adequately* known. Short-time action cannot be reasonably grounded. The absolute whole together with the dialectic in its Hegelian form is simply not *relevant* to finite purpose, convenience or need. For Marx there are wholes not *the* whole. (3) The third respect in which the Hegelian dialectic is mystical is already involved in the above. It is unable to explain the detailed mechanisms of the activities which it purports to describe in *ad hoc* fashion. It offers no clue to empirical approach or control. History is an illustration. The dialectic method assures us that the spirit of freedom will realise itself. But it does not tell us when, where and how.

2. *Dialectic as the Logic of Totality in Marx*

Once the Hegelian dialectic is freed from its mystical form, its place and importance in Marx's methodology appear sharp and clear. For purposes of exposition it is necessary to distinguish between the influence of the category of *totality* on Marx's thought—which corresponds to the static aspect of the Hegelian dialectic—and the category of *activity* which reflects its dynamic aspect. The notion of " active totality " in Marx differs from the " absolute whole perpetually renewing itself " in Hegel in that the Marxian totality is social and limited by other totalities, while the Hegelian totality is metaphysical and unlimited,

[1] *Introduction to Critique of Political Economy*, p. 293.

For Marx as for Hegel the social system constitutes a whole. Its various cultural aspects—educational system, religion, art— are parts of the whole. The real character of any of these aspects cannot be grasped when we isolate it from the context of tradition and living energies which define the culture of an age. A system of law, for example, can only be understood in the light of its function in relating different social activities such as the economic relations whose character substantive law expresses, the ethical practices of the community whose ideals it seeks to incorporate, and the political mechanism of repression and control whose stability it tends to sustain. But the nature of the whole is such that it cannot be studied *as a whole* any more than the physiologist can study the human body as a whole. We must begin with a tentatively isolated part. In order to understand the part, however, we must go on to other parts. As we extend our investigations and as the relationships which the part has to the whole become clearer, we are compelled to modify our original conclusions about the nature of the part when it was considered in relative isolation. Whatever we know about the hand or the eye as a consequence of analysing its structure in isolation assumes a different significance when it is studied as an instrument of the organism as a whole. The mutual determination of function and structure becomes intelligible only from the point of view of the whole system. This involves a continual revision of our knowledge as it goes from part to part until the systematic nature of the whole is revealed. The development of knowledge, in the language of Hegel and Marx, is from the abstract to the concrete. The part is an abstraction, the whole is concrete. In the social discipline this insight has now become almost a commonplace. It is well known that a history of religion or of theology merely in terms of the doctrines which men have believed does not possess the same degree of intelligibility as a social history which shows how these religious beliefs were bound up with other aspects of the culture-complex. This was the nub of Marx's criticism of Feuerbach's psychological interpretation of religion. It is even more obvious that the same logic holds for the structural relationship of any specific subject matter, e.g. political economy. The analysis of the " economic cell-form " of capitalist production—the value form of the commodity as discussed in the first volume of *Capital*—must be modified by the analysis of the body of " capitalist production as a whole," as discussed in the third volume.

It is just at this point that the categories of Hegel's doctrine of Essence appear prominently in Marx. The nature or essence of the system studied does not exist behind or beyond the appearances but is expressed in them. The whole exists in its parts; the parts in the whole. The contingency of the initial starting point is rationalised by the insight into the necessity of the organised whole; the necessity of the whole appears in the contingency of all possible starting points. For Hegel and for Marx, whole and part, necessity and contingency, continuity and discontinuity, are polar categories—one term cannot be intelligibly used without the other. The material and formal elements in the natural process, the active and the passive factor in the historical process, capitalist and proletariat in existing society—all are inseparable distinctions within organised wholes whose continuous existence demands the presence of both. So long as we at any given moment preserve the structure of a differentiated whole, it is impossible to accept the consequences of one of the polar categories and to reject the consequences of the other. Just because " the relations of production of every society constitute a whole,"[1] it is impossible to eliminate the periodic crises, the unemployment, and mass of proletarian misery, that is, the *bad* side of production, and still retain *on the same plane*, the *laissez-faire* philosophy of operation which provides an open field for talent and initiative, that is, the *good* side. The bad and good are opposite faces of the same situation. Just because the capitalist in virtue of his position *must* produce for profit, " he ruthlessly forces the development of the productive powers " (*Capital*, I, 649), and lays the material foundations for a different society. The principle of polarity discloses the *structural opposition* of whatever has systematic unity.

3. *The Dialectic as the Principle of Activity*

So far we have considered the principle of dialectic as it applies to a system at rest. But the system which Marx was analysing was a *social* system in *movement*. The logic of *co-ordination* must

[1] *Poverty of Philosophy*, English trans., p. 120.

be modified by the logic of *succession*. The whole at rest must be regarded as a limiting case of the whole in movement. The key to the development of a whole is to be found in the specific character of its structural opposition. At any given moment, the structural opposition must be such that its mutually supporting elements are *not* of equal strength. The elements within the structure interact upon one another in a way which threatens to upset the precariously established equilibrium which appeared at first analysis. In this tendency to disturb the equilibrium one can recognise incipient development. Gradually there results a qualitative change and equilibrium is restored. The extent, the strength and the rate of interaction between the polar elements within any situation depend upon the specific factors involved. They cannot be *deduced* from the general formula of dialectical movement. That means that the equilibrium which is analysed in the present cannot be regarded in complete independence of the equilibrium which preceded it; and that it already contains within itself indications of the general character of the equilibrium to be realised in the future.

Formally, the dynamic aspect of the dialectic method may be presented in abbreviated fashion as follows:

(1) *The Fluidity of the Fact.* If logic is to be relevant to existence it must do justice to one of the fundamental characters of existence, viz. movement and flow. " The object," writes Hegel, " is in its essential nature movement."[1] The analysis of its nature, then, will consist in distinguishing the various phases of an object as integral moments of a process, and unifying them in some synoptic concept. In our analysis we begin with concepts and meanings that are fixed and unchangeable. But how can these meanings which are constant and timeless be significantly applied to an existence which is variable and temporal (for Hegel read " finite ")? Meanings must develop with the objects of which they are the meaning. Otherwise they cannot be adequate to their subject matter. The retort comes that meanings cannot develop at all. By *definition* they do not change. When we speak of the development of meaning we mean the succession of *new* meanings. None the less the situation is not altered by regarding

---

[1] *Phänomenologie des Geistes,* Lasson ed., p. 75.

every development in meaning as a *new* meaning. For first, the old meaning is included in the new, and secondly, the series of meanings which are generated by the subject matter in question are knit together by a *qualitative unity* which distinguishes them from all other series. For example, we may define capitalism, with our eye on the seventeenth century, as a system of commodity production which arises whenever labour-power appears on the market as formally free. Yet as we analyse the development of the capitalistic system through the industrial capitalism produced by the technological revolution in the eighteenth and the nineteenth centuries, and the financial capitalism of the twentieth, we enrich the significance of the meaning of capitalism by including the various phases through which it has passed as differentiated aspects of the same *type* of social organisation. We study slavery and feudalism in the same way but do not confuse the continuities established in our investigation by distinguishing between the three different *types* and redefining them in relation to all available material.

(2) *The Logic of Development.* Every meaning has an objective reference. It is controlled by that objective reference. The discovery of the nature of the objective reference—which in its systematic connection with other things is revealed as a process —gives the meaning a richer connotation. It is invariant only as the unity of the different determinations it includes. No meaning applicable to things is a mere identity. Man is man (A is A) does not tell us the meaning of man. Man is rational (A is B) does. But man is also mortal (C), animal (D), social (E), etc. Man can always be the subject of another predicate. His nature is not something *behind* these predicates but is revealed *in* them. Every one of these predicates tells us something new about man and with each one the *system of predicates*—or the *meaning* of man—changes. Where thinking is relevant to existence we may define a dialectical situation as one in which we are compelled, with the progress of knowledge, to redefine our terms. Since " the *content* of knowledge and the *form* of knowledge are inseparable," says Hegel,[1] the growth of one entails a corresponding growth of the other. And since for Marx the content of knowledge can never be boxed within any closed system, logic

[1] *Science of Logic*, 1929, I, 54.

itself, as the study of the *order* of things, can never be a finally
closed system.

(3) *The Schema of Development.* The driving force in the
development of a dialectical situation is derived from the conflict and opposition of the elements within it. The nature of a
thing is disclosed in its relation to other things. Every relation
may be viewed from two opposite aspects, i.e. from the point
of view of the two terms it relates. Each term regards the relation as internal to itself and the other term as external to itself.
An antinomy results which can be solved only by *reinterpreting*
the situation and by looking at both terms and their relation
from the point of view of a wider relation (whole or system).
But one antinomy is solved in order to make way for another.
Opposition breaks out between the terms on a higher level. It
is this opposition which Hegel calls the principle of *Negativität*.[1]
It is the self-moving soul of all physical and spiritual life. Noth-
ing is sacred to it, nothing immune to its negations. It is " *der
Geist der stets verneint*."

Marx's analysis of capitalist society begins with an examination of the actual economic relations in which men find themselves. These relations take the form of opposition between
proletariat and capitalist, between the necessities of production
and the needs of consumption, between the expansion of industry
and the contraction of purchasing power, etc. All of these oppositions constitute a whole.[2] They cannot be solved without changing the whole. At a certain point in the interaction of the opposite
elements, the equilibrium is destroyed and reconstituted by
human *action*. Marx's *Capital* is a description of the mechanism
of production of the objective forces making for opposition.
Within it, the dialectical principle appears as class activity.

(4) *The Levels of Development.* Dialectical resolution of conflict and opposition is the motor-power of all development. It
is a *productive* synthesis of the conflicting elements within a
situation and not a deductive analysis of what both have in
common. A true synthesis is more than the logical addition of
this *and* that. It is this and that *taken* in a definite way. The

---

[1] " The Negative in general contains the ground of Becoming, the unrest of
self-movement " (*Science of Logic*, 1929, I, 180; cf. *Encyclopædia*, Sec. 81).

[2] *Aus dem literarischen Nachlass*, 1902, II, 132.

specific way in which they are taken can never be predicted in advance. For Marx, since the developmental process is temporal, the manner of synthesis depends not only upon the subject matter within which development takes place but upon the shifts and realignments of human interests in time. No matter how the specific synthesis may be effected, its general character may be indicated. A genuine synthesis is more than a simple *destructive* process which removes the possibility of further development and conflict (as when a community goes down to a common doom as a result of class-struggles). But neither is it a simple *additive* process which by fusing and compromising opposing elements produces a new situation—one in which the original elements can still be discerned and, by some inverse operation, precipitated out again (as when we mix a white sand heap with a black sand heap to get a grey sand heap). Nor is it a simple *transformative* process in which the qualities of the different elements are no longer discernible in the new quality created (as when water emerges from the union of oxygen and hydrogen). Nor is it finally a simple *repetitive* process in which the elements remain unchanged. A dialectical synthesis is all this and more. Thesis and antithesis are resolved in such a way that the pretensions of each to constitute the whole of a relation are *denied*; yet aspects of each are retained or *conserved* in every new whole or situation; and are reinterpreted or *elevated* (*aufgehoben*) as subordinate moments in a more inclusive whole. As Charles Peirce realised, what Hegel is groping to express in this way, is the logic of natural *continuity*.

Hegel alleges this continuity to be purely logical; for Marx it is primarily historical and social. Out of it arises the succession of social systems in determinate order—primitive communism, slavery, feudalism, capitalism and socialism. The necessity of development is natural (on this plane, more accurately, *socio-historical*), not logical. Any two of these stages exhibit the relations described above, e.g. socialism and capitalism. Socialism affirms the social nature of the productive process under capitalism, denies the anti-social character of its distribution and reinterprets both as the condition under which socialised man uses his knowledge of natural necessity to attain cultural freedom (*Capital*, English trans., III, 954).

(5) *The Rôle of Consciousness in Dialectic.* In Hegel the dialectical process is expressed not only in the realm of objective spirit but in the realm of nature as well. Indeed, most of the illustrations of the natural dialectic which Engels cites in his *Anti-Dühring* and which are so popular in socialist literature are to be found in Hegel's *Logic*.[1] Now there can be no question but that Hegel is justified in terms of his own system in extending the dialectic to nature. Does he not tell us that " self-consciousness and existence " are absolutely one and the same?[2] If they are, then nature as implicit self-consciousness can be legitimately analysed as a continuous series every term of which is in some sense aware of the subsequent terms within the series. Without this thread of awareness, the relationships within the series would be contradictory. It supplies the principle of unity. Only by virtue of the activity of consciousness can Hegel write a *Naturphilosophie* in which every aspect of the physical world is represented as seeking dialectically to transcend and fulfil itself in the continuous whole whose systematic interconnection is both objective meaning and mind.

That consciousness is essential to the dialectical process in nature is apparent at almost any stage in the succession of the categories in the first two books of the *Logic*. But for purposes of illustration we may take his discussion of the category of " limit " (*die Grenze*).[3] Whatever has determinate being must be differentiated from something else. All determination is negation; any something has character because it is not its other. A meadow that had no bounds, a sea that had no shore, would be neither meadow nor sea. A thing (*Etwas*), then, must be given together with its limits. Its character may be defined as the negative unity of its limits. But Hegel's problem is, so to speak, to get the thing over and beyond its limits. Otherwise there can be no movement, no development, no dialectical synthesis of the balanced tension between the positive and the

---

[1] e.g., the development of the plant from seed, through flower to fruit, which serves as Engels' stock illustration of natural dialectic will be found in Hegel's *Logic*, I, 147. How close a student Engels was of Hegel's natural philosophy may be gathered from his recently discovered manuscript, *Dialectik und Natur*, edited and published by Riazanov in *Marx-Engels Archiv*. 1926–7, II, 117–395.

[2] *Phänomenologie des Geistes*, 1907, p. 158.

[3] *Logic*, 1929, I, 147.

negative aspects of every something. How can something transcend its own limit ? This can be done only when the something
in question senses that its nature is involved in another *possible*
something which cannot be *actualised* without destroying its own
original limits. Hegel's own language reveals a continual implicit
reference to consciousness and the activity of consciousness.
When something, he tells us, realises that its own deeper nature
is involved in some systematic whole which extends further than
its own limits, then those limits become " fetters " (*Schranken*).
They impede self-development and growth. They must be burst.
" In order that the limit applying to something in general
should also be a fetter, something must pass over into itself
beyond the limit; it must, referring to itself, relate itself to it as
something which is not."[1]

To a naturalist who denies that nature is implicitly spirit,
the above must sound like sheer mythology. Yet it needs only
to be translated out of its technical jargon and illustrated with
examples drawn from the proper fields in order that its profound
insight be apparent. The proper fields from a naturalistic point
of view would be psychology and sociology. We may briefly
mention the development of personality and the growth of
social institutions as illustrations of what Hegel means. The
development of personality can be understood as a process of
overcoming the obstacles which have been created by past
achievements—achievements which are as genuine an expression
of personality as the effort necessary to prevent them from cramping and routinating new experiences. The growth of institutions
may be described as a process of liberation from the restricting
influence of rules and principles which at an earlier time were
essential for proper functioning. Wherever we protest that means
have become goals, that the forms of justice have become the
ends of justice, that the letter killeth the spirit, the situation

---

[1] *Logic*, 1929, I, 145–6. Struthers and Johnson, following McTaggart, unfortunately translate *Schranke* by " barrier " instead of " fetter." The problem which
puzzled McTaggart as to why Hegel should contrast " the ought " of Something
(*das Sollen*) with its limit as fetter (*die Schranke*), and which he solves by introducing Hegel's desire to score on Fichte, seems to me to be better illuminated
when we emphasise the spiritual presuppositions of the whole dialectical process.
If all being and existence is implicit self-consciousness, then all their modes must
literally *strive* to transcend their partiality. Striving is only possible when there
is something to be overcome. What is to be overcome is the " fetter "—the past
progress which stands in the way of present progress.

presents the pattern unfolded in Hegel's discussion of the limit.

Marx is a naturalist. Spirit is not the source of matter but rather its highest product. And since the social is primary to the individual psyche, the dialectical relation is primarily a social relation. Its synthesis must consequently always be effected by human *activity*, for the human will is part of the social whole. Within this whole the moments of opposition are the objective conditions (*thesis*) which are independent of immediate consciousness (but not of history) and the human needs and desires (*antithesis*) which project possibilities on the basis of those conditions. At a certain point, as a result of the pressure of objective conditions on the will and thought of a definite class, action (*synthesis*) results. An attempt is made to actualise the objective possibilities generated by the interaction of the social environment and human needs. By means of class action the "moments of opposition" are transformed into "phases of development."

It is clear, then, that consciousness is an integral part of the social process. It is amazing that critics should have overlooked the place and function accorded to class consciousness in Marx's thought. Perhaps the explanation is to be partly found in the fact that the emphasis upon the presence and efficacy of class consciousness shifts gradually from explicit assertion in *Die heilige Familie* to implicit statement in *Capital*. In the latter work Marx is primarily interested in analysing the mechanism of the social system which produces the *conditions* of revolutionary class consciousness. There can be no consciousness without mechanism and no social mechanism without consciousness. In none of his writings does he withdraw from the position he took in earlier philosophical works. His historical writings illustrate concretely,[1] the abstract propositions already formulated in *Die heilige Familie*, where he considers the factors which drive the proletariat to a realisation of the inhuman character of its existence.

[1] It is incomprehensible on purely methodological grounds that those critics who have so much to say about Marx's fatalism should neglect his historical writings, especially *The 18th Brumaire of Louis Napoleon* and *Class Struggles in France 1848-50*, in which the Marxian theory of class consciousness finds definite application.

" The proletariat senses in its position in society its own destruction, becomes aware of the character of its inhuman existence and of its own helplessness. To use a phrase of Hegel's, in this infamy it is the expression of indignation against infamy, an indignation to which it is necessarily driven by the contradiction between its human nature and the living conditions which represent the crassest, most inclusive, and decisive negation of that nature. Private property abolishes itself only in so far as it produces the proletariat *as* a proletariat, whose physical and spiritual misery becomes conscious misery, and which in becoming conscious of its inhuman condition succeeds in abolishing it."[1]

(6) *The Criteria of Dialectical Thinking.* If the dialectical process controls dialectical thinking and action, what are the criteria enabling us to determine whether we have thought validly and acted properly ? *Formally* we may answer in terms of the category of *coherence.* Only when that whole or unit or continuity which has been destroyed by the presence of conflicting factors has been restored or re-established in another whole (or resting point) can we claim validity for our procedure. All thinking as well as the need for all philosophy begins, says Hegel, " when unity has disappeared from the life of man, and when its oppositions, having lost their vital relations and interactions, assert themselves as independent."[2] We go on from whole to whole by bridging the gaps which arise in our experiences and integrating external relations into an ever larger systematic unity. And where, short of the absolute, do we stop ? From a *finite* point of view Hegel admits that the process comes to completion whenever the finite purpose of our inquiry is satisfied. But as distinct from his naturalistic followers, he insists that all logical purposes must themselves be systematically unified and that the dialectical relation between different purposes drives us to the one all-embracing purpose of absolute self-consciousness. Marx refused to admit that all the purposes and needs of inquiry constitute an organic system, that there is any absolute whole under which they can all be subsumed.

[1] *Nachlass,* 1902, II, 132, freely translated.
[2] " Differenz des fichteschen und schellingschen Systems " (*Werke,* 1832 ed., I, 174).

As a naturalist he holds that there is no limit to the series of *new* purposes generated by the fulfilment of past needs and desires. What logically unites Hegel and Marx here is the belief that the *specific criteria* of correct thinking must vary with a developing subject matter. Hegel is always looking away from the finite standard to the self-certifying absolute One; Marx is content to remain on the ordinary level of experience and examine each standard on its own claim. But both deny that standards are given once and for all time. They are to be tested by the subject matter to which they are applied. Only because they are continuous with their subject matter can standards be significantly applied at all. Standards have histories. In their development they are evaluated by other standards which are themselves conditioned by different subject matter and purpose. Hegel in a sense would have agreed with Ranke's dictum *Aus Absicht und Stoff entsteht die Form.* He leaves no doubt that the forms of knowledge in finite experience show a definite growth.

> " The standards of testing change when that whose criterion the standard was supposed to be, no longer remains in the course of testing what it was. The test is not only a test of knowledge but of its standards as well."[1]

Hegel emphasised the relativity of our evaluating categories in order to point to the necessity of an Absolute which swallowed them all; Marx did so in order to win the possibility of new institutional activities in a changing world. " Categories are historical and transitory products," Marx urges against Proudhon. Quite so, answer the formal philosophers, but these are only social and economic categories. Surely, the same cannot be true of the categories of thought itself by virtue of which we distinguish changes in the categories of other phenomena. But from the standpoint of Marx's evolutionary naturalism (dialectical materialism) the categories of thinking must develop together with the generic traits of the existence thought about. " Der Denkprozess selbst ein *Naturprozess* ist," he writes.[2] As a natural process it is comparatively invariant in relation to the process of social and economic change. But with the gradual

---

[1] *Phänomenologie des Geistes*, p. 61.
[2] Letter to Kugelmann, July 11, 1868.

change in things and the increasing complexity of the organ of thinking, new forms of thought are produced. Standing in the present, we necessarily regard our categories as invariant for all time. The history of thought shows, however, that man has been driven from one invariant to another until the only thing that he can declare invariant for all time is the barest, formal logical relation. To hold that the logic we know is invariant for all possible existence is to utter a proposition which we cannot test, for the very meaning of " all possible existence " depends upon what we discover actuality to be. For Marx any material which is the subject of man's activity generates its own normative ideals in relation to the way it succeeds in fulfilling human needs. From the reciprocal influence and interaction between the ideal and the actual a new subject matter is produced out of which in turn are born the means by which it will be changed. This is the heart of the dialectic.

4. *Dialectic as the " Algebra of Revolution "*

It is in the field of history, however, that the principle of dialectic becomes vitally relevant for Marx. It is in relation to history that it has been significantly called the "algebra of revolution." [1] Through *class* consciousness society attains self-consciousness. Consciousness implies activity. As a result of the activity of class consciousness the interacting social whole becomes transformed. The class is the subject of the historical process, the carrier of the transformative principle. The social environment is the object of the historical process, the matter transformed. In changing the historical object, the subject changes itself. " By acting on the external world and changing it," says Marx, " man changes his own nature " (*Capital*, I, 198). Human nature, then, far from being a *constant* in world history, definable in terms of fixed instincts and desires, becomes a *variable* which within limits can be modified by man's social and historical activity. " All history," he proclaims, " is the progressive modification of human nature." The gradual changes in human nature which are the result of the evolution of the forces of production produce sudden changes in the social relations of production. Sudden changes in the social relations of production

[1] By Herzen, I believe.

can be effected only by political revolution. In class societies
social evolution is impossible without political revolution at
some point in the process.[1]

5. Dialectic and Nature

Upon the foregoing interpretation, the attempt to apply
the dialectic to nature must be ruled out as incompatible with a
naturalistic starting point. Marx himself never speaks of a
Natur-Dialektik, although he was quite aware that gradual
quantitative changes in the fundamental units of physics and
chemistry result in qualitative changes. Engels, however, in his
Anti-Dühring and in his posthumously published manuscript
Dialektik und Natur openly extends the dialectic to natural
phenomena. His definition of dialectic, however, indicates that
he is unaware of the *distinctive* character of the dialectic as
opposed to the physical concept of " change " and the biological
concept of " development." " Dialectic," he writes, " is nothing
more than the science of universal laws of motion and evolution
in nature, human society and thought."[2] Practically all of knowledge, therefore, falls within its scope; and every thinker from
Thales down could claim to have in some sense advanced the
science of dialectic. Only an idealist can adhere to the distinctive
connotation of dialectic expounded above and still believe that
nature, independent of man, is an illustration of it. Galileo's
laws of motion and the life history of an insect have nothing to
do with dialectic except on the assumption that all nature is
spirit. Here as elsewhere, Engels swallowed more of Hegel than,
as a naturalist, he could properly digest; and one is tempted to
say that it kept coming up throughout his work.

Some Marxists have so generalised the meaning of dialectics
that it refers to the sudden emergence of new qualities in *any*
field. Plechanov, e.g., holds that the transition from 9 to 10, or
90 to 100, in the process of counting is evidence of dialectic
at work.[3] Confusion has arisen because of the multiple and ambiguous references to the term "*Natur-Dialektik.*" Sometimes it

[1] *The Poverty of Philosophy*, English trans., 1910, p. 180.

[2] *Anti-Dühring*, 12th ed., p. 144.

[3] Cf. his " Sudden Changes in Nature and History," in *Fundamental Problems
of Marxism*, English trans., p. 97.

means no more than the commonplace fact that change is observable in all fields of thought and activity. Sometimes it means that every account of physics must operate with contrasting and complementary principles in order to do justice to the polarities and oppositions in the structures of nature. But in these senses it is foreign to Marx's conception of dialectic, which is historical and restricted only to a consideration of the causes, nature and effects of human activity that destroys the equilibrium of a polarised society and redetermines the *direction* of the movement of society. In this last sense, the dialectic is the principle of social activity, its medium is the class struggle, its spearhead, in class society, the social revolution. Whatever the natural dialectic may be it is not the basis of the class struggle. There is no need to show that there are sudden leaps and jumps in *nature* to justify revolution in *society*. Whether natural phenomena are continuous at all points or discontinuous at some is an empirical question. It is strictly irrelevant to the solution of any *social* problem. The mistaken conception that they are relevant is bound up with a cognate confusion between the truth-character of the findings of science and the social motives and conditions of scientific investigation. The results of physics may be used by the bourgeoisie but there is no such thing as bourgeois physics. To read the class struggle back into science and nature is to imply that all nature is conscious—a proposition which only an Hegelian idealist can accept.

The dialectical principle in Marx expresses primarily the logic of *historical consciousness* and *class action*. The natural objective order is relevant to dialectic only when there is an implied reference to the way in which it conditions social and historical activity. And as a materialist, Marx believed that although activity is impossible without nature, nature itself has existed, can exist and will exist without social activity.

CHAPTER II

THE YOUNG-HEGELIANS
AND KARL MARX

IF INSIGHT into a man's thought is furthered by an appreciation of the doctrines which he contended against in his struggle for clarity, then we must trace in detail Karl Marx's relationship to the radical Young-Hegelians. Here we shall find one of the most significant sources of his intellectual development—a development from a " critical " philosophy of *self-consciousness* to a revolutionary philosophy of *social activity*. This chapter of Marx's intellectual biography began with an acceptance of the left-wing Hegelian philosophy of religion, proceeded to a penetrating sociological criticism of the roots of all religious belief in general and of the philosophy of Christianity in particular, and ended with the first groping formulations of historical materialism in *Die heilige Familie*. The period coincided with the rising movement on the part of the liberal bourgeoisie to bring the political forms of the German state into line with the changed social relationships of the post-Napoleonic period. As the movement gathered momentum, the first stirrings of the German proletariat made themselves felt in the revolt of the weavers and in the spread of utopian and religious socialism. But the opening shots in the struggles between the liberal bourgeoisie and its proletarian allies against the imposing army of semi-feudal landlords, absolute monarchs in Germany and Austria, a bureaucratic officialdom, and a reactionary church, were fired on the field of philosophy and of religion.

This early period of Marx's development has more than an historic and academic interest. For, as we shall see in the course of the exposition, the doctrines and attitudes which Marx opposed in the forties of the last century still flourish to-day in distorted form as essential parts of influential contemporary ideologies.[1]

[1] This study, and subsequent ones, ought to be useful to readers of Marx's early essays, and of his *Heilige Familie* and the *Deutsche Ideologie* who are desirous of familiarising themselves with the ideological background of the period. Marx

I

THE PANTHEISTIC HUMANISM OF STRAUSS

Marx was probably the first thinker to characterise the philosophy of Kant as " the German theory of the French revolution." It set the individual self up against traditional social institutions, conscience against the church and state, practical reason over theoretical reason, the will over the idea. But lack of political unity, the slowness with which the industrial revolution took hold, the strength of the absolutist states prevented the German bourgeoisie from accomplishing, or even attempting, what the revolutionary bourgeoisie had done in England and France. The critical philosophy of Kant ended not with a call to action but with a theory of " the good will ": the discrepancies between the dictates of the moral ideal and the material class interests and needs, out of which the ideal developed, were harmonised in some transcendental sphere.

Hegel continued the work of Kant. But with an important difference. He sought to justify bourgeois society not on the basis of the " good will," " abstract reason " and " the rights of man "—for, taken seriously, this meant bloody business, as the French terror had shown—but on the basis of a metaphysics of history. According to this metaphysic, as we have seen in the preceding chapter, the development of the natural and social world reveals a plan which is both necessary and reasonable. True freedom consists in submitting to the inner necessities which are gradually working themselves out in social institutions and not in attempting to force matters by revolutionary action. In this way Hegel sought to reconcile the objective antagonism between the developing bourgeois society in Germany and its out-moded semi-feudal political system.

The Young-Hegelians at the outset regarded themselves as orthodox Hegelians. But by stressing the element of continuous dialectical change, they drew political consequences from Hegel's system which were closer to the revolutionary philosophy of the

himself supplies the socio-economic analysis of this ideology, but since he was writing for contemporaries, he assumes familiarity with the doctrines he is criticising. Stenning's translations of some of Marx's early essays under the title of *Selected Essays* (1926) are incomplete and inaccurate.

French Enlightenment than to the official conservatism of their master. Their great theoretical advantage over the Enlightenment was their historical approach to all social institutions, especially religion. Whereas the French materialists sought to refute religion and the absolutistic state by " logic," the Young-Hegelians attempted to show that traditional religions and political institutions—once historically justified—had become irrational in virtue of their own historical development.

Their historical approach, however, suffered from a threefold defect. First, it was abstract: it considered the development of theological doctrine in independence of (a) the institutional activities of the church with which church dogmas were often closely connected, and (b) other bodies of doctrine—jural, philosophical, social—which were pervaded with religious notions. Second, it was idealistic: it did not search for the origins of religious thought and practice in the material culture of the age; and where it did recognise the relation between religion and the social order, it did not inquire into the linkage between the elaborate techniques of religion and the material wants of the everyday economic life of man. Third, it was fatalistic: it regarded the historical process as automatic, carried on either (a) by no men at all but by pure Spirit, or (b) by certain individual leaders, the key to whose appearance in world history was a secret of Spirit.

The ideological struggles of the Young-Hegelians against the whole array of post-Kantian philosophies were first fought out on the field of religious criticism before the combatants grasped the social and political implications of their respective positions. It was only when Feuerbach and Marx came on the scene that it was fully realised that the criticism of religion could only be completed by radical social criticism.[1] Questions apparently so remote from the needs of daily practice as the relative priority of the Gospels, their historical credibility, and the roots of religious belief in general, were shown to involve in their chain of assumptions and consequences, definite attitudes to the existing social and political order. It was not accidental that Metternich met the first attempt at higher criticism of the

[1] *Zur Kritik der Hegelschen Rechtsphilosophie*, Marx, *Gesamtausgabe*, Abt. I, Vol. I, p. 607.

Bible with political persecution. For he believed that the challenge to the principle of authority, when generalised, involved the collapse not only of the sacredness of the church and the absolutism of the state—but what was more dangerous—the sacredness of property rights as well.[1]

Religion had always professed a metaphysical dualism. Its chief concern *seemed* to be with other-worldly affairs. The Young-Hegelians charged that this concealed the way in which religion's threefold emphasis upon authority, tradition, and renunciation strengthened the political and social props of the existing order. How could religion function in this concrete manner, the Young-Hegelians were later to ask, unless it was in some definite way continuous with past and present forms of social activity ? The primary objective of the Young-Hegelian movement, as a philosophy of religion, was to discover the character of this continuity by submitting the specific texts, doctrines, and practices of organised religion to a searching immanent criticism. On the basis of investigations which will be discussed in detail below, they concluded that religion was a fantastic and compensatory expression of the nature of man; and that it arose and endured in the course of a prolonged and unconscious struggle on the part of human beings to adjust themselves to an irrational and inhuman social environment. A critical analysis of religion, then, was at the same time a radical criticism of the world out of which it had arisen. For in the words of Marx, when he was just breaking away from the circle of Young-Hegelian thought, religion was an inverted expression " of the general theory of this [social] world, its encyclopædic compendium, its logic in popular form, its spiritualistic *point d'honneur*, its enthusiasm, its solemn completion and moral sanction, the fundamental source of its consolation and justification."[2]

[1] Metternich was a more astute statesman than is commonly realised. He maintained that the real struggle was not between the conservatives and the liberals, who thought they could stop with the introduction of religious freedom and political democracy, but between the conservatives and the revolutionists who wanted to carry liberal principles to their logical conclusion. In refusing the demands of the liberals Metternich believed that he was defending their own best interests against those who stood behind them—the social revolutionists. Cf. his *Nachgelassenen Papiere*, Bd. 4, p. 90 *et passim*; Bd. 7, p. 402 *et passim*. He would have agreed with Marx's statement: " The mortgage, held by the peasant on the heavenly estates, guarantees the mortgage held by the bourgeoisie on the peasant estates " (*Class Struggles in France*, 1848–50, Eng. trans., p. 112).

[2] Marx, *Gesamtausgabe*, Abt. I, Bd. 1, p. 607.

But this emphasis on the political and social implications of religious criticism marked the last phase of a development which began much more innocently, though with sufficient repercussions, with the writings of David Friedrich Strauss. Strauss published his epoch-making *Leben Jesu* in 1835. This was the same year in which the railway was introduced into Germany,[1] and in which Gutzkow, the leader of Young-Germany, issued his sensational novel of social doubt and revolt, *Wally oder die Zweiflerin*. Each one of these events was a different storm centre of the same general movement against the entrenched authority of the semi-feudal teutonic states. Controversy raged fiercest, however, around Strauss. Railways could justify themselves by profits as well as by their extreme usefulness in military service; the writings of Young-Germany were really more amusing than dangerous. But there was nothing in Strauss' work to compensate for his devastating critique of the sacred dogmas of Christianity.

Strauss cut under the prevailing interpretations of the Gospel by raising questions which neither the rationalistic nor the ethical schools, which were still working with the " common sense " assumptions of the Enlightenment, dared to ask. The rationalists were striving to gloss over the discrepancies between our ordinary experience and the deliverances of the " sacred book " by interpreting the latter in terms of common-day knowledge. The fall of man, for example, was explained as the natural consequence of eating poisoned fruit which fundamentally impaired the human digestive system. Christ's raising of the dead was explained as resulting from his superior medical knowledge, etc. The ethical interpretation sought to show that the incidents reported in the Bible were the expression of profound and eternal moral truths. Thus, Kant in trying to explain away the Psalmist's prayer of violent hatred against one's enemies, maintained that enemies here referred to our own unruly passions. Of both these uncritical ways of abusing

---

[1] After he had taken his first railway journey, Strauss wrote to his friend Rapp, " Five hours in half an hour. Impressive significance of the modern miracle, dreamy consciousness during the modern flight. *No fear but a feeling of inner kinship between my own* principles and that of the discovery " (*Ausgewählte Briefe*, herausgegeben von Zeller, p. 103). In one of his interesting letters to Græber in 1839, Engels draws a picture of a locomotive and labels it *Zeitgeist* (Marx-Engels, *Gesamtausgabe*, Abt. I, Bd. 2, p. 524).

clear texts, Strauss made short shrift. Let us examine, he declared, what it is the writers of the Gospels actually said before we go on to assert what it is they " really " meant. The sober task which he set himself in his *Leben Jesu* was " to investigate the internal grounds of credibility in relation to each detail given in the Gospels and to test the probability and improbability of their being the production of eye-witnesses, or of competently informed writers."[1]

1. *The " Mythical " Interpretation of Religion*

Strauss' conclusions were radical, cogent, and clear. With brilliant critical acumen and monumental learning, he proved that the gospel accounts were so inherently contradictory that there was not the slightest logical grounds to regard them as credible historical narratives. But then how explain the *existence* of these narratives ? In his answer Strauss develops his philosophy of religion. The gospels are the result of the *myth-making consciousness* of the Christian community reared in the tradition of the Old Testament. They were constructed on the models of the miraculous tales and prophecies which were part of that tradition. Until now the orthodox Christians had maintained that what distinguished Christianity from all other religions was precisely the fact that *it* was historical while the others were mythical. But Strauss showed with unanswerable logic that its historical dogmas, as history, had no more justification than the superstitions of the Hottentots. He did *not* say that the evangelical myths were intentional fictions, nor that the *essence* of Christian faith was affected by his criticism. Like the good Hegelian he was, he pronounced Christianity the most adequate and intelligible symbol of the ideal truths of philosophy. He differed from Hegel in denying that the religious symbol or myth could be rationally deduced, or that formal truth could be intelligibly predicated of it. According to Strauss, whoever asked whether religious myth is true or false must put the same question to poetry.

It is clear that on this interpretation, the myths themselves

---

[1] p. 70. All page references to *Leben Jesu* are to the English translation by Miriam Evans (George Eliot), 6th ed., London, 1913.

are not so important as the source and carrier of the myth, i.e. the community. The secret of the myth is to be found in the way the community lives, in its hopes, traditions and fears. The history of the religious myth is the history of the community which has nurtured it. Out of it religious doctrines are born. The doctrines can only be understood and criticised in the light of their development. In both his *Leben Jesu* and in his even more brilliantly philosophical *Die Christliche Glaubenslehre in ihrer geschichtlichen Entwicklung und in Kampf mit der modernen Wissenschaft* (Thüringen, 1840) he traces that development, defending as his main thesis, the proposition that: " The true criticism of dogmas lies in their history." Using the history of Christian theology as the specific foil to his general argument, he sketches in bold strokes the way in which the diffuse and amorphous folk-lore of the community hardens into definite doctrines.

The community begins with naïve beliefs, expressed not so much at the outset as belief, but as vague myth. Just as in youth we poetise our feelings rather than clarify our ideas, so the community as a whole when *it* is young and not yet weighed down by the tyranny of formulated tradition. And just as the obscure imaginings of the youth are a clue to the nature of his personality, so do the characteristic strivings of the community, its national ambitions, traditional experiences, its burden of sorrows and songs of hope, express themselves in its religious myths. Each individual as a member of the community feels streaming through him this " mythical " consciousness. It serves as a guide, a model, an inner conscience until the world at length becomes too complex for it. Something more definite is needed to integrate conduct. Then these myths are written down and appear as naïve *beliefs*. But as beliefs, since they are expressed in loose terms which, in a changing world, of necessity become ambiguous, they have a way of altering their character. In order to fix their meaning, beliefs are fastened to set *symbols*. But man with the first gleam of sophistication cannot worship symbols without striving to understand what it is they symbolise. These fixed symbols are now attached to clear, simple, naïve *doctrines*. The germ of a system of religious thought is born. The naïve doctrine becomes a fixed church *dogma*. The growth of knowledge in other fields tends to challenge dogma. Dogma follows dogma. In that succession, the dogmas receive their real criticism. It is a history which is impartial in virtue of its successive partialities. Finally the critical spirit revolting against the dogmas in one field which contradict its experiences in another, becomes conscious of another path by which the truths of religion may be saved. It rejects the *idea* of dogma. It distinguishes between the letter of the text and the spirit, the form of the ritual and its ideal content, the visible and the temporal in the life of man as opposed to the invisible and the eternal. The process of criticism becomes central. At this point, the substance of belief is subordinated to the subject who believes. The subject who believes realises that his beliefs do not come from the blue, that they have a history and that he himself has an origin in a metaphysical substance or unity— the human species—which renews itself through perpetual activity. And so in the course of time, the ancient Hebrew myth or legend of a god of thunder and lightning standing outside of the world, develops into the belief in an immanent process of development of a supreme logical Idea; the whims and humours of Jehovah become metaphysical attributes and then natural laws; a thin ascetic morality of non-participation becomes an allegiance to ethical use and wont, to a social morality; the glorification of the church gives way to the glorification of the state. We have begun with Genesis and ended with Hegel.

2. *The Social Absolute and Man-God in Strauss*

As an Hegelian, Strauss was compelled to reinterpret the traditional concept of divinity. Its locus could no longer be found in something transcendant to the social process. Creative power must arise from within the existing world. It cannot be breathed in from without. In his attempt to convert the term, divine, from a description of man's presumed origin, into an attribute of his goal, Strauss was struggling against the disastrous effects of religious dualism—a dualism which begins by separating human nature from the divine and then fruitlessly seeks ways of bringing them together again. Metaphysically, such dualism cuts the cord of connection between the ideal and the real, the descriptive and the normative, time and eternity. Strictly taken, it narrows the sphere and influence of human activity. Of course no religious dualism has ever been absolute, that is to say, metaphysically consistent. The notion of reward and punishment establishes at least one relation between this world and the next. Its conception of Heaven—which is built up by moving to it the furniture of earth—is another.

Christianity, so Strauss maintained, was the first great religion to claim that it had overcome metaphysical dualism. This was the purport of its doctrine of the unity of human and divine consciousness in the person of Christ, the God-man. The divinity and humanity of Christ were the foci of intersection, so to speak, between heaven and earth. For many centuries philosophical apologists accepted this as a solution of the traditional difficulties. But it gradually became clear that from a standpoint genuinely opposed to dualism, it was necessary to regard the divine and human spirit as one and the same, not only in *essence*, but in *existence*. From which it followed that if Christ, the divine, was human, then all humans were divine or Christ-*like*. Yet the Bible and the church doctrine taught that the human spirit and the divine spirit were two distinct things and were held together in Christ only by the tie of his personality. Christ alone was both the God-man and the Man-god.[1] The only way to conquer the dualism in this connection, urged Strauss, was to substitute humanity, the species, the race as the exemplification of the Man-god. The apotheosis of the God-man then becomes the apotheosis of humanity.

" If reality is ascribed to the idea of the unity of the divine and human nature, is this equivalent to the admission that this unity must actually have been *once* manifested, as it never had been, and never more will be in one individual ? This is indeed not the mode in which the Idea realised itself; it is not wont to lavish all its fullness on one exemplar, and be niggardly towards all others—to express itself perfectly in that one individual and imperfectly in all the rest. It rather loves to distribute its riches among a multiplicity of exemplars

[1] *Glaubenslehre*, Vol. I, p. 30.

which reciprocally complete each other—in the alternate appearance and suppression of a series of individuals. And is this no true realisation for the Idea? Is not the idea of unity of the divine and human natures a real one in a far higher sense, when I regard the whole race of mankind as its realisation, than when I single out one man as such a realisation? Is not an incarnation of God from eternity, a truer one than incarnation limited to a particular point of time? "[1]

But this was curing matters with alarming means. It seemed to be saving Christianity from dualism by converting it into an unchristian doctrine. It destroyed one of its most vital beliefs— the belief in a personal, active, creative Deity. Strauss was skating here on thin ice, especially for one who still professed himself a Christian. He defended himself by showing that from the standpoint of philosophy the objections which the Greeks had raised against the conception of an active God were insurmountable. A God who creates by an act of free will, rests and then creates again, is at the moment of creation a different creature from what he is at the moment of rest. He falls under the category of the mutable, the finite, the temporal. It is not an escape from the difficulty to say that his activity must be understood as an eternal activity. For even so, how could it explain why God operated with natural laws at one time, and with miracles at another? No philosopher could pretend to *prove* the dogma of original creation.[2] He could only interpret it —could only save verbal appearances by altering the essential meaning. So Hegel. So Strauss. But Strauss called attention to what he was doing. And he claimed that Hegel had done the same.

It is no exaggeration to say that Strauss irretrievably bankrupted the Hegelian stock in the German market and contributed, as one contemporary remarked, to driving Hegelians from " the paradise of German university appointments." Here was a lineal descendant of Hegel using the Hegelian method and Hegelian arguments to prove the presence of the divine in the carnal, to show that sin is necessary to the highest beatitudes of virtue, and to interpret holiness as a rational worldliness, not as a preparation for heaven. There was a social challenge behind all

[1] *Leben Jesu*, pp. 770–80.   [2] *Glaubenslehre*, Vol. I, p. 59.

his arid exegesis. It would sometimes break forth like a tongue of fire in a pall of smoke. " The earth is no longer a vale of tears through which we journey towards a goal existing in a future heaven. The treasures of divine life are to be realised here and now, for every moment of our earthly life pulses within the womb of the divine."[1]

3. *Strauss' Philosophy of History*

Strauss' philosophy of history can easily be read off as a corollary from his philosophy of religion. It is an idealistic variety of evolutionary optimism closely patterned on Hegel's model. The meaning of history is cumulatively revealed in the succession of empirical events. It shows that man is coming of age, or in the jargon of the period, that humanity is progressively attaining self-consciousness. Strauss, however, had not yet given an empirical interpretation of consciousness. He was yet to write *Der alte und neue Glaube* in which he whole-heartedly embraced naturalism. But there is a greater sensitiveness to detail in Strauss than in Hegel. There is no *Vergewaltigung* of inconvenient historical fact. And there is a greater emphasis on the absolute process than on the absolute result.

Nevertheless the three fundamental principles of Strauss' philosophy of history indicate how close Strauss is to Hegel, despite their differences on specific questions of theology. (1) History is a record of the conquest of the human spirit over intractable material. The historical process consists in humanising ever wider fields of social life on ever higher levels. (2) An adequate explanation of any specific expression in which this process realises itself cannot be found in one particular factor but in the *system as a whole*, in the " substantial," the universal pattern. This pattern is like the structure of a melody without which the notes (particular acts) would be so many noises (meaningless). (3) The efficient agent of historical development is the community. Individuals, without being conscious of it, are carriers of historical ideas. Their subjective interests cancel each other in the objective rhythms of social development.[2]

---

[1] *Glaubenslehre*, Vol. I, p. 68.
[2] Strauss, *Streitschriften*, Vol. III, pp. 125 ff.; cf. Koigen, D., *Vorgeschichte des modernen philosophischen Socialismus*, 1901, pp. 33–4.

The community both creates and criticises " objective mind " or the cultural absolute.[1]

4. *Strauss and Marx*

Marx, as distinct from Engels, was never an enthusiastic follower of Strauss.[2] In fact he criticises him in *Die deutsche Ideologie* as one of the Young-Hegelians who had mistaken the limits of religious criticism, as one whose criticism, because it did not eventuate in practice, was still pervaded by a religious spirit. Strauss, according to Marx, believed that the struggle for a new world had been won once it could be established that the dominant views in law, politics and culture were expressions of a religious attitude. Both the Young-Hegelians and their opponents shared a fundamental premise which was more significant than their differences. They both believed " in the supremacy of religion, of Ideas, of the universal, in the existing world. Their only quarrel was whether this supremacy was a usurpation or whether it could be recognised as legitimate. . . . It never suggested itself to any of these philosophers to inquire as to the connection between German philosophy and the existing realities in Germany, to ask what was the relation between their own criticism and the material environment."[3]

We shall return to this important line of criticism in our discussion of the relation between Marx and Bauer, Stirner and Feuerbach. Here we wish to point out that Marx owed an indirect debt to Strauss in that the latter's critical use of the Hegelian philosophy of religion prepared the way for Feuerbach's later work. Both Feuerbach and Marx transcended Strauss' position but they did so by using his methodological principle of monism more widely, consistently, and critically

[1] " The subjective criticism of the individual is a fountain spray which any child can stop for a while; but the criticism which objectively develops in the course of centuries dashes on like a mighty swirling torrent against which all sluices and dams are in vain " (*Glaubenslehre*, Vol. I, p. x).

[2] Up to 1844 Engels never lost an opportunity to declare his allegiance to, and admiration for, Strauss. His early letters are full of exclamatory eulogy. *See* Marx-Engels, *Gesamtausgabe*, Abt. I, Bd. 2, esp. pp. 546, 538, 525, 562, 555. I quote a typical passage. " I have sworn fealty to the flag of D. F. Strauss and have become a first-class mythologist. I tell you Strauss is a grand fellow (*herrliche Kerl*). His genius and subtlety are beyond comparison " (p. 546).

[3] *Gesamtausgabe*, Abt. I, Bd. 5, pp. 9, 10.

than did Strauss himself. Strauss, to be sure, was an idealist. But he later confessed that he had always regarded the opposition between materialism and idealism as verbal. The decisive question was, and is, " dualism or monism." Both consistent idealism and materialism have a common opponent, he writes, " in the dualism which had become the ruling conception throughout the whole Christian era, a dualism which split man's soul from his body, divorced his existence in time from his existence in eternity, and set over against the created and transitory world, an eternal creative God." Both idealism and materialism are monistic, in that they explain things on the basis of one leading principle. One operates with material forces, the other with ideas and ideal relations. The weakness of idealism is that it refuses to descend from its heights of abstraction and submit its insights into how the world is put together to the controlled tests of physical sciences. Materialism cannot be regarded as a satisfactory philosophy until it provides an adequate account of man's cultural and spiritual life.[1] Such was Strauss' position. Marx carried this programme further by attempting to develop a critical materialism which would explain man's social and historical behaviour as adequately as scientific materialism explained the behaviour of man as a physical body or biological organism.

5. *The Revolutionary Theology of Bruno Bauer*

If Strauss was responsible for discrediting Hegel in the eyes of educational authority, Bruno Bauer, the friend and teacher of Karl Marx, was the man who compelled the Prussian State to issue a secret decree forbidding Hegelians to lecture on all subjects but æsthetics. Starting out as an orthodox Hegelian of the extreme right and as a conservative critic of Strauss, Bauer developed so far to the left that he was soon saying of Strauss what Strauss was saying of the fundamentalists. His *Kritik der evangelischen Geschichte der Synoptiker* (3 vols. 1841–2) represents the high-water mark of the higher biblical criticism of his day. Its doctrines will be best appreciated when compared with those of Strauss.

[1] Cf. *Der alte und neue Glaube*, Sec. 66. Also *Ausgewählte Briefe*, p. 542.

The chief weakness of Strauss' *Leben Jesu,* in the light of his own assumptions, was that he had not evaluated his sources. Instead of critically weighing the documents as such and assigning relative values of credibility to them, he had taken them all on their face value, catalogued the many contradictions between them and introduced the myth-making consciousness of the community to explain how these contradictions arose. Bauer pointed out that Strauss had operated with a conventional assumption that anything which seemed to violate the rule of natural law could not have occurred. But the Gospels also reported significant events which did not involve miraculous intercession, e.g. that there was a man Jesus, who lived in Galilee and was crucified at Golgotha. Why believe this if it is recorded in the very same documents which contain an account of extraordinary events rejected as incredible? Either all the documents must be accepted or rejected and all the reports declared true or false; or else a critical evaluation of the texts themselves must be undertaken to determine where they could be believed and where not.[1]

Since Strauss had neglected to do this, Bauer branded his mythical point of view as " mysterious," illogical, and tinctured with not a little religiosity.[2] Bauer's own approach to the gospels was as critically matter of fact as the approach to any other important *human* document. The only presuppositions he brought to his work were that the same canons of historical criticism which enable us to determine, say, whether or not Diogenes Laertius' *Lives of the Philosophers* is an accurate or credible report of the history of its subjects, could be applied here, too. Strauss should have taken as his point of departure, said Bauer, the work of Weisse and Wilke on the relative priority of the different gospels, instead of introducing the idea of saga or tradition. He should have sought the key to the constructions of early Christianity in the personalities of the evangelists themselves—in their personal interest, aims and character. " He who speaks of the Saga and tradition in the manner of Strauss

---

[1] It is interesting to note that the famous Tübingen theologian, Ferdinand Christian Baur, who had been Strauss' teacher, passed the same immanent criticism upon Strauss as Bauer did. Cf. his *Kritische Untersuchungen über die kanonischen Evangelien*, Tübingen, 1847, pp. 147 ff.

[2] *Synoptiker*, I, p. vi. ff.

. . . deprives himself of the right to raise the question . . . how in the world was it possible for tradition to accomplish what was attributed to it."[1] Bauer's own conclusions were that the gospels had not been written independently of one another, but that the writer of the Fourth Gospel (John) had borrowed from Luke, and that both Luke and Matthew had themselves merely elaborated upon Mark. In other words we had really only one account and three imitations. Of these imitations, Bauer remarks, " Here not the saga has ruled but simply and solely the writer."

Strauss had been careful enough to say that " the controversial problems as to whether the myths proceed from the individual or community, from the poet or the people is not essential." But Bauer vigorously protests that this makes textual criticism impossible, since "the community possesses no hands with which to compose, no power of judgment to fuse relevant details into a unity."[2] It is only the individual who has creative power and not the brooding mystical consciousness of the community. Tradition plays only a subsidiary rôle.

Why were Bauer's conclusions so startling? (1) Because on the basis of documentary analysis, and not on metaphysical dogma, he denied the *historicity* of Christ as well as his divinity. " In the prophecy as well as in the fulfilment, the Messiah was only an ideal product of religious consciousness. As an actually given individual he never existed."[3] (2) Because he rejected the idea of an unconscious mythical creation as superstitious; instead of going back to the early Jewish tales of the Messiah for the tradition of the Christ legend, he investigated the purposes of the individual evangelists. (3) Because he maintained that the evangelists were to be classed with men like Hesiod and Homer, of whom Herodotus had said that they created the Greek Gods. These conclusions were defended by the most toilsome of labour, in a manner which, although lacking the literary brilliance of Strauss, was more scholarly and judicious.

A concrete example will best illustrate the difference between the methods of Strauss and Bauer. All the four gospels relate

[1] The best statement of the methodological issues between Strauss and B. Bauer will be found in the latter's criticism of the 4th edition of *Leben Jesu* in the *Deutsche Jahrbücher*, 1842, p. 664.

[2] *Synoptiker*, I, pp. 27, 71, 162. [3] Ibid., III, p. 14, cf. p. 247.

that Jesus was anointed by a woman. Each one, however, gives a different version of the incident—on the assumption that it is the same incident. In treating of the problem which grew out of these discrepancies, Strauss takes the position that the variations in the evangelical account can only be explained on the supposition that they had been unconsciously transformed by the successive traditions of the community. The critic's duty was to establish " which one of these accounts is nearest the original fact." What fact ? asked Bauer. We have not yet reached a fact. We are confronted only with four different historical *accounts*. Why should the assumption be introduced so suddenly that the communal tradition acted as a refracting medium upon the reported fact ? You must first catch your fact before you can distort it. Is it not more logical, inquires Bauer, to examine these conflicting reports in themselves to see *what* it is they report and *how* they report it ? And what does our examination disclose ? That in the written reports, the structure of the sentences, the turn of the phrase, the very words chosen, are so similar that in all probability the reports were not written independently of one another. Instead of four independent observations we have on key matters only *one* original report and three poorly concealed paraphrases. The critic's task is to distinguish between them and the original, which happens to be Mark. Once he has done this, the variations in the other three paraphrases are to be explained by the character of the persons transcribing from the original report. We find that the same type of variation is consistently present in all three paraphrases. If we take a central incident from Mark we can almost anticipate the kind of deviation—if there are deviations—which we shall find in Luke or John. The same technique must be adopted towards emendations and omissions. After we are through with all this preliminary work, and *only* then, are we logically entitled to raise the question which Strauss tackled at the very beginning, viz., the relation between the original report and the actual incident, if there was an actual incident. Bauer completed his argument by asserting that the gospel of Mark must be dismissed as inherently incredible— so glaring were the internal contradictions, so artificial the constructions, so strained the interpretation.

6. *Bauer's Radical Atheism*

The difference between Strauss and Bauer involved more than disputes between two learned exegetists. Essential questions were in issue. Strauss felt that he was fulfilling the spirit of Christianity by making it philosophically more liberal; Bauer was convinced that he had destroyed the historical basis of Christianity and uprooted all religion root and branch. Strauss soon won a following among theologians, Even the orthodox could accept some of his conclusions. For although he played off against one another the contradictions in the four gospel accounts, he had to admit that on some matters there was unanimous agreement among them. And these facts upon which there was agreement, coming on Strauss' own presupposition from four *independent* sources, carried great logical weight. Christianity could content itself with believing those things on which all four gospels agreed. But Bauer, by showing that we are dealing with one report and three distorted versions, pulled the logical prop from under the facts of agreement. We are dealing with the tale of one "eye-witness" whose inconsistencies, credulities and ignorance we now judge in a significantly different way.

Then, too, Strauss' "mythical" standpoint opened the door to a higher mysticism, to another type of reconciliation between faith and reason. Bauer, as far as his method (in contradistinction to his metaphysics) was concerned, was soberly naturalistic and could legitimately criticise Strauss' position for not being critical enough. "Strauss' mistake was not that he set a general force into movement (tradition) but that he conceived it to operate in a purely general way. Such an attitude is still religious and miraculous, the reassertion of a religious point of view in a critical position. It is religious ingratitude and cruelty towards self-consciousness."[1] A Christian might make peace with Strauss but from Bauer he was separated by an abyss. Strauss had left a back-door open to theology. And it was the very nature of a theologian, the Young-Hegelians said, to keep an eye open for a back door. But Bauer was a Samson straining at the pillars of theology. Strauss' attack cost him at most an academic post. Bauer's works were matters for the police. And not without

[1] B. Bauer, *Die gute Sache der Freiheit und meine eigene Gelegenheit* (1842), p. 118.

reason, for though, as we shall see, the main impact of Bauer's thought, as a whole, was reactionary, his criticism of religion was a revolutionary force.

The open implication of B. Bauer's position was atheism. Hegel had undermined the philosophical basis of religion; now its historical justification had been exploded. Nothing was left but critical method and the free spirit which was to wield that method against the reign of religious principles in every branch of culture. We know that Bauer together with Marx planned to found a society of atheism. Voices were soon heard protesting that the negative results of Bauer's philosophy of religion, even if justified, were only valid against the *specific content of a specific religion*, and that he failed to appreciate the importance of a religious *need* and the necessity of gratifying it. One critic wrote, " It is foolishness to attempt to set up a philosophy in place of religion. . . . He who wants to destroy religion must supply another."[1] Bauer realised, however, that the use of the critical method alone could never justify a positive creed in the realm of faith. Complete negations were easier to defend than half-hearted assertions. Especially when those assertions had to serve both as literal truths and poetic symbols depending upon the exigencies of the controversy. He set about to ground his refusal to be positive. " If I dissolve one limit must I erect another ? " he asked. " Must he who atones for one crime forthwith commit another ? If I have revealed the lies and hypocrisies of theology is it necessary for me to invent new ones ? "[2] It is not a question of abolishing one particular limitation upon the human spirit but all limitations; not one religion but all religion. Nor is it a case of substituting philosophy or art or poetry for religion. Nothing has to be substituted, for nothing has been taken away save an illusion. An illusion is a psychic disease. But when a man is cured of one disease, the cure is certainly not produced by infecting him permanently with another. As a critical philosopher Bauer is wary of committing himself to principles which are not self-affirming. The only principle to which he can pledge categorical allegiance is the principle of criticism itself.

Marx was right when he pointed out in *Die heilige Familie*[3]

---

[1] Gruppe, quoted by Bauer, *Die gute Sache* . . . , p. 201.
[2] Ibid., p. 201.   [3] *Gesamtausgabe*, Abt. I, Bd. 3, p. 315.

that the differences between Strauss and Bauer were a family quarrel among absolute idealists. What Bauer had done was to seize upon the element of activity in the Hegelian system and attempt to deduce from its cyclical convolutions the historical facts of nature and society. Strauss, on the other hand, had started with the Hegelian system and explained activity as a progressive revelation of an antecedently existing logical pattern. If we regard the Hegelian philosophy as a synthesis of the Spinozistic doctrine of substance and the Fichtean principle of activity, then we are justified in considering the work of Strauss as marking a reversion to Spinoza, and the philosophy of critical and creative self-consciousness in Bauer as a return to Fichte.

7. *The Terrorism of Reason*

Bauer proceeded to carry over the critical attitude to other fields. He called his method atheistic because it denied any kind of doctrinal and institutional authority. The critic has no presuppositions. " *Reine Kritik heisse Voraussetszunglos*," wrote the brother of Bauer. The laws of logic and the principle of consistency were to be the instruments of human liberation. They were not themselves presuppositions which needed testing, but self-evident propositions. The critic's task is to reveal the inevitable inconsistency between what we think and how we behave ; to show that all existing human institutions function inhumanly; to suggest that things could be different without trying to make them different; in fact to demonstrate that any kind of action, except intellectual analysis, uncritically neglects other possible ways of acting equally legitimate *logically*. Not that Bauer did not believe that the world should be changed. Indeed he tried to prove that since it was logically inconsistent it *must* be changed. But changed by taking thought ! " The true and pure critic," he wrote, " never puts his hand to anything (*legt ja niemals selbst Hand an*)."[1] His task is to struggle for the consistency of our ideals and to oppose all attempts to compromise their immaculate purity by realising them in action. " The ideal is already realised in itself. Its reality consists in being an ideal in and for itself. It is the only reality which can

[1] *Allgemeine Literatur Zeitung*, Heft 11–12, p. 44.

exist in the realm of thought. The ideal is thought and *as such* first elevates things to their true reality."[1]

What is this ideal? And how could Bruno Bauer conceal from himself the fact that he had his own presuppositions? The ideal is freedom. Bauer denies that freedom is an uncritical prejudice since it has no definite meaning. Anyone can define it for himself. And for Bauer, it is sometimes mere self-consciousness, sometimes the separation of the state from the Christian church, sometimes social reform, and most often, merely the right to assert the principle of freedom. Once dissolve the dogmas of religion in the mordant solution of criticism and all things human will develop freely.

> " Once religion is overthrown it is not a question of philosophy but of humanity. The several goods of humanity— art, science, and the State—form a systematic whole in which no particular one rules absolutely and exclusively. . . . They cannot so rule if they are to avoid new evils. All of them, after having been fought by religion to the death, will become finally free and develop without restraint."[2]

This rather vaguely foreshadowed free development of human nature and institutions—unhampered by anything external to the natural processes of life and mind—is presented as the logical consequence of the principle of critical atheism. Human struggle will no longer be a clash between the blind, opaque forces of tradition on the one hand and the logic of criticism on the other; it will represent an unvarying process of conscious development, social and personal. Struggle there must be, for else the life of criticism will be over. But it will be a struggle between what *has* already been achieved and what *can be* achieved; between the consciousness of the present and our desire to live in it, and the urge to prepare for a present to come. Self-knowledge will be man's first and last virtue. And since man is always developing, complete self-knowledge becomes an eternal yet unattainable ideal. The critical processes grind on for ever. Whenever the institutional expressions of the self-consciousness of yesterday resist the attack of the critical self-consciousness of to-day, a fever arises in the body politic. There

[1] *Allgemeine Literatur Zeitung*, p. 40.   [2] *Die gute Sache . . .* , p. 203.

is confusion and delirium. "Criticism is the crisis which breaks man's delirium and brings him again to a recognition of himself."[1]

There was a sound empirical kernel obscured in this transcendental mythology. It needed a social, materialistic base. But Bauer was unable to develop it. As a consequence, his refusal to recognise the essential unity between theory and practice made his sweeping negations not only harmless to existing social iniquities but even positively dangerous to the attempts to begin actual reform. From his standpoint of theoretical intransigence, he hurled charges of inconsistency against all those who accepted the existing order to be better able to change it. The more violent his declamatory tirade against authority, the more impatient he was with those who had begun to forge from the weapons of criticism, real weapons of social combat. Unwittingly he became a practical social force, giving direct aid to the reactionary tendencies of his day even when mouthing the most revolutionary phrases. " The terrorism of pure theory," he wrote to Marx in 1841, " must clear the ground clean."[2] In the following chapter, we look a little closer at what that terrorism accomplished.

[1] *Die gute Sache* . . . , p. 204.   [2] *Gesamtausgabe*, Abt. I, Bd. 1, Pt. 2, p. 247.

CHAPTER III

BRUNO BAUER AND KARL MARX

I

THE REVOLUTIONARY POLITICS OF BRUNO BAUER

KARL MARX prefaces his excoriating attack upon his former teacher—an attack which he significantly entitles *Kritik der Kritischen Kritik*—with the following words:

> " Realistic humanism has in Germany no more dangerous enemy than that variety of spiritualism or speculative idealism which in place of real individual human beings has set ' self-consciousness ' or ' spirit,' and taught with the evangelists that the spirit is life and the body of no account. It is clear that this bodiless spirit has spirit only in its imagination. What we oppose in the criticism of Bauer is the speculation which reproduces itself as a caricature. It seems to us to be the completest expression of the Christian-Germanic principle which is attempting to retain its supremacy by transforming ' criticism ' itself into a transcendental power " (Marx-Engels, *Gesamtausgabe*, Abt. I, Bd. 3, p. 179).

What was there in Bauer's position to call forth these words and a book of several hundred large, closely printed pages of refutation ? It was not only the *consistency* of Bauer's doctrines which Marx questioned. What interested Marx primarily was their impact upon the central political and social problems of the day, their relation to Marx's own gradually maturing revolutionary purposes and their bearing upon the possibility of organising a mass movement. We must therefore examine some of the views upheld by Bauer and the members of his school.

1. *Bauer's Anti-Liberalism*

Marx somewhere says of the Germans of his day, echoing a remark of Heine's, that out of pure respect for the Idea they did not attempt to realise it. A *cult* grows up around the idea, not a social movement. The characterisation is quite apposite of Bauer. " Be critical of all things but do nothing," expressed his attitude towards the church, the state, and society. He had proved that religion was an expression of man's uncritical consciousness trying to feel at home in a world it did not understand. He had claimed that the church was the chief obstacle to developing the critical consciousness which was man's greatest good. We should expect that in conformity with his theories he would at least urge the immediate withdrawal of critical spirits from the church, and the official separation of the church and state. But with a strange dialectical twist which comes from operating with concepts that are not related to social experience, far from advocating such measures, he discourages them. Withdraw from the church ? A mere half-measure ! The church is part of the state. It is merely the external expression of the unfree Christian State which uses the church sacraments to strengthen its secular power (*Die gute Sache der Freiheit und mein eigene Gelegenheit*, p. 219). The *state* is the enemy. Withdraw from the state ? That has no meaning. How then combat the state sup-ported church and the church supported state effectively ? By proving in accordance with the strictest demands of theory that the state, too, is foreign in principle to the essence of freedom and critical self-consciousness. It is an external expression, an out-moded appearance of the human spirit. In fact the spirit of the age—an age in which the final philosophy of critical self-knowledge has been promulgated—has left the empty shell of the state far behind. True, it is therewith by no means deprived of its *power*. But what is more important, its nature is *understood*. Its essential life is over even if those who exercise state power do not know it. " Theory which has enlightened us about our own nature and which has given us the courage to be ourselves . . . has reduced the Christian state to an unessential appearance " (Ibid., p. 224).

But there were other groups in Germany who, not content with theoretical proofs that the *essence* of the state had been destroyed, attempted to modify its *existence*. In South Germany and in Königsberg a liberal bourgeois movement had arisen which demanded constitutional reforms and parliamentary privileges from the absolute Prussian state. Bauer and his group instead of making common cause with this liberal movement proved that such a demand was internally inconsistent. It accepted the existing state form and was willing to participate in it, when on its own principles, it rejected the very idea of a monarchical state.[1] True representative government could not be reconciled with the rôle of a personal sovereign even on the English model. Pure theory was compromised by such tactics. Critical self-consciousness could not stop short of anything but a radical republican democracy. Unless an *absolutely free state* could be had at one stroke, Bauer would have nothing at all. Similarly, when demands were made for the reform of the educational system in Prussia, the " pure " critics cried out that the system must be abolished, not reformed. To reform it meant to acknowledge it. Again, when agitation made itself felt for the liberalising of the marriage laws, the followers of Bauer had no difficulty in pointing out that the free spirits (Bauer's club in Berlin called itself *die Freien*) could accept nothing else but the abolition of legal marriage. The free spirit accepts and dissolves its own ties.

The whole line of attack now shifted from the theoretical discussion of first principles and the refutation of all authority to bitter criticism of those who had taken up the struggle against authority. The guillotine of pure criticism was brought to bear upon the necks of former friends and allies. It became a *perpetuum mobile*. A contemporary watching its operations wrote, " It worked by day and night and made unceasing progress over a road strewn with the corpses of former friends."[2] The liberals were muddled ! They were corrupted by practical issues ! They had betrayed their principles ! So ran the charges against them.

2. *Bauer and the Jewish Question*

A genuinely radical attitude can avoid the two extremes of " practical " reformism and revolutionary phrasemongery. Marx's searching criticism of Bauer's views on the Jewish question may well serve as an excellent example of true revolutionary

[1] Cf. *Das Juste Milieu* (E. Bauer, *Das Rheinische Zeitung*, Aug. 21, 1842).
[2] " Die Deutsche Philosophie seit Hegel's Tode " (*Die Gegenwart*, Bd. 6, 1851, p. 304).

method which seeks neither half a loaf nor a sterile ideal. All the
more so because Bauer's views on the Jewish question reveal
his position at its strongest.

For centuries the Jews had been denied political rights in
Western Europe. After the French Revolution and the German
Enlightenment, their intellectual spokesmen demanded the
removal of political and social restrictions. Napoleon had
elevated them to citizenship in France but Germany was slow
to follow. In the early forties, with the growth of commerce
and industrial expansion, the agitation on the part of reform
Judaism for political enfranchisement was again resumed. It
was caught up by all liberal elements as a good talking point
against the government. Bauer took the field against this campaign on the ground that since the demand for the extension of
civic rights to Jews still recognised in principle the difference
between Jew and Gentile, it was patently inconsistent and
infected with religious prejudice to boot (*Deutsche Jahrbücher*,
1842, p. 1094).

The Germans themselves, Bauer asserted, were politically
unfree. They were *subjects* not citizens. How then could the
Jews legitimately demand emancipation for themselves unless
they ceased claiming sectarian privileges and joined in the
common task of establishing a free and human state ? The
Christians to whom the Jews appealed for support were either
religious or not. If they were not religious, their interest was in
liberalising the entire state in the name of humanity, not in the
name of a few chosen people. Why should these free-minded
Christians aid the Jews in retaining their own religious movement when the Jews refused to aid them in their radical struggles
against the state which was the *source* of *all* discrimination ?
But if the Christians to whom the Jews appealed were themselves religious, then the Jews were asking them to surrender
their religious prejudices while clinging all the more tenaciously
to their own. As genuine Christians they *must* believe that their
religion is the true religion. Else why should they be Christians ?
But if they must believe this, then they are consistent in exclud-
ing from Christian social life those who have a different religion.
In asking them to grant to the Jews the same rights Christians
enjoyed, the Jews were asking them to cease being Christians.

But the Jews were not willing to cease being Jews. This was a peculiar asymmetrical logic and ethics.

The Jewish problem, Bauer went on to say, can only be solved when the religious problem is solved. The religious problem can only be solved by overthrowing the logical foundations of faith and destroying the Christian state. The Jews can only become truly human by first becoming atheists. It is only as atheists that they acquire the capacity of being free citizens.[1] The church must at least be separated from the state before the Jews can be emancipated. But they must demand that separation as human beings, conscious of the community of their political interests with other human beings, and not as Jews.

Marx begins his critical discussion by pointing out that Bauer has confused several important issues. What is *political* emancipation after all ? And why does it demand religious emancipation as its precondition ? Does not political emancipation in France and especially in America show that even when the state is nominally free and separated from the church, religion still flourishes like a green bay tree ? There is no inconsistency on the part of the Jews in demanding political privileges and the right to retain their Judaism. For even the democratic, atheistic state of Bauer recognises, as an inalienable human right, the freedom to worship as one pleases. Bauer's error is that he does not see that it is not the so-called Christian state but rather the so-called free and democratic state which permits the whole of social life to be pervaded by religious principles. The essence of religion is the dualistic organisation of human life, the splitting up of individuality into isolated cultural spheres, the dislocation of the creative centres by subjecting man to inhuman circumstances, the fetishism of what were once valid techniques into magic rites and symbols. Organised religion is not the cause of social maladjustment and discrimination but its effect; *religious* belief arises from some form of *social* maladjustment. There is only a limited usefulness in preaching to people to give up their religious prejudices before they can be politically or socially emancipated. Those religious prejudices will disappear when their source in social fear, irrational organisation, and arbitrary

[1] " Die Fähigkeit der heutigen Juden und Christen, frei zu werden " (*Einundzwanzig Bogen aus der Schweiz*, 1843, p. 56).

frustration will disappear. It is not enough then, to argue against religion, although such argument has its uses. The argument to be truly radical must dig down to the social roots of political and religious life; it must involve some reference to a method of social action which will remove the evils of religion at their source. The emancipation of human beings from the recognised state form of religion, at which point Bauer stops short, is not the emancipation of human beings from the domination of religious principles in real life—principles which are expressed in the worship of money, fear of uncertainty, condemnation of the flesh, etc. Only when the latter are destroyed will the religious attitude towards society and human nature be destroyed.

In the so-called Jewish spirit—commerce—the Jew reflects only the character of the society in which he lives, a society which enforces upon the part of most of its members, anti-social activity as the necessary means to a successful livelihood. The Jewish problem is an aspect of the social problem. Those who seek to liberate the Jews from political discrimination should not be *opposed* on the ground that their position is logically inconsistent; they should be criticised because they do not see where the locus of the real problem lies. There is no inconsistency in advocating the extension of civil rights to Jews before society itself has been freed from its worship of Mammon. What is downright stupidity is to imagine, as Bauer does, that the Jewish problem can be solved short of solving the social problem. " The social emancipation of the Jews means ultimately the emancipation of society from Judaism " (*Gesamtausgabe*, Abt. I, Bd. 1, p. 606).

3. *Bauer and the Social Problem*

Bauer's social philosophy was modest, unambitious—and dangerous. It never appeared in the open save on the heels of gigantic metaphysical constructions which towered so high that it was difficult to see how far they reached. No one could understand his social philosophy in the light of his metaphysics but once the leading feature of his social philosophy was grasped then everything else could be understood, even his metaphysics.

Bauer, despite his anti-religiosity, held fervently to the belief that the world could be changed only if men first changed their soul, their heart, their mind. No theory of social causation was advanced to explain how it was possible, by purifying one's heart and cultivating one's mind, to abolish the material evils of social life. But where knowledge failed, conceptual dialectic and poetic imagination came into play. In order to make intelligible the causal influence of spiritual self-improvement, Bauer projected a metaphysics according to which the material world itself was an unconscious creation of our transcendental mind. On this view, that which was material in the world, was merely the opaque, the unillumined, the unclarified. The more we understood the material world, the easier it was to realise that it was a complex of ideal, logical relations and principles. For to understand anything, according to Bauer, meant to grasp it in terms of logical relations and principles. Matter thus becomes synonymous with the ever diminishing surd of the process of critical discovery. What are these logical relations and principles out of which the material world seems to be built up ? Bauer held that they could have no existence by themselves. They were not Platonic universals. They were the principles by which our minds—our transcendental minds—operated. In order to understand the world, then, we had to understand ourselves. *The only objective knowledge was self-knowledge.* From Bauer's philosophy of self-consciousness, it followed that the nature of the world depended upon the activity of the ideal mind and the ideal will which was involved in the very attempt to understand anything.

Applied to society, these principles generate the characteristic features of Bauer's social philosophy. The material aspects of life—because they have not been illumined by critical analysis —are specific expressions of the principle of evil. Human ignorance, the fixations of habit, a blind, because uncritical, intellectual technique, produce in different ways and on different levels confusion, suffering and disaster. And at the root of all these dogmatisms there lies the unregenerate (unconscious) will. Bauer and his school did not deny that specific social evils such as pauperism, crime, prostitution, etc., arose out of the material conditions of social life. But in consonance with his metaphysics, the material conditions of social life were themselves regarded as the product of a set of uncritical principles. It was only because those who ruled the destinies of the social world, as well as those who suffered this rule, were limited by their ignorance and ill-will, that social evils arose and persisted. The real source, then, of social evils was the lack of a rational, idealistic and critical attitude on the part of individuals. It was futile to attempt to revolutionise things before people's ideas, souls, or spirits were revolutionised. Indeed, things and all their evils were what they were *because* of human attitudes. Their significance and very existence depended upon consciousness. Things could be genuinely changed only by a revolution in human evaluating attitudes and not merely by reforms in the material structures and mechanisms of social life. What good would the latter do, if the old uncritical attitudes still persisted ? At best a new set of evils would replace the old.

In developing his social programme, Bauer reveals the class bias of this metaphysics. The function of the social philosopher was to bring people to critical self-consciousness and to demonstrate that the evils of the world arose from false ethical values. And, according to one of Bauer's fateful and uncritical definitions, all values were false which were not universal. Those like Proudhon or even Flora Tristan, who sought to organise the working class on the basis of their concrete interests, were mistakenly appealing to the very same values—individual self-interest, preferential rights, class needs and loyalties, etc.— which were at the root of the social problem. If poverty is the result of private property, how can poverty be abolished if those who suffer from poverty are organised into trade associations to snatch more private property for themselves ? Private property is really the result of the poverty of the spirit. The trouble with Proudhon is that " he writes only from the standpoint of the interests of the proletariat." His categories are historical not logical; his values partial and limited, not truly critical and ethical. The proletariat is oppressed by the same lack of critical insight as the rest of society. " The worker to-day thinks only of himself," complains Bauer. Personal and social salvation can only be found through " critical love " and the " serenity of knowledge."

This was the social evangelism of Bauer and his followers. It necessarily led them into opposition against those whose appeal was not to critical self-consciousness but to resolute mass-action.

4. *The Critical Spirit* versus *the Masses*

The critical insight which is necessary for social reform, claimed Bauer, is no easy thing to acquire. An arduous intellectual discipline had to be undergone in order to attain that degree of disinterestedness and freedom from presuppositions which were essential to drawing fine distinctions. In the very nature of the case those who had been deprived of the opportunities to engage in self-critical activity—the masses in the workshops—could not be expected to rise to the high level of critical probity demanded by the philosophy of self-consciousness. Indeed, because of their numbers, because of the diversity of their background and training, the masses cannot grasp and defend ideas in their purity. Ideas are vulgarised, their meanings altered and subordinated to irrelevant purposes. " The masses," wrote Bauer, " desire nothing but simple ideas in order to avoid the trouble of coming to grips with things ; shibboleths to settle all matters in advance; high sounding phrases with which to destroy all criticism " (*Allgemeine Literatur Zeitung*, Heft 5, p. 23). He complained that the ideas of those critical philosophers who are concerned with liberating the masses are first emptied of their critical content, then filled with foreign matter in the guise of economic interest, and finally turned dogmatically against the philosophers themselves. The real critic must resign himself to being misunderstood in the turmoil of party strife. Concerned as he is only with absolute truth and that which concerns all parties, the critic is essentially a lonely and solitary spirit. " The critic," writes Bauer, " does not take sides (*macht keine Partei*). Nor does he want to take sides with any party. He is lonely—lonely in that he loses himself in the object of criticism—lonely in that he sets himself up against it. Criticism separates itself from everything (*löst sich von Allem ab*) " (Ibid., Heft 6, p. 33).

The masses, for Bauer, are a social expression of the metaphysics of matter. They are driven by ignorance and passion. They are enslaved to the tyranny of the practical, to the temporal duties of bettering their lot. They are sunk in preoccupation with their material interests. They try to clip the wings of critical thought by making it concrete, by narrowing the impact of its critical force to class action. Indeed because the masses are such a refractory medium for pure ideas, they represent the principle of evil. The ideas of critical philosophers must *struggle through and against* mass inertia and distortion. All the significant deeds of history have been performed despite, not because of, the support of the masses. "All great acts of previous history were doomed to failure and to remain without significant influence because the masses became interested in them and enthusiastic in their behalf; or they came to a miserable end because the Idea—which was the central thing—was of a kind such that it had to content itself with a superficial expression, and consequently depend upon the favour of the masses." The masses are not the carriers of ideas but their destroyers. Whoever appeals to the masses is appealing to the passive material element to harness the active ideal element. The masses cannot even be trusted to be an effective *instrument* of the critical spirit. Still less its guide! In fact Bauer confesses that sad experience has taught him that " in the masses and not elsewhere is the true enemy of the spirit to be found. . . . The spirit now knows that it must seek its only opponent in the phrases, self-deception, and unprincipled character of the masses " (Ibid., Heft 1, p. 2).

But yet the masses must be saved and social evils abolished. Consistent with Bauer's opposition, in his religious psychology, to Strauss' belief in the creative power of the community, and with his political opposition to the masses, we should expect that wherever Bauer discusses concrete methods of social reform, the appeal would be to purely personal agencies. We are not mistaken. Bauer, like Carlyle, invoked the great man, as the representative of the critical spirit, to reform society. But unlike Carlyle the great man to whom he appealed was not the fervent prophet or enlightened despot, but the sentimental philanthropist—a philanthropist drawn on the order of the literary prototypes contained in the novels of Eugene Sue, George Sand and Dickens.

5. *Sentimental Philanthropy as Social Reform*

The modern reader of Marx's *Die heilige Familie* is amazed to discover that almost one half of the book is devoted to a discussion of Sue's *Mysteries of Paris*. But the significance of this novel in Germany of the early forties can only be grasped by a first-hand study of the social literature of that day. It is no exaggeration to say that through it the German critical philosophers discovered the social problem.[1] It proved, wrote Herr Szeliga, one of Bauer's staunch band of followers, that " the critic, when he desires, can be a poet also." The tale it unrolls recounts the adventures of Rudolf, Prince of Gerolstein, who becomes the incarnation of the critical spirit of justice. In a bloody and maudlin series of intrigues he is represented as the friend of the weak and distressed, the consoler of the poor, and the dispenser of ethical medicaments to a sick society. Marx takes up the story in detail to prove that Rudolf is just as confused on the social problem as *die Freien* who have apotheosised him, and that the whole story with its cry—*Ah! si le riche savait!*—is only a variant of the feudal slogan of supine suppliance—*Ah! si le roi savait!*

This naïve conception of how the social problem is to be solved expressed the attitude of one whose spiritualistic sociology was a continuation of a metaphysical and religious myth. The spirit of divine philosophy, effulgent with justice and charity, was to pervade the dark, oppressive places of the earth. The pure critic was the saviour of the fallen. He confounded the mighty with logic and solaced the weak with soup kitchens, work farms and tracts on critical self-consciousness. He reconciled the opposition between the spirit and the flesh by proving that the flesh exists for the spirit, and dissolving it into another form of spirituality. And he explained evil as a necessary stopping place of the critical spirit on its unending journey towards absolute self-consciousness.

6. *Bauer's Historical Fatalism*

Bruno Bauer did not conceal from himself that critical logic solved none of the concrete problems which were agitating the less critical of his fellow-men. It did not even restore him to the

---

[1] Engels' own description of the significance of this work for the thought of the early forties will be found in a brief notice in the *New Moral World*, Feb. 3, 1844, reprinted in Marx-Engels, *Gesamtausgabe*, I, 2, 455.

university post from which he had been removed by uncritical academic authorities. He was consequently compelled to fall back upon the quietism latent in every cosmic idealism. It was a quietism which could be expressed in very revolutionary language extremely terrifying to the censor; it was a quietism which compensated for one's helplessness before the tragic events of history; and it was finally a quietism which combated on principle any attempt to offer a realistic interpretation of history in terms other than ideas and personalities.

How strikingly an idealistic fatalism can dress itself up in war-paint and emit blood-curdling cries for revolution, is best illustrated in the writings of Edgar Bauer, Bruno Bauer's most faithful disciple. Hegel and Schelling had used the argument from history for conservative purposes. The Young-Hegelians, especially Edgar Bauer and Köppen, used the argument from history for radical purposes by pointing out that most recorded history is a history of successive revolutions. They agreed with Hegel that history had been made by ideas, and argued that since whatever had been brought into existence by ideas, must, on the Hegelian position, be reasonable, revolutions and the consequences of revolution—no matter how bloody—must be part of the organic pattern of the one, Absolute Idea. Of the French Revolution, Edgar Bauer wrote:

" It is true that the revolution shed much blood. But has there ever been a theory which when carried over into practice has celebrated a bloodless victory ? Christianity, Moham-medanism, the Reformation—did not the goddess of destruc-tion stand over their cradle ? . . . Once the revolution is re-garded as a struggle of ideas, the blood which it cost does not seem to us to have been shed in vain. . . . Every theory once carried over into practice will call forth a flow of blood in direct proportion to its own strength and intensity " (*Deutsche Jahrbücher*, 1842, p. 1195; pp. 1186–7).

Dangerous doctrine indeed—were it not so harmless. For even the censor soon learned that for the Bauers theory and practice were distinctions within spirit; that where they wrote blood, they meant ink ; and that their furious struggle with ideas was a struggle to make themselves free from the struggles actually going on.

The critical process, taught Bauer, accomplishes its own ends in its own ways. But the logic of the process gives us the comforting assurance that it will sweep the earth clean of traditional evils.

The iron broom which will sweep the earth clean of the Christian state, the social evil and the annoying censor, will not, taught Bauer, be wielded by human hands. History itself will provide the motor-power with its own logic. Human beings who have merely historical and not logical existence must cultivate the necessary patience and the insight to endure existing evils. Above all they must conquer the temptation to action.

> " The theory which has helped until now, still remains our only help in the struggle to free ourselves and others. History over which we have no control and whose decisive turns lie outside the scope of our deliberate calculation, will destroy the appearance and . . . transform the world. . . . Criticism is the only power which can enlighten us about the self-deception of the existing order and give us the upper hand. History will take care of the crisis, and its outcome " (*Die gute Sache*, pp. 224 ff.).

With this religious assurance, there is no longer any necessity to risk something in action to settle the immediate crises of our life. In fact, we have a standpoint from which to combat such action. And when such a standpoint is combined with revolutionary programmatic intransigence, then there is further justification to reject any other theory of the historical process which introduces material factors as conditioning or determining factors.

That was exactly the position in which the Bauers found themselves. At this time the first tentative gropings towards a realistic historiography appeared. Hegel had already stressed the importance of the geographical environment in tracing the autobiography of the world spirit; Buckle had impressed Europe with the far-reaching consequences of climate, topography, and quality of the soil upon the character of cultural life; French historians like Michelet were writing the political history of their country in terms of class-struggle, and the English and French Utopian socialists were emphasising the pervasive effect of the mode of property relationships upon the law and social morality of the day. All of these were rival interpretations to the historical fatalism of the current idealism. They challenged the philosophy of self-consciousness. The critical spirit in the person of the Bauers took up the challenge. And with one amazing dialectical thrust it brought the opposition low!

The critical philosophy declared these realistic interpretations to be nothing more than an " aristocrat's consolation and defence " against genuine revolution. If such material factors as the influence of the unlimited plains, proximity to the sea, and the wealth of fortified cities were to be introduced as explanatory causal factors of history, then human beings were not free to assert their essential freedom. Controlling material conditions, indeed! Reference to them was an excuse for not making history as we want it made at any definite moment. If the ideas which make history are determined by something not ideal, then man loses his freedom and history is no longer human.

> " The ordinary rebel says that freedom is the essence of man. It finds its expression in the course of history. All restrictions which limit and hinder the assertion of his essential nature must be destroyed so that the freedom which was at the outset only a natural right becomes a securely acquired, inalienable possession. . . . The aristocrat makes freedom depend upon accidents [i.e. natural conditions] in order to be able to prove that so far as any specific case of the absence of freedom is concerned, it is entailed by these accidents " (*Deutsche Jahrbücher*, 1842, p. 1188).

We are now in a better position to appreciate the grounds, occasion and implication of Marx's criticisms of Bauer and his philosophy of critical self-consciousness.

II

MARX'S CRITICISM OF BAUER

Marx was firmly convinced that it was impossible to develop a genuinely revolutionary doctrine and movement on the theoretical basis of philosophical idealism. The more consistent idealism was in theory, the more dangerous it was in practice. Its practical consequences led him to challenge its fundamental assumptions. For he discovered that it either ran out into a futile and extreme philosophical anarchism like Bauer's or else adopted a shameless expediency like Hegel's towards the concrete issues of the day. Events in his own political experience confirmed him in his conviction that philosophical idealism inevitably evolved into a philosophy of escape or a philosophy of compromise. And if he could have witnessed the careers of men like Bax, Bernstein, Jaurès, the Fabian Socialists, the Italian Neo-Hegelians, and the German Neo-Kantians—all of whom sought to base their socialism on the postulates of idealism —he would have found additional evidence for his view.

In his criticism of Bruno Bauer, Marx himself was not yet, so to speak, a full-fledged Marxist. He was writing from the standpoint of a radical follower of Feuerbach, but none the less with an historical insight and logic which were completely beyond the power of Feuerbach himself. In fact he had already essentially transcended the position of Feuerbach—as his *Deutsche Ideologie*, written a year after his published attack on the Bauers, shows. But the framework, phraseology, and historical assumptions of his book against Bauer were still Feuerbachian. Its very title, *Die heilige Familie*, is derived from Feuerbach. It is a reference to the sixth chapter of *Das Wesen des Christenthums* in which Feuerbach shows that the " holy family " is a sublimated expression of the material lacks and needs of the early Christian community; that it is a mystical compensation for the suppressed sexual desires of the early anchorites, and of their inexpugnable craving for some form of social participation. And since there were three Bauers—Bruno, Edgar, and Egbert— all of whom professed a consolatory theory of pure criticism, the choice of the title was not inappropriate. Its sub-title was *Kritik der Kritischen Kritik, gegen Bruno Bauer und Konsorten.*

1. *Bauer's Defective Social Psychology*

Marx had accepted from the very outset Bruno Bauer's extremely acute criticisms of the gospel. But he was more dubious about Bauer's theory of religious consciousness. In accordance with his personalistic speculative idealism, Bauer had claimed that religion as such, and Christianity in particular, was the result of the intellectual activities of outstanding personalities. The social character of religion was neglected in the attempt to show how individual motives accounted for the presence of certain doctrines and ritual forms. His philosophy of religion was really a sophisticated expression of the belief prevalent during the French Enlightenment that religion is an *invention* of the priests, or leaders of the community. At best he could explain why some one belief rather than another was imposed upon the community; but he could not explain, on the basis of his methodological assumptions, (a) *why the community believed at all*; (b) the *general* patterns of belief within which the specific religious ideas of specific religious leaders were set. Nor could Strauss; for when Strauss spoke of the " communal consciousness " as the source of religion, he was invoking vague spiritualistic concepts and not empirically verifiable psychological and social factors. It was Feuerbach who began the movement to discover the roots of religious behaviour and sacred belief in the "profane" socio-psychological environment. He did not, as will be seen below, go very far in his social probing. But Marx embraced his starting-point with enthusiasm. He called upon the speculative philosophers of religion and higher critics of theology to abandon all temporising with symbolic Biblical patchworks in the fashion of Strauss, and to continue along the lines laid down by Feuerbach in reducing supernatural belief to an inverted expression of the natural and social wish. Even before he had broken with Bauer, Marx addressed the radical left-Hegelians with punning levity: " There is no other way for you to truth and freedom except through the bath of fire (*Feuer-bach*); Feuerbach is the purgatory of the present."[1]

---

[1] " Luther als Schiedsrichter zwischen Strauss und Feuerbach," *Gesamtausgabe*, I, 1, 175. Written 1842 for Ruge's *Anecdota*, etc. (In the interest of literary usage I have translated *bach* as bath instead of stream.) Marx signed this piece " Kein Berliner," no doubt intending a thrust at Bauer and *die Freien*, whose critical proclamations were given to the world from the Berlin cafés.

In *Die heilige Familie* Marx proves that Bruno Bauer—despite the loose use of some phrases picked up from Feuerbach—is still confined within a religious conception of the world. His very philosophy of self-consciousness shows it. Instead of the "Holy Ghost" guiding the pen of the evangelists, it is the infinite self-consciousness, albeit, still somewhat uncritical, which writes itself out through the individual minds of religious leaders. "We make no secret of it," writes Bauer in the preface to his *Kritik der Synoptiker*, "that the correct conception of evangelical history has its philosophical foundations in the philosophy of self-consciousness" (Bd. 1, p. 15). And this concept of self-consciousness, we need not remind the reader, is a thin abstraction of what Hegel had clothed with flesh and blood in the *Phänomenologie*. Yet Bauer's own criticism of Hegel was that Hegel had not yet cut himself free from theology, that his philosophy was still dressed up in the terminological frills and ruffles of Christianity.

2. *Bauer's Creative Idealism*

Philosophy and religion have so often been associated that there never was a revolt against religion which did not conceive itself to be at the same time a revolt against philosophy. Why? Because historical philosophy for the most part has been idealistic philosophy—and all idealism, when it does not run out into an ineffable solipsism, is either a disguised or vestigial supernaturalism. No better illustration could be desired than Bauer's philosophy of self-consciousness. And no illustration could be more impressive because Bauer himself, as well as the authorities who persecuted him, declared his philosophy to be out-and-out atheism. How was this possible? The answer is suggested in Marx's analysis.

The sophisticated consciousness starts with itself as the most significant and indubitable fact of existence. In the ordinary course of experience, it discovers that there are certain intractable elements which seem to be foreign to consciousness, and which compel or control it. These elements go by the name of matter. But the self realises that this matter is not so hostile and foreign to it as it had at first assumed. Cannot this matter be

understood? Has it not intelligible connections which enable us
to order and control it for our *own* purposes? But how is it
possible for consciousness to *know* matter unless it has something in common with it? Like can only know like, said the
Neo-Platonists. The mind can only know mind; and if matter,
by definition, is that which cannot be known, how can we know
that it exists at all? And if once more, we change our definition
of matter, and define it as the source, or cause, of consciousness,
how is it possible for that which is conscious to proceed or
evolve from what is totally unconscious and inert? Consciousness
must at least be involved potentially or implicitly in what is
called matter, or else science and logic must confess that they
are confronted by a miracle, which they cannot of course do.
The only solution plausible to the facts of consciousness is to
assume that matter is dead spirit or mind which gradually comes
to life. But the nature of consciousness as such is self-activity.
Consequently all of nature can be viewed as something which
has come into existence as the result of primal active self-
alienation of the One or Absolute (or whatever it is which we
substitute for the idea of God). The next step is to see nature
as a process in which what has been alienated strives by perpetual self-activity to win its way back to the untroubled inno-
cence of the Absolute. The two insoluble immanent problems of
this philosophical myth are: why is it necessary for the Absolute
Mind to alienate itself into the apparently material? And
exactly *how* does matter evolve into explicit self-consciousness?
The philosophy of Bruno Bauer is an attempt to answer these
questions. Bauer's success may be gauged by Marx's incisive
summary and criticism of his system.

In *Das Entdeckte Christentum*[1] Bauer had criticised the one-
sided metaphysical materialism of the French philosophers.
" The French materialists have interpreted the development of
self-consciousness as the development of the universal substance,
matter; but they could not see that the development of the
universe only became real in and for the development of self-
consciousness " (p. 115).

[1] Bauer's *Entdeckte Christentum* is his most radical work. It was suppressed
by the censor immediately upon publication. Marx quotes it twice in *Die heilige
Familie*. It has been reissued with an interesting introduction by Barnikol, Jena,
1927.

" So ! " comments Marx, " The truth of materialism is its very opposite, i.e. absolute, exclusive, pretentious (*uberschwängliche*) idealism. Self-Consciousness, Spirit is everything. Nothing exists outside of it. It is the almighty creator of the world, the heavens and the ·earth. The world is a living expression of self-consciousness, which must alienate itself and take on an enslaved form. But the difference between the world and self-consciousness is only an apparent difference. The latter distinguishes nothing real from itself. Indeed the world is only a metaphysical distinction, a ghost of the ethereal brain and imagination of self-consciousness. It dissolves the impression which it had let prevail for a moment that something really existed outside of itself. It does not recognise as real anything which is produced thereby. Through development, however, self-consciousness produces itself as absolute; for the absolute idealist must necessarily, in order to remain an absolute idealist, go through the following process: first, to transform the world into an appearance, into an arbitrary notion of his brain, then to declare this fantastic notion to be what it really is, a pure fantasy, in order, finally, to be able to proclaim its sole, exclusive existence unembarrassed by even the appearance of an external world. . . .

" Herr Bauer who introduces his philosophy of Self-Consciousness or Spirit into all fields in opposition to the idea of substance or matter must consequently concern himself in all fields with the ghosts of his brain. Criticism in his hand is the instrument to sublimate into pure thought everything which still maintains its finite material existence outside of infinite self-consciousness. He struggles against the idea of substance not as a metaphysical illusion but against its kernel—nature—nature as it exists outside of man as well as within him. When Bauer says he refuses to take substance or matter as a starting point in any field, what he means is that there is no existence separate from thought; no natural energy different from the spontaneity of consciousness; no human power which is not reason; no suffering which is not activity; no influence of others upon us which is not a form of our own influence; no feeling or will distinct from knowledge; no heart without a head; no object without a subject; no practice without theory; no human beings who are not pure critics ; no real community which does not possess abstract universality; no ' thou ' which is not at the same time ' me.' It is quite consistent, therefore, that Herr Bauer should proceed to identify himself with the spirit of self-consciousness, and in the place of his creation to put its creator. He is still consistent when he goes on to condemn the rest of the world which selfishly persists in regarding itself as something other than a product of self-consciousness, as stubborn mass and matter. . . . He construes the revolt of his own critical principles against the development of mankind, as the mass revolt of humanity against his criticism, against the spirit, against Herr Bruno Bauer and company " (*Gesamtausgabe*, Abt. I, Bd. 3, pp. 317–319).

3. *Solipsism and the Social Problem*

It was not illogical for Bauer to conceive of himself as a critical saviour of the world of his own imagination. But it was the height of confusion to offer himself as a saviour to those who did not share his philosophy. At best, claimed Marx, he could reform or corrupt people's logic. He could not solve their problems. For these problems arose not from their failure to attain philosophic clarity but out of the mechanisms of social life. In Bauer's eyes all of these problems were aspects of *the* problem of evil—a problem of evil which, as we have seen, is essentially metaphysical and religious. Metaphysical, because it admitted the existence of matter which could not be derived by pure logic from definitions of the absolute; religious, because as the source of division, strife and suffering, it had to be justified as a disguise of the good. For Marx there was no problem of evil. As a naturalist, he accepted the material world as a fact not as an ethical problem. Evils arise only with development of human consciousness. But their locus was not always psychological. All human evils that were at all remediable were regarded by Marx as *social*. As social they were challenges to action and organisation, not occasions for prayer or religious apologetic. Not that Marx believed—as most social reformers—that social problems could be solved independently of each other. He held that in any society the complex problems with which it was faced—be they educational, vocational, legal or matrimonial—received their specific point and context from the system of property relationships which distinguished one society from another. At this period in his development Marx saw *the* social problem as a question of the relation between the *conditions of work*, and the human *needs* of those engaged in work. All social problems were facets of it.

To such a point of view, it was inevitable that Bauer's philosophy of idealism should appear as a kind of magical wish thinking. On Bauer's principles, it was easier for the workers by taking thought to add a cubit to their stature than by taking thought to eliminate the degrading conditions under which they were forced to work. They need but become clear on the nature of existence, the nature of the self, and the nature of felicity to realise that each was a critical monarch unto himself. Above all was it degrading to think in terms of *interests* or *needs*. These could not be critically thought about. One could only uncritically fight for them. To which Marx responds:

" According to the critical critics the source of the entire evil lies with the 'thinking' of the workers. . . . But the mass of communist workers who are active, for example, in the workshops of Manchester and Lyons do not believe that by ' pure thought ' they can reason out of existence their industrial masters and their own practical degradation. They have a very painful realisation of the difference between existence and thought, between consciousness and life. They know that property, capital, money and wage-labour are by no means ideal figments of the brain, but very practical, very objective products of their own enslavement; and that consequently they must be abolished in a practical, objective way in order that man become truly human not only in thought, in consciousness and in social existence (*massenhaften Sein*), but also in life. Critical criticism teaches them, on the contrary, that in reality they cease to be wage-workers when they have transcended in thought the idea of being wage-workers, when they cease to regard themselves in thought as wage-workers, and, in accordance with this exaggerated fantasy, refuse to accept payment for their persons. As absolute idealists, as ethereal creatures, they can after that live naturally on the ether of pure thought. Critical criticism teaches them that they abolish real capital whenever they conquer the category of capital in thought; that they can really change themselves and become truly human when they change their abstract *self* in consciousness, and scorn as an uncritical act any real attempt to change their existence, that is to say, the real conditions of their actual self. ' Spirit ' which sees in existence only categories, naturally reduces all human activity and practice to the dialectical thought-process of critical criticism. That is how its socialism is different from the socialism and communism of the masses " (*Gesamtausgabe*, Abt. I, Bd. 3, pp. 223–4).

4. *Historical Dynamics and the Masses*

Already in his criticism of Bauer, Marx reveals that deep understanding of the historical process which was later to come to full fruition in his systematic theory of history and in his detailed historical studies. In those very masses in whom Bauer saw the " matter " of history, Marx saw the " power " of history. In the " ideas " in which Bauer saw the power of an abstract historical process, Marx saw the instrumental aids of a concrete historical struggle. The history of ideas itself becomes for Marx, in a sense, the history of mass action. The purpose of history is no longer, as with Bauer, the progressive discovery of objective truths but, in so far as we can speak of the purpose of history, the realisation of *class* needs.

The philosophy of Bauer is really a worship of the absolute significance of " ideas." In attacking this worship Marx does not substitute for it a worship of the masses. On the contrary, since for him dominant social ideas are, from one aspect, an expression of class purposes, those who are unconscious of the purposes which dominant attitudes and values serve, are really supporting the class which uses them as its slogans. Uncritical devotion to ideas is often tantamount to uncritical acceptance of the class whose power they tend to sustain. It is only when the relation between class interests and abstract ideas is grasped that real social criticism can begin. The conflict of social ideas and ideals is part of the conflict of social interests and classes. It is in the light of class *interests* that the appropriateness and " validity " of class ideals are to be judged. Marx never worshipped the masses; he gave them a theory on the basis of which they could criticise themselves. Those of his disciples who have erected the slogan, " The working class can do no wrong," have betrayed both the spirit and the sense of his position. For that was precisely what Bauer charged his radical friends with believing, and it was that charge, among others, which Marx was concerned in answering.

Marx begins his discussion of Bauer's worship of ideas and his systematic underestimation of the rôle of the masses in history by pointing out that ideas of themselves—no matter how revolutionary—can never change existing conditions. At best they can only refute or destroy the ideas which have grown out of existing conditions. They can nullify and undermine the influence of dominant attitudes and produce a state of affairs which is usually called " a period of transition " or of " ideal revaluation." But to accomplish a concrete social change they must be translated into action. " In order that ideas be realised, human beings are necessary who can exercise a practical force " (Ibid., p. 294). It is only when ideas are illustrated in human behaviour, when men risk their lives and fortunes in activity, that the world's work gets done.

Marx misses no opportunity to deflate what he calls the " windy pretensions " of Bauer's historical fatalism with its amorphous notions of " progress," " development," and " freedom." Bauer could believe that ideas made history because he had personified history into a metaphysical entity. History, therefore, becomes " a Person separate and apart, a metaphysical Subject, while human beings are its mere carriers." The so-called truths of history (" *Wahrheiten, die sich von vornherein von selbst verstehen,*" Bauer actually called them) become hypostasised ideas waiting in a subsistent heaven to descend into men's consciousness. Man exists for history. He exists to illustrate an historical truth in the same way as the hero of a Greek play exists to illustrate the decrees of fate. This means, Marx claimed, that there really is no such thing as the realm of history. At best, history is the domain of poetic myth. It answers no question of *why*, *where*, and *when* things have happened. It does not even make intelligible the rise, fall and succession of ideas. It is a *reductio ad absurdum* of Bauer's initial assumptions. Bauer forgets that no human being thinks or acts by himself; he is always a member of a group whose language, tradition and needs have moulded his outlook upon the world. Bauer forgets that the empirical history of his own time is largely the result of conflicts between groups. He does not investigate the nature, conditions, and causes of group conflicts. He consequently overlooks the specific character of historical causation and reads it in terms of an arbitrarily construed, poetic or logical, necessity. He does not see that the various forms of his own philosophy of historical fatalism, by attempting to construe history as something apart from the passions, interests, wills, and minds of men living in society—have served, both in the past and present, a definite class purpose. Bauer's philosophy suggested that the organisation of society and the succession of historical events reflected an ideal pattern of social perfection already stored up in a heaven of antecedent being—and that our inability to see the logical justification of the existing order is due to the distortions produced by our own subjective interests. It is necessary, therefore, to examine more carefully the non-ideal basis of ideas.

5. *Ideas and Interests*

Bruno Bauer had taken a clear position on what has always been regarded as the central problem of the philosophy of history: do ideas make history or does history make ideas? Marx was not content to answer with a simple negative Bauer's positive affirmation of the creative power of ideas. For him the very way of putting the question involved a mistaken conception of the nature both of ideas and of history. To ask whether ideas make history or vice versa was to assume that they stood over against one another as abstract and fixed entities, awaiting in their ready-made finality the definition and dialectic which would bring them together. Ideas are always a part of history; their relationship to other aspects of the historical process can be revealed only through a study of their organic connection with human *needs* and *interests*. The place of ideas in the history of the French Revolution is taken as the spring-board of the discussion.

Like most philosophers whose professional concern with the formal relations between ideas has weakened their grasp of the social conditions within which these ideas functioned, Bruno Bauer regarded great historical occurrences as affairs rationally undertaken for the sake of an objective end. " The French Revolution," he wrote, " was an experiment which was definitely specific to the eighteenth century." And on the analogy of an experiment, he described its deeds and criticised its outcome. An experiment is meaningful only when there are objective criteria, accepted by all competently informed critics, which determine whether the experiment is to be regarded as a success or failure. For Bauer these criteria were logical and ethical. In his analysis of the French Revolution, then, it was inevitable that he declare it a failure—a failure attributable to the fact that the irrelevant question of *class material interests* had been introduced into the experiment. History, which exists to discover objective truths by experiment, cannot make progress when irrational desire or need interferes with the experimental process. Ideas must be completely divorced from our interests or feelings about them. Otherwise they cannot be objectively tested. History presents the sad record of the bad logic and disastrous consequences which result from mixing up our subjective desires with objective truths.

Marx takes up the challenge and refuses to dissociate historical ideas from material interests. No matter how progress is defined, if we say that history has revealed a progressive course, it is only because the historical ideas which have triumphed have been bound up with definite historical interests, richer and more inclusive than those interests over which it has triumphed. Historical values are the objects of historical class interests. Before a revolution can be called a failure, we must know what and whose *interests* it tried to fulfil. Our historical analysis will be confusing if we are unaware of what these interests really are, and what means and actions were necessary to carry them out. Marx writes:

" ' Ideas ' always fail only in so far as they separate themselves from ' interests.' It is of course easy to understand that
every historically effective mass ' interest,' when it first makes
its bow on the stage of world history dressed up as an ' Idea '
or ' Ideal,' goes much further than the real limits of its part
and identifies itself with human interests in general. This
illusion constitutes what Fourier called the ' tone ' of each
historical epoch. The interest of the bourgeoisie in the revolution of 1789, far from having in any way ' failed,' succeeded
in ' winning ' everything, even though the ' enthusiastic '
flowers of rhetoric with which its interests garlanded the
cradle of the revolution have long since withered. These
interests were so powerful that they victoriously overcame
the pen of a Marat, the guillotine of the terrorists, the sword,
crucifix, and bloodbath of Napoleon. The revolution was a
' failure ' only for the masses whose real ' interests ' were not
represented in the ' political ideas ' of the bourgeoisie—ideas
which expressed not the living principles of the masses but
the living principles of the revolution. The real conditions of
their emancipation are essentially different from the condition
within which the bourgeoisie can emancipate itself and society.
If the revolution has failed, it has failed because the masses,
whose living conditions it represented, constituted a limited
and exclusive mass [i.e. the bourgeoisie] and not the entire
mass. If it failed, it was not because the masses enthusiastically supported it, but because the greater part of the masses
—that part which is distinct from the bourgeoisie—instead
of having its real interests expressed in the principle of the
revolution, instead of having its own characteristic revolutionary principles, attached itself to an ' empty idea ' and
experienced a transient elation in an object of momentary
enthusiasm " (*Gesamtausgabe*, Abt. I, Bd. 3, pp. 252–3).

6. *The Beginnings of Historical Materialism*

Ideas can only be historically effective when they are an
expression of class interests. That is the secret of their life-
history. If it does not explain their birth, it at least explains
their acceptance, their modification, their victory and defeat.

But Marx pressed his investigations further. What kind of class *interests* are here involved ? How do they arise ? How do they assert themselves ? How are they translated into ideologies ? Marx raises these questions in *Die heilige Familie*. He does not answer them all; but, none the less, he gives emphatic expression to the leading principle of historical materialism.

In all historical activity classes are dominated by many interests, religious, psychological, legal, economic, etc. Which of all these interests is central ? And if all of them enter into the motives of class action, which predominates and makes the course of subsequent history most intelligible ? Marx projected his answer on the basis of a study of why different classes *failed* to win and hold power during the French Revolution, why some ideas fell on barren soil and were embalmed in dusty tomes or lost in the cheap tracts of the day, and why, finally, still other ideas received a lip allegiance from all and practical support from none.

> " Robespierre, St. Just, and their party went down to destruction because they confused the realistic-democratic community of antiquity, which rested on the foundations of real slavery, with the modern spiritualistic-democratic representative state, which is based upon the emancipated slavery of bourgeois society. What a colossal contradiction to recognise and sanction in the abstract the rights of man, modern bourgeois society, the society of industry, universal competition, the unrestricted pursuit of the ends of private interest, of anarchy, of degraded natural and spiritual individuality, and yet, at the same time, to attempt to wipe out the expression and effects of the very life of this society upon its separate individuals, to attempt to construct the political façade of this society upon the model of antiquity ! " (*Gesamtausgabe*, I, 3, 298.)

The dominant interests are those which grow out of the organisation of the mode of production. Already in *Die heilige Familie* Marx gives intimations of the revolutionary social psychology he was later to develop. The methodological starting point of all human history is the character and intensity of man's needs. Out of these needs arise the division of labour, specific vocational activity, class status and allegiance. These express themselves in a set of volitions and attitudes which develop into a systematic ideology. The latter in turn tends to preserve or modify the objective conditions which have produced the original needs. The historical process is an interesting whole of objective economic order, the socio-psychological needs which this generates, and the conscious ideals in whose behalf man reacts upon his conditioning social environment. In his subsequent work, Marx analyses the nature of the objective economic order to show its threefold root in the historical development of culture, the social nature of man, and the character of his productive tools.

It is not unfair to say that Marx used his critical *Auseinandersetzung* with Bauer's philosophy of self-consciousness to attain a critical self-consciousness of his own position. It is marred a little by his Feuerbachian phraseology, especially in the use of the term " human " where he later wrote " class." But it definitely marked his repudiation of every type of philosophical idealism. Among the problems ahead of him was to show how the kernel of sense in idealism—the appreciation of the essential activity of human consciousness—could be fitted into a materialistic context. His more immediate problem, however, was to convince those Young-Hegelians who in behalf of political democracy had broken away from Bauer, that true political democracy could be fulfilled only in a social democracy.

CHAPTER IV

ARNOLD RUGE AND KARL MARX

ARNOLD RUGE was the central figure of the Young-Hegelian movement. As editor of the *Hallische Jahrbücher*, the *Deutsche Jahrbücher*, and the *Deutsch-Französische Jahrbücher*, he brought to mature and vigorous expression the political aspirations of the rising bourgeoisie in Germany. On the basis of a broad philosophy of culture, he sought to formulate the views of the Young-Hegelians on specific political issues and to prepare a policy of action for a bourgeoisie which was more ready to compromise with feudal reaction than to fight it.

Ruge's philosophy of culture was Neo-Hegelian; he attempted to reform Hegel in the name of a liberal Hegelianism. Successively a follower of Strauss, Bauer, and Feuerbach, he exhibited neither originality nor consistency in his philosophic doctrines. But he was much more alive than his teachers to the political relevance and social impact of ideas. In the early forties he was, in a sense, a fellow-traveller of Karl Marx[1]—never quite so radical and analytical but always in the van of the critical war which the Young-Hegelians waged on the German cultural front. When the final break between Ruge and Marx came in 1844, it was over the nature of the state and its function in modern society. Ruge himself never advanced beyond radical political democracy; even where he professed to accept some of Marx's social ideals, he believed that they could be realised by the ordinary methods of political action. Communism he regarded not as the fulfilment of democracy but as its negation.

The periodicals which Ruge edited contain the most important source material of the intellectual history of Germany during the period of Marx's formative years.[2] Beginning with the most

---

[1] Marx was co-editor of the *Deutsch-Französische Jahrbücher*, Paris 1844. It was suspended after two issues had appeared.

[2] *Hallische Jahrbücher für Wissenschaft und Kunst*, founded 1838, was suppressed in 1841. The *Deutsche Jahrbücher für Wissenschaft und Kunst*, founded in Dresden in 1841, was suppressed in January 1843. The form of these two magazines was the same. They appeared, as a rule, six times a week as a large, closely printed, double-column four page sheet. For the first three years the pages were numbered according to the columns.

faint-hearted political liberalism and ending with the extremest theoretical radicalism, they provide not only an indication of the ideological *milieu* in which some of Marx's early attitudes were formulated but also definite clues to important cultural doctrines which he retained and strengthened after he had outgrown Ruge and his other Young-Hegelian associates.

I

THE PHILOSOPHY OF ARNOLD RUGE

When the *Hallische Jahrbücher* made their first appearance in 1838, intellectual Germany was abuzz over Strauss' *Leben Jesu*. Politically, however, hardly the faintest liberal murmur had made itself heard. The only important political movements which had manifested themselves were conservative; they grew out of the secondary effects of a twofold fundamentalist reaction in religion. An aggressively orthodox Catholic movement in the South and a narrow evangelical pietism in Prussia demanded guarantees that the religious foundations of the state would be preserved against the " wormy exegesis " of the biblical critics. The Catholics were explicitly ultramontane; the Protestant pietists declared that they preferred a theocracy to a liberal or constitutional monarchy. So strong was this current of orthodoxy, that sometimes the Prussian government, in order to counteract the potential danger to its own political autonomy which flowed from religious fanaticism, came forward in the rôle of a neutral arbiter between the heretical theologians and the orthodox churchmen. It was at this time that the *Hallische Jahrbücher* appeared. Quick to seize the first opportunity to ingratiate itself with the suspicious censor it pretended to be the champion of Protestantism—identifying Protestantism with the spirit of freedom in general and with the essence of the Hegelian philosophy (which had not yet been discredited) in particular. Ruge later confessed that the fast and loose way in which he played with the idea of Protestantism was due in part to political expediency and to a desire to win tolerance for ulterior political and social views.[1]

Looking back upon this period, Rudolf von Gotschall, a literary historian and poet, who was himself a sympathetic contemporary of the Young-Hegelians, remarked, "The *Hallische Jahrbücher* marks the fall of the Hegelian philosophy from divine grace, and its expulsion from the paradise of the Prussian government appointments."[2] But the important reservation must be made that the fall from grace was very gradual and gathered momentum only as the *Jahrbücher* turned from playing at re-defining Protestantism to an open advocacy of political insurrection in behalf of a democratic republic. In this development three definite stages may be distinguished. (*a*) In its first stage the *Hallische Jahrbücher* steps on the scene as the champion of the *spirit* of Protestantism. The implicit ideal of the Prussian state is defended against the ultramontane tendencies of the Catholic dissidents and the dogmatic obscurantism of the pietists. Frederick the Great is apotheosised as the incarnation of the philosophy of civil freedom in high places and held up as an ideal to contemporary Germany. The Prussian war of liberation against Napoleon, it was claimed, had to be refought against the domestic powers of cultural reaction. This war, as well as the wars that were still to be fought, was announced as the practical corollary of the ethical philosophies of Kant, Fichte, and Hegel.[3] (*b*) In the second stage the magazine began a spirited attack upon the cultural presuppositions of the Romantic movement in Germany. It regarded this literary movement, correctly enough, as an expression of the social and

---

[1] *Aus früherer zeit*, Vol. IV, p. 445. Such sentences as, "The light of Protestantism is the light of the world, its spirit, its rule, its future" (*H. J.*, 1839, p. 238), were not uncommon in the early years. They were often intended as a sleep-inducing incantation for the censor; for in the same article Ruge would go on to say that by Protestantism he means "only the protest against the congealation (*Erstarrung*) of the spirit" (p. 289). Later this enabled Ruge and Echtermeyer to conceal radical attacks on the Protestant Prussian state on the ground that it was not Protestant enough.

[2] *Die deutsche Nationalliteratur des 19.Jahrhunderts*, 5th ed. Breslau 1881, Bd. 2.

[3] Ruge did not blind himself to the contradiction between the ethical philosophies of Kant and Hegel but he maintained that the apparent political accommodation which followed as a corollary from the Hegelian ethics was extrinsic to the system. Hegelian ethics for Ruge meant the "conscious activity (*Praxis*) of the historical dialectic." It was in this spirit that the magazine was conceived and developed. Cf. Ruge, *Sämmtliche Werke*, second ed., Vol. 6, Pt. 2, p. 75. Mannheim, 1848.

political power of feudal Germany struggling against the industrial revolution. It followed this campaign with a devastating
criticism of the historical school of law and its two foremost
protagonists, Leo and Savigny. In the name of a " free " Protestantism, Ruge and his contributors began a crusade against
what they called " the principle of romanticism " in social life.
Professing to see the romantic attitude dominant in politics,
religion, and education, they thus were able, before the censor
awoke, to inject in the guise of allegiance to the " genuine "
Prussian tradition, a stringent criticism of the existing Prussian
state. (c) The third period began with the suppression of the
Hallische Jahrbücher and its reappearance under a new name at
Dresden.[1] It now let loose one broadside after another against
bureaucracy and oppression throughout Germany. It declared
itself to be constitutional, democratic and republican. It referred
openly to the Prussian state as the brutal embodiment of the
Polizeistaat of the restoration—unfaithful to the vision of its
own philosophers, to the ideals of its greatest sovereign and to
its solemn pledges to its own people. With the suppression of
the *Deutsche Jahrbücher*, Ruge, with the aid of Marx, continued
his work in Paris.

1. *Philosophy as Politics*

Ruge was among the first to see that once the Hegelian-dialec-
tic method was separated from the Hegelian system, conclusions
could be derived which undermined the orthodox allegiances to
the existing state and culture. The first step was to interpret the
dialectical method as an instrument of *reflection*. In reflection
no object can be thought about without negating it, or going
beyond it. This is done by viewing the object in the light of the
possible alternatives into which it might develop. In natural
things which are unaffected by human interest or activity, such
as the movements of the heavenly bodies, these alternatives are
limited by the structural interrelationships of the objects themselves; analysis can only discover which of these alternatives
will probably be realised. In society, although the alternative

[1] On the occasion of the removal of the *H. J.* to Dresden, Ruge wrote to Köppen
(June 10, 1840): " No further subterfuge or moderation will help us. They will
never forgive our attack upon romanticism " (Dresden collection of Ruge's letters,
from the photostatic archives of the Marx-Engels-Lenin Institute, Moscow).

paths of development are limited, human consciousness enters into the determination of these alternatives. In some sense, then, human thought—in matters historical and social—creates the possibilities between which it chooses. The dialectic method of thinking becomes a method of *criticism* comparing "what is" with "what might be." It is also a method of *action*, since it fulfils itself by developing some one alternative rather than another. " The true content of the Hegelian *Geistes-philosophie* is *humanism*, its true method is *criticism*," wrote Ruge. For the abstract " absolute spirit " of Hegel, the Young-Hegelians read the abstract historical activity of abstract Man. They regarded the *Phänomenologie des Geistes,* with its description of the progressive development of different phases of individual and social consciousness, as Hegel's most important work, and boldly identified his metaphysical concept of freedom with political, religious, legal, and intellectual freedom as occasion demanded.

We shall not stop to inquire into the legitimacy of this interpretation of Hegel. Let us rather examine its consequences. It is sufficient to point out in passing, however, that the technique by which the developmental metaphysics of Hegel was converted from its intended explanatory and descriptive function into a normative and reformative one, was simple and clear. Marx expresses it pithily as follows: " Reason has always existed, but not always in reasonable form. The critic, consequently, can take his point of departure from every form of theoretical and practical consciousness, and out of the given (*eigenen*) forms of existing reality develop the true reality as its ' ought-to-be ' (*Sollen*) and goal."[1]

The consequences of this interpretation of the dialectic method were startling. Absolute idealism was transformed into practical idealism; the philosopher, now no longer " with Brahman wisdom sits calmly on his haunches absorbed in idle speculative gaze " but is " the apostle of the future." The processes of history and the processes of consciousness cannot be separated. Philosophy, then, as the criticism of consciousness is also the criticism of history. " Here there is no realm of blood-less ash-grey shadows which have no relation to the world;

[1] *Gesamtausgabe,* Abt. I, Bd. 1, p. 574.

philosophy is related to the whole, vital movement of life."[1] Nothing is foreign to it which has any significance in the life of man. The problems and difficulties of social life, practical interest in which Hegel was inclined to disparage as preoccupation with things merely temporal, were declared, in their broader aspects, to be as much a concern of philosophical consciousness as that which appeared eternal. Indeed, the problem was to make over existence in such a way that out of temporal experience significant life would be born. It is not really a question between losing oneself in time or losing oneself in eternity, Ruge argued, for pettiness and degradation as well as grandeur and nobility have their eternal aspects. The choice is between *significant* and *consciously* made history on the one hand, and confused, unconscious historical processes on the other. The philosopher is the one who must lead in making history humanly significant. Ruge appeals from Hegel to Plato in his emphasis on the rôle of the philosopher in history. " Philosophical criticism contributes to the movement of world-history. . . . It is the philosopher who knows when the situation is ripe, who sits at the loom of time."[2]

Ruge differed from Bruno Bauer, who had expressed similar sentiments, in that he honestly went on to tackle specific problems in the concrete. As we have seen, Bauer's theoretical intransigence was so extreme that he refused to demand immediate reforms on the ground that they involved a betrayal of first principles. But Ruge believed that piecemeal reform was better than none. The first specific use to which he put his conception of philosophy as politics was to demand a *legal* status for political opposition. Refusing to distinguish between society and the state, he tried to prove that the very conception of a developing society involves the presence of a legally recognised political party which expressed the principle of opposition as such. The state was an *organic* whole; a political opposition party was just as much an integral part of that whole as the administration or government itself. As in every organic body, once destroy the negative element, the element of opposition, and you destroy the very possibility of development. " *Without criticism there is no development and without development no life.*" A state without an opposition party is not an organism but a dead machine serving private purposes.

Having justified in theory the *right* of a political opposition to exist, Ruge went on to draw up the kind of programme the opposition would need *were* it to exist. From abstract philosophical premises and by an illicit appeal to what a rationally interpreted history has proved, and in an amusing philosophical jargon (the sugar-coating for the censor) he claimed to have established the necessity of popular representative institutions, disestablishment of the church, the jury system, and freedom of the Press.

In their concrete proposals as well as in their appeal to rationally interpreted history, the Young-Hegelians came into conflict with the two dominant cultural ideologies of the day— the historical school of law and the literary philosophy of Romanticism. To the first, the emphasis on reason instead of tradition was anathema; to the second, the universalism and internationalism implied in the use of reason appeared hostile to the national, mystical, and irrational mythology at the heart of romanticism. In the eyes of the Young-Hegelians these dominant ideologies had definite political import. So long as they prevailed, the battle for immediate reforms—even when these reforms reflected the interests of the rising bourgeoisie— could not end in a clear-cut victory. It was inevitable that the Young-Hegelians begin their attack by submitting these and similar movements to a searching critique. There was a double advantage in their eyes in beginning here. Politically, it was safer; and in this field the philosopher could bring more effectively into play his professional accomplishments.

2. *Literary Romanticism as Political Reaction*

" It is remarkable," writes Engels in one of his early essays in literary criticism, " how in art and literature, as well as in life, reaction manifests itself . . . and how the cry of modern German obscurantists on the one side, correspond to a phase of modern German poetry on the other."[1] To Ruge, however,

---

[1] *Gesamtausgabe*, Abt. I, Bd. 2, p. 66. These essays of Engels contain a brilliant description of the contemporary literary scene.

belongs the merit of having revealed the intimate connections
between the resurgence of romanticism in Germany and insur-
gence of new political and social forces upon the cultural scene.
During the reconstruction period which followed the Napoleonic
wars, liberal ideas acquired a new momentum. They were imported into Germany from France by the enthusiastic members
of the Young-German and Young-Hegelian schools. Although
no overt political movement resulted from them, they caused
a considerable stir in intellectual and academic circles. The
official spokesmen of semi-feudal German society sought to find
a more stable base for public morality and cultural authority.
Hegel, they discovered, was too ambiguous in his positions.
His reliance upon reason was a double-edged weapon. Kant
and Fichte were too close to the Enlightenment; some of their
doctrines smacked of the French Revolution. The quest for an
escape from the shock of new experiences and the challenge of
new ideas found an outlet in the glorification of the culture of
the past. The pietistic character of German life made it impossible whole-heartedly to revive the Greek and Roman tradition.
The only other possibility open was the mediæval synthesis.
Accordingly those who feared the rise of new industrial and
cultural forces defined the good, the beautiful, and the holy in
terms of the Christian heritage. The inevitable result was that
the creative art and literature of the day tried to translate the
significance of this imaginatively reconstructed culture into a
contemporary idiom. The Schlegels and their circle, Jean Paul,
Tieck, Baader and others of the South German school illustrated
the forms of escape which those who feared the French Revolution were willing to take to find emotional security.

By romanticism, Ruge meant, in the first instance, the
literary German tradition of the first few decades of the nineteenth century which were characterised by lyrical other-
worldliness, philosophical mysticism, arbitrary æsthetic sym-
bolism, and mediæval political and social ideology. In its more
general sense, romanticism denoted in the minds of the Young-
Hegelians all varieties of religious dualism, all intrusions of the
authoritarian principles into public life, all escape from present-
day evils by imaginative flight into the past. Ruge opposed this
romantic tendency not on the grounds that it was not art, but

rather that it was not significant art. Poetic mysticism which tries to suggest the truths of another age he declared to be a prolonged hymn to superstition. The distant was not synonymous with the magical, nor the strange identical with the poetic. Fairy tales, ghosts, miracles, dreams, night, longing, moonshine—surely these were not the only themes which could be sung. The interests of the profane world, the workaday struggle, the forces liberated by the industrial revolution were just as legitimate subject matter of true poetry as the transcendental longings of the lonely soul. Especially did he oppose the romanticists' aversion to what they called the " gallic principle "—which emphasised the place of reason and analysis in æsthetic criticism as well as in general education. If " wonders " there must be, he cried, the important thing is not to believe in them but to accomplish them.[1]

In the catechism of the romantic school which Ruge, Echtermeyer, and the other Young-Hegelian critics drew up as a target for attack, the following beliefs were taken as central :

" (a) Allegiance to the ideals of the middle ages; a return to Catholicism in its mystic, not rational form; devotion to mediæval art, especially pre-Raphaelite painting.

" (b) An enthusiasm for the poetry of superstition in all times and a contempt for the poetry of reflection; cultivation of folk-song, folk-lore, folk-legends accompanied by the assumptions that they transmit the spiritual character of the national soul and that their ' deeper ' significance cannot be conveyed in words.

" (c) An attempt to make the categories of myth, magic and creation central in all expository accounts of the nature of the world and man.

" (d) A preference for the beauty of the wilderness to the beauty of civilisation: opposition to the industrial revolution on æsthetic grounds.

" (e) Addiction to the rhetoric of rhapsody; the use of terms like ' profound ' and ' mystical ' at every third word; studied avoidance of words like ' utility.'

[1] *Hallische Jahrbücher*, 1840, pp. 413, 436, 446.

" (f) Violent hatred of the Enlightenment, the French Revolution, and all their cultural effects.

" (g) A conviction that the ' end of the world ' is near; and that in the arts it has already taken place.

" (h) A belief in ' spirit ' as the only reality—aside from the existence of the devil and ghosts.

" (i) Apparent political indifferentism to the present, expressed in the slogans, ' All is vanity,' ' There is nothing new under the sun.' "[1]

This opposition to the Romantic school and its reactionary politics was a continuation, on a more critical plane, of the earlier opposition of the school of Young-Germany to the antisocial obscurantism of Novalis and his associates. But it was more sustained. It differed from the attitude of the Young-German school in two ways. It was motivated by a livelier appreciation of the social forces involved in the clash of principles (there were fewer apostasies among the Young-Hegelians than among *das junge Deutschland*) and it was characterised by a nicer discrimination between valid æsthetic forms which could be filled with a varying content and æsthetic forms which were completely integral with the social significance of their content. Later, however, some of the Young-Hegelians and " wahre Sozialisten," especially those who had been influenced by Börne, shifted all literary discussion to a political plane, and in the interest of immediate social action turned upon Goethe as well as Heine for their pure æstheticism and detachment. Marx came to the defence of both. But this phase of Young-Hegelianism we shall treat below.

3. *The Anti-Historicism of the Historical School*

The romantic movement in literature buttressed its position with arguments supplied by the " historical school " in law,

[1] This last was the subject of a special attack by Engels writing in Gutzkow's *Telegraph für Deutschland*, 1840, No. 26–8, under the pseudonym of Oswald. The title of the article is " Retrograde Zeichen der Zeit," reprinted in Marx-Engels, *Gesamtausgabe*, Abt. I, Bd. 2, pp. 66 ff. Later Engels broke with the school of Young-Germany to which Gutzkow belonged. The best criticism of *das junge Deutschland* from the standpoint of the Young-Hegelians was written by Engels in the *Deutsche Jahrbücher*, 1842, pp. 640–7, apropos of a critical analysis of A. Jung.

philosophy and culture study. It was necessary, in order to complete the task of criticism, to settle accounts with the pontifical authorities who had made "the argument from historical authority" (read "piety," "folk-consciousness," "national tradition") intellectually respectable and persuasive. Indeed one of the most fascinating chapters in the development of European thought in the nineteenth century is the struggle of the Young-Hegelians to wrest the "argument from history" out of the hands of the official representatives of the historical school and use it as a weapon in behalf of their own revolutionary purposes.

The appeal to history on the part of the post-Kantian philosophy and the historical school of law was the German answer to the French Revolution. The humiliation which Germany suffered at the hands of the French armies, the danger to political stability which flowed from the French ideals of republicanism, the "revolutionary" doctrines in law, education, religion, and even in love—were all laid at the door of the cult of reason. Reason (*Räsonieren*), in the form of the critical understanding which set up abstract principles to test all things and guide social action, was declared to be responsible for the liberation of the hellish forces of revolution and terror. Schelling and the early Hegel on the one side, Savigny, Leo, and their camp-followers on the other, sought in different yet related ways to undermine the autonomy of critical Reason—of that "Reason which the butchers of the French Revolution had elevated to the throne of God to pass criticism upon the ways of the Almighty." (Leo.)

The logical *schema* of the argument was briefly as follows: a distinction was introduced between "understanding" (ordinary reason referred to as *Verstand*) and "Reason" or "Spirit" (*Vernunft*, and in the terminology of the historical school, *Geist*). Understanding recognises distinctions: reason is the completed pattern of all the relations which the critical understanding distinguishes. The completed pattern of reason unwinds itself in time. As it unwinds it gives us empirical history. The human understanding exists not to create these patterns or to attempt to change them but to recognise them. The secret of the present is the past. Its meaning has been revealed in the past. But at this point the argument of the different schools diverges. The Hegelians professed to believe in a *developing* history which could be made by human beings once their critical understanding was informed by the spirit of reason (read " piety " and " tradition "); the historical school of law believed that no development in the present could be conscious development, that the life of the community was expressed and advanced in the cultural institutions which had come down from the past. For the historical school, there was no more sense in enacting laws than in legislating the kind of fruit a tree is to bring forth. Like the ripe fruit of a tree, the necessary social measures will drop from the tree of history whenever the proper time will have come. Woe to man if he feels that it is within his power to set the proper time ! The attempt to do so means a *Sundenstrafgericht* like the French Revolution. Savigny did make an effort to distinguish between the letter of the law and the spirit. But better than elaborate citation and commentary upon his doctrine is the following sentence from his chief theoretical work: " Of course it is not the letters [that matter] but the spirit, yet one can only learn what the original spirit is out of the old letters."[1] The spirit of the law is nothing but the old letters, the old texts, the old laws.

The Young-Hegelians, as the self-declared inheritors of the Hegelian philosophy, glossed over the ambiguities in Hegel's position—all the more readily because Savigny had attacked the equivocal rationalism of Hegel's philosophy of law. They addressed themselves to the leading principles of the historical school such as "the historical foundations of society" in order to show how glaringly inconsistent the protagonists of this doctrine were even in terms of their own system. The political roots of this philosophy were too obvious to be examined. But the sophistry, specious pleading and downright falsification of the historical record demanded a fundamental analysis. Ruge concerned himself primarily with Savigny; Köppen and Engels with Leo; and Marx with the founder of the school, Hugo.

(a) *Ruge versus Savigny.* For an entire decade, Wienbarg and the Young-Germans had protested against the tendency of the historical school to nail the present upon the cross of the past.

[1] *Vom Beruf Unserer Zeit für Gesetzgebung und Rechtswissenschaft*, 1814, p. 72.

But they had restricted themselves to stinging satire and bitter raillery against some of the paradoxical conclusions which followed from the historical view. They could marshal neither the arguments nor the information necessary to make an impression upon the mountains of irrelevant erudition which the historical school had laboriously built up in defence of its views. The questions which Ruge's group put to Savigny were themselves cogent arguments against the historical position. Their logic is so clear and sound that I shall cite them all, summarising the argument whenever necessary:

(1) " What do the supporters of the doctrine of *historical foundations* understand by that phrase ? What are the essential characteristics of its presence at any given time ? In what way is it distinguished from eternal, or purely human factors in the foundation of the state ? And what justifies its presumption to superiority over these others ? "

(2) " What is understood by the phrase historical *right* or law ? In what way is it distinguished from purely human right which at any given period the spirit of the age . . . brings to light and invests with validity ? "

(3) " What span of time is necessary and what other general conditions are essential to elevate a factor to the rank of *historical foundation* and *historical* right ? "

(4) Since what claims to have historical validity to-day has not existed from eternity, and has at some time in history replaced institutions which made the same claim to validity in *their* day, it follows that some kind of force must have been used to destroy the previous historical foundations. The question is what force or power has the right *to-day*, to overthrow the historical foundations of the *present* ? (argument summarised.)

(5) " When, as is notoriously the case, an historical foundation no longer serves *satisfactorily to maintain* the state but in the course of changing relationships becomes a *burden to it*, what is to be done to cut oneself loose from this nightmare (*Alpdruck*) in order not to sacrifice the present to the past ? Is there any means besides the organic vitality of development (*die constitutionelle Lebendigkeit der Entwicklung*) or the

realisation of reason and freedom in the state and its institutions ? "

(6) What is to be done to free those countries from the oppression of unreasonable and barbarous practices which make no pretext at being justified by historical foundations ? Slavery, for example (argument summarised).

Those questions are so framed that the historical school is practically compelled to yield a justification for reform, and at times, even for violent revolution. The article concluded with the observation that to appeal to history to preserve the past was illogical, since history was the record of change, i.e. of past ages which have not maintained themselves. " We very much fear," the article said, " that *history* as well as its *foundations* is an infinitely active thing; that it is an eternal revolution in comparison with which Mt. Vesuvius with all its eruption is a monotonous bore."[1]

(b) *Köppen and Engels on Leo.* Savigny was not the man to spend time in answering the attacks of the Young-Hegelians. Leo it was, who, as a professional historian rather than as a jurist, felt called upon to defend the faith. Indeed, he had begun the defence with an attack upon the Young-Hegelians in an influential work which he called characteristically enough, *Hegel und die Hegelingen.* But it was in his *Universal Geschichte* that Leo indicated how the ideas of the historical school of law could be used to interpret the great historical movements of the past. Typical of his attitude was his justification of Alva's suppression of Protestant Netherland, his attack upon the German reformation, and his denunciation of the French Revolution as the second fall of man. Wherever men had tried to make history according to reason, the result was disaster and a blood bath. Köppen, in reviewing the fourth and fifth volumes of this work, took a bold step forward and accepted the revolutionary consequences which Leo claimed were involved in the attempt to make reason practical. If reason is to be condemned on the ground that it leads to bloodshed, then at least its praises must

---

[1] *Deutsche Jahrbücher*, Dec. 8, 1841, p. 548. This article was written under the pseudonym of Balticus. I have ascribed it to Ruge not because I have evidence that he is the author, but because as editor of the magazine Ruge was personally responsible to the censor for everything which he published.

be sung on the ground that it has resulted in less bloodshed than the forces of unreason which Leo glorified. If historical events are to be evaluated from the standpoint of the amount of bloodshed or suffering they produced, then all movements—those which Leo called good as well as bad—stand judged as immoral and wicked. But such an interpretation is preposterous. It is not bloodshed as such which condemns an event but the conditions, purposes, and consequences of its use.

Anticipating later historians, Köppen points out that the French " reign of terror " had a twofold necessity. It was an instrument of national preservation and the means of consolidating the gains of 1789. If the history of the French Revolution was to be written from the standpoint of its innocent victims, as a chronicle of intrigue and decapitations, then it would naturally appear to Leo as an abomination. But Köppen reminded him that in the same fashion it was only too easy to write a history of the church in terms of *its* massacres, burnings, and heresy-hunting. If such histories struck Leo as "degenerately one-sided," then his own interpretation of the French Revolution must be regarded just as degenerate. " If the revolution is to be abominated because it snatched the lives of several thousands, so must many periods of the Christian era . . . be abominated. What is sauce for the goose is sauce for the gander." Köppen went further. Accepting for the nonce the ethical standard involved in Leo's attitude, he maintained that tradition, reaction and clericalism have always been more brutal and bloodthirsty than revolts conducted in the name of freedom and reason. Enthroned power resorts more readily to violence than oppressed minorities. In words which show that the speeches of St. Just and others before the Convention were still echoing in his head, he wrote:

" Yes, the tree of freedom has been watered with blood and fertilised with corpses. But what are all the crimes of the Jacobins compared with the crimes of the priests, the court favourites and royal tyrants ? Neither in respect to quality or extent are they on the same level. . . . What is the guillotine against the Inquisition, what the reign of terror against the wholesale extermination of the

Albigenses, the massacre of St. Bartholomew, the dragonades? What are the wildest of terrorists compared to Alva, Guise, Torquemada? What is a Robespierre to a Philip II? "[1]

As a pietist, Leo was compelled to explain how it was possible if the finger of God could be seen in all events, for these revolutionary excesses to have taken place at all. He falls back upon the time-honoured device of visiting the sins of one generation upon the heads of another. Desert and reward are asymmetrical. Because of the sins of the French Revolution, mankind is visited with a Young-Hegelian movement. The whirlwind which the Young-Hegelians are sowing now, will be reaped by their own descendants. Not only is this true in history, but also in one's personal life. Leo calls medicine to witness. One man's pleasure may mean disease to his children unto the third and fourth generation. It is at this point that Engels takes up the idea in a humorous skit on Leo in *Die Rheinische Zeitung*. He shows that if this " ethical " principle of justice were consistently acted upon, that if one were to be punished for another's sins and rewarded for another's virtues, utter absurdity would be the result. It was just as intelligent to attempt to found jurisprudence and medicine on Christian principles as to write a German grammar by them.[2]

(c) *Marx on the Historical School.* Marx never minced words about the historical school. In his *Critique of the Hegelian Philosophy of Law* he denounces it, in an aside, as a school which "legitimises the contemptible practices of to-day by the contemptible practices of yesterday, a school which stamps every cry of the serf against the knout as treasonable once that knout is an ancient knout, an indigenous knout, an historical knout; a school to whom history reveals, like the God of Israel to his servant Moses, only its posterior side."[3] But wherever we find denunciation in Marx we are sure to find it as the outcome of critical analysis and not as a substitute for it. That analysis is contained in an article in *Die Rheinische Zeitung* entitled, " Das philosophische Manifest der historischen Rechtschule." It is

[1] *Deutsche Jarhbücher*, 1842, p. 515.
[2] Marx-Engels, *Gesamtausgabe*, Abt. I, Bd. 2, p. 305. Engels here is undoubtedly under the influence of Feuerbach.
[3] *Gesamtausgabe*, I, 1, 609.

one of the most penetrating and suggestive criticisms of the methodological presuppositions of the historical school of law which has been written. It has been strangely neglected by professional scholars.

Marx's thesis is a paradoxical one and can only be understood in light of his Hegelian antecedents. The historical school of law, he says, is not merely a *reaction* to the abstract reason of the French Enlightenment; it is a consequence of it. This may best be seen in examining the manifesto issued by the father of the school—Hugo. The doctrines of Savigny, Stahl, Haller, Leo and the other representatives of the historical school are variations upon the inverted natural law theories of Hugo. The occasion which Marx took for his " higher criticism " of the sources of the historical school was the appointment of Savigny in 1842 as Minister of Legislation. A few years before there had appeared a *Festschrift* to Hugo in which Savigny himself acknowledged his indebtedness to the author of the *Lehrbuch der Naturrecht*. Marx, therefore, could with justification regard it as the " old testament " of the historical school.

But how can the traditionalism of the historical school be derived from the rationalism of the Enlightenment ? Marx's answer is that both shared the fiction of the existence of a natural man whose fixed original nature provided the standard for what was reasonable or unreasonable, possible or impossible in social institutions. But whereas the rationalists believed that man's original nature could express itself consistently, and be ruled by reason, Hugo believed that man's original nature was such that no rational organisation of social life was possible upon it as a basis. Whatever social organisation existed was irrational. And in its irrationality, in its very positivity—its justification was to be sought. For that irrationality was merely the expression of a " higher Reason " whose specific productions must be *accepted* and not tested by ordinary critical reason. " If Kant's philosophy," wrote Marx, " is regarded with justification as the German theory of the French Revolution, then Hugo's natural law is the German theory of the French *ancien régime* " (*Gesamtausgabe*, Abt. I, Bd. 1, p. 254).

Hugo had taken as the primary postulate of his jurisprudence the proposition that " the only jural differentiating character

of man is his animal nature " (Sec. 40 of his *Lehrbuch*). In other
words, a strictly legal and rational justification of an institution
can be found only when the institution in question can be
derived from man's animal impulses—monogamy from sex,
private property from physical power, etc. Using this postulate
as his criterion of rational validity and a conception of human
nature which would have shamed Hobbes, he examines the
nature of social institutions and the positive law of those institutions. He shows that property, the state, marriage, etc.,
cannot be rationally derived from man's animal nature, that,
in fact, they contradict the assumptions of the rationalists
who believe that all of these institutions can be proved to be
convenient and *necessary*. No, maintains Hugo, if they have any
validity, they cannot have *rational* validity. An abstract
ethics and logic based on human needs can only establish the
fact that all social institutions are irrational. But this scepticism is only a transitional phase in Hugo's argument. Social
institutions, he argues, are none the less in existence. If logic
does not sanction them, our feeling does. This feeling does not
derive from nature but from society and history. If social
institutions are to have any validity, it must be the *historical*
validity of tradition, custom, and authority—sources which are
autonomous and above the shallow canons of *logical* validity.
Marx writes:

" Hugo does not seek to prove that the positive [institutions
and law] is *reasonable*; rather he seeks to prove that it is
unreasonable. He drags together evidence from all parts of
the world with the most near-sighted industry to prove that
positive institutions, property, marriage, the state, etc.,
possess no rational necessity, that in fact they even *contradict*
reason, that at best they serve as occasions for idle chatter.
One cannot attribute this method to the accidental fact
of Hugo's personality. It is rather the logic (*Methode*) of his
principle, the *naïve, ruthless logic* of the historical school.
If the positive is to be *valid* merely because it exists, then
I must prove that wherever what exists is *invalid,* it is invalid because it is *reasonable.* And how can I prove that more
simply than by showing that whatever is positive exists not

because of reason, but in spite of it ? If this is madness, there
is method in it ! " (p. 252.)

The method is to vindicate the *status quo* against all attempts
at reform. It is to employ the argument from relativity to
produce scepticism and lack of faith and then fly to revelation
or tradition to assure a basis for faith in whatever institutions
happen to be at hand. It is cynically to decry all ideals as un-
practical and irrelevant in order to hold on more securely to the
material goods and power possessed by the dominant class.

For Marx, of course, to appeal to abstract ethical ideals, to
insist upon their absolute validity independently of a specific
biologic, psychologic, historical, social and class context is the
reverse face of reactionary historicism. Abstract idealism and
extreme historicism differ not in principle but in the specific
things they declare to be good or evil. Whoever proclaims that
valid ideals are independent of existence is in the same logical
position as he who maintains that all existence is ideal. Ideals
cannot be identified with things, but they grow out of things—
have significance, relevance and effect only in relation to things.
The manner in which ideals operate in history, their conditions
and consequences, Marx was later to describe in his theory of
historical materialism.

4. *Poetry as Politics*

In all times of close political censorship, the ideas of the opposition find their way into *belles-lettres*. This was true of eighteenth-
century France with its satirical drama, of nineteenth-century
Russia with its sociological novel, and of Germany from 1830–
1850 with its *tendenz* novel and social-political lyric. The age
of Metternichian reaction was one in which those " who sang
because they loved to sing " sang of the past in a romantic,
religious, and mystical vein; while those who longed for some
form of participation in the new social movements which were
surging over Europe sought, with the school of Young-Germany,
to convert " *die Kunstkritik zum Organ des Zeitkritik.*" Börne,
the head of the school, had graphically stated that his purpose
was " to pull the bed-cover off the sleeping Germans "; and after
him all the members of the school had filled their works with

criticism of their age and proclamations of the new social and political evangelism.

A critical reaction soon made itself felt against this tendentious literature. Even Freiligrath, who later became the chief singing strength of the *Rheinische Zeitung*, attacked the propagandist attitude. In one of his poems he exclaims: " The poet stands on a watch-tower higher than the battlements of party." Other voices were not wanting to take up the refrain. The argument was very simple. Poetry treats of the eternal, the universal and the absolute; in so far as it is political, it becomes temporal, limited and partial. Good politics is no excuse for bad poetry and good poetry is completely indifferent to the special interests of the time. It is above politics. The only question appropriate to it is whether it conforms to certain immutable æsthetic categories of coherence, economy of means, and fidelity to subject matter.

The Young-Hegelians lost no opportunity in coming forward in defence of the view that literature and politics are necessarily connected. If poetry is above politics, they asserted, it is above life, too, for in a broad sense politics determines the character of life, explains its specific cultural expressions and changes. " The dogma has long enough prevailed among Germans," wrote Stahr, one of the leading spirits among the Young-Hegelians, " that poetry and politics have nothing to do with one another, that political stuff can never serve as poetical material. But why ? Shall it be maintained that the point at which the life of man culminates is not poetic ? That the histories of nations and peoples . . . the development of man . . . does not lend itself to, or is unworthy of, poetic expression. Have not the masterpieces of epic and the dramatic poetry of all ages sprung from such soil ? "[1] The cult of the eternal in poetry is an expression of a metaphysical dualism which tries to separate eternity from time. The task of the poet, the Young-Hegelians held, is not merely to select for emphasis that aspect of his age which has significance for all time but also to *make* the immediate aspect of his age significant. As the child of his age, the poet should seek to make his parent immortal. He should bring his age to self-consciousness by articulating its hopes and integrating its activities in poetic

[1] *Deutsche Jahrbücher*, 1842, p. 1077.

vision. " Poetry and life stand in the closest reciprocity to one another. All true poetry is a child of its time expressing its loves and hates, its activity and suffering. . . . The age gives birth to the poet and the poet transforms the substance and spirit of the age into forms in which we recognise our own flesh and blood."

The time for *Weltschmerz* was over; the hour for social action had come. The poetry of social action had no place for the liquid rhythms of nostalgia and romance; it hammered out its iron measures in the white heat of indignation against social evils. There was blood in it and the beat of marching feet. In the forties when the flaming lyrics of social revolt burst forth in the works of Herwegh, Beck, Dingelstedt and others, the Young-Hegelians were the first to greet them as the harbingers of a literary and political renaissance. Upon the appearance of Herwegh's *Gedichte eines Lebendigen,* the *Deutsche Jahrbücher* officially applauded him as the poet of freedom, cried with him *guerre aux chateaux, paix aux chaumières,* quoted the most violent of his poems and called upon the other poets of the dead age to join the voice of the " living." " Political freedom," it wrote, " is the poetry and religion of our time."[1] Before many years had elapsed lyricists like Herwegh and Freiligrath were playing an active rôle in the political and social struggle of the day— even more so than Ruge who was wont to remind them, " mit dem Blumenstangel ihres Zauberstabes schlägt man keinen Schädel ein."[2]

It was natural enough that the introduction of a political axis into the evaluation of works of art would produce some bizarre judgments. Books were often damned simply because of the politics of their authors. The formal achievements of a work of art were subordinated and sometimes totally ignored in the emphasis upon its moral tendency. In this the young radicals were sharing the critical premises of the orthodox and conservative whose politics they so vehemently opposed. The attitude towards Goethe was symptomatic of the state of criticism at this time. The Romanticists and other political conservatives who were devoted to the ideals of a Germanic and Christian fatherland attacked him because of his cosmopolitanism and philosophical pantheism. The priests were bitter against him

---

[1] *Deutsche Jahrbücher,* 1841, p. 263.   [2] *Werke,* Bd. 6, 2ter Teil, p. 100.

because they believed that the Young-German cry for "*die Rehabilitation des Fleisches*" had its roots not only in "French degeneracy" but in Goethe's frank paganism and his ethics of beauty. But Goethe fared no better at the hands of the young radicals. Most of these dissident spirits resented his detached æsthetic attitude to affairs of political moment. They missed an explicit social note in all of his writings and were revolted at the notion of a *Geniemoral*. His Olympian serenity was denounced as a false neutrality. They were pitiless in revealing his personal frailties—especially the weakness of his knees in the presence of the mighty. Börne had been the first to couple him with Hegel, the apologist of the existing order, in an oft-quoted quip : "*Goethe ist der gereimte Knecht und Hegel der ungereimte.*"

Interestingly enough, the first voices which made themselves heard against the excesses of this radical literary criticism were those of Karl Marx and Frederick Engels. The attitude of the Young-Hegelians towards literature in general and Goethe in particular had been carried to extremes by the "*wahre Sozialisten,*" especially Hess and Grün. The last had even published an entire volume against Goethe. In 1847, treating of the vagaries of these "real Socialists" in *Die Deutsche Brusseler Zeitung*, Engels (in an essay until recently ascribed to Marx) protested against this judgment upon Goethe. He insisted that it was possible to distinguish between Goethe, the philistine and Goethe, the poetic genius.[1] Politics was relevant to art as subject matter : but it could not determine æsthetic taste or lay down the standards of significant expression.

5. *Above-the-Battle Neutralities*

Closely allied with their political interpretation of literature was the impatience of the Young-Hegelians with all attitudes which sought to retain a critical neutrality towards the social issues of the day. Nothing indicated more clearly the rapid development of sectarian tendencies in the Young-Hegelians than their denial that there could be middle ground between the forces of "critical progress" and those of "uncritical

[1] "*So ist Goethe bald kolossal, bald kleinlich; bald trotziges spottendes, weltverachtendes Genie, bald rücksichtsvoller, genugsamer, enger Philister*" (Mehring, *Aus dem Literarischen Nachlass Marx-Engels*, Bd. 2, p. 388).

conservatism." Sometimes they mistook a mediate view for political indifferentism. But the two forms of political indifferentism which the Young-Hegelians expressly opposed were (a) complete devotion to abstract pursuits coupled with the refusal to regard one's social position in the community as the source of social duties and responsibility; and (b) the tendency to find peace and safety from political struggle in some form of unnatural seclusion.

Ruge made no attempt to carry over the same political attitude that he took to poetry to the more technical sciences. Politics was not constitutive of pure science. In fact he was willing to make the grandiloquent and inconsistent admission that "science constitutes a realm which is not of this world." But he insists that the historical career of science as well as the individual life of the thinker is very much bound up with this world. It is an artificial and selfish isolation for the "educated to refuse to participate in social affairs . . . and to regard the evolution of the state as completely foreign to their interests." The excuses they offer are inadequate. Politics is one-sided; it corrupts intellectual integrity; truth is irrelevant in party-strife—were some of the reasons advanced for refusing to enter into political struggles or for withdrawing from politics after one had been active. Ruge protests that this is merely a "superior way" of dodging responsibilities to one's fellow-men. To seek refuge in an intellectual or artistic vagabondage which does not salute any social ideals because it is above all social ideals, to cling to neutrality as a pretext for concealing our fear of taking sides, to boast of devotion to universal values and yet refuse to act to make those values really universal, to convert the standpoint of criticism which is conscious of everybody's faults into the position of political indifferentism in which there are no degrees of fault—all this is at best a justification for weakness, and at worst, a confession of insincerity. The nature of man demands fulfilment in political life and activity. " It is only the participation of the individual in history which gives him his true significance, and when his science or art . . . leads him away from the movement of ideas and political activity that is a sign of its abstract, and sadly inadequate position."[1] As we shall see below, Ruge meant by political activity not only

[1] *Hallische Jahrbücher*, 1840, p. 1423.

interest in social affairs but definite allegiance to a political *party*.

Another tendency—more literary than practical—against which the Young-Hegelians took the field, found expression in the belief that personal seclusion or retirement from social life was the most effective means of personal salvation and that the major evils of social life were due to worldliness and needless complexity. This was not a form of religious romanticism. Neither its motivation nor goal were political. It was not attached to the ideas of the past but dreamed of a simple and idyllic life in country and village where each could live his own life without dictating his neighbour's. It touched those who had felt the futility of ambition and the hollowness of fame; those who were indifferent to wealth, but sensitive to beauty.

The Young-Hegelians characterised this attitude—it was in the main only a theoretical point of view presented in some of the contemporary novels—as a mixture of strength and weakness. " Strength in so far as the individual desires and seeks deliverance; weakness in so far as he seeks it through flight."[1] To escape life in order to preserve our individuality is to forget that our individuality becomes different in virtue of that escape. Society, to paraphrase Danton, is not something which exists merely under the soles of our feet. It has its tendrils in our very speech, our very thought and mind. We cannot escape life by changing our residence. The temporary good which comes from isolation—the easing of psychological tension—is a *personal* good which of itself can never appease our sense of social justice. The life of man in society must be taken as it is and made the basis for reform. Nothing is changed by shutting one's eyes or running away.

6. " *Partei ! Partei ! Wer sollte sie nicht nehmen !* "

There were German liberal elements who were willing to go as far as Ruge in emphasising the importance of *discussing* central political issues but who stopped short at the idea of taking a part in a definite political organisation. They clung to the ideals of freedom and tolerance, pointed to the inevitable discrepancy between abstract principles and party

---

[1] *Hallische Jahrbücher*, p. 1919, in a review of Dingelstadt's *Unter der Erde*, Pt. I, 1840.

attitudes, and pinned their faith to the possibility of *logically convincing* those who possessed the state power that the reform of the political system would really serve the interests of all. Ruge was compelled to dissociate his position from those who called themselves *philosophical* liberals. In the very same month in which the *Deutsche Jahrbücher* was suppressed, he characterised philosophical liberalism as the faint-hearted aspiration for freedom on the part of a people stuck fast in theory—a theory of fantasy because it did not know that its true end was practice. The reform of consciousness, the liberation from abstract dogma, the true religion of freedom could only be realised through political organisation—political organisation not under the ambiguous slogans of liberalism but of republican democracy.

For the purposes of exposition we may regard Karl Rosencranz, Hegel's biographer and the leader of the Hegelian centre, as the representative of philosophical liberalism. His views on the philosophy of politics were epitomised in a very interesting essay " Über den Begriff der politischen Partei " (written January 1843, the month in which Ruge's magazine was finally suppressed).[1] He addresses himself here directly to the question of the relation between the state and political parties. But in passing he discusses the relation between philosophy and politics. It is his answer to this latter question, however, which determines the answer to the former. A political party is defined as a limited organisation aware that it represents special interests in the general conflict of interests within the state. Rosencranz's liberalism consisted in his insight that, so defined, the existence of *one* political party demanded the existence of *another*. This established the legal right of an opposition party to exist. If the opposition party were destroyed there was no longer any political party at all in the sense defined. Affiliation with any political party, therefore, definitely committed a person to one-sidedness, since its professed aim is to destroy the opposition. But how can any critical minded man bind himself to any one side—even to the side with whose general aims he is sympathetic ? Sensitiveness to new ideas, even freedom of criticism are checked in the face of party triumph. The interests of political expediency too often demand an open disregard of the truth. And since it is a

[1] Reprinted in *Neue Studien*, Vol. II, p. 50 (Leipzig, 1875).

good Hegelian dictum that no one has all the right on his side is it not hard to tie up with organisations which act as if they have ?

This difficulty is solved by Rosencranz's distinction between the philosopher as such and man as such. Man as a philosopher cannot take sides; man as a human being must. Philosophy is no sister to politics—indeed, it has no relatives in the existing world at all, though the philosopher himself may have. But how can the two be separated ? They cannot, Rosencranz admitted. But although the philosopher is a human being and in so far partial, he insists that philosophy is more than human. The philosopher in politics must struggle against his own humanity.

> " Philosophy in and for itself is partyless, or, to put it better, impartial. And the philosopher too should be impartial ! Should be ! But in mortal affairs there is a deep cleft between what is and what should be, between the idea and its reality. Only God is absolutely impartial. Yes, but the striving after impartiality is still left for us. This striving after impartiality is neither weakness nor arrogance, but a necessity. The partiality of the philosopher as such consists in his striving after impartiality." [1]

We are now in a position to understand Rosencranz's answer to the question of the relation between the state and political parties. The state is an expression of the impartial philosophical principle; the political party is the expression of erring, one-sided humanity. The state was not to take political sides. It should not represent a party interest but the interests of all parties. It was like an umpire or judge watching the political play carefully and closely, penalising here and there but always conscious of the fact that it was not a player itself. " Were the state to take sides with any party," said Rosencranz, " it would inevitably fall into political onesidedness and as a consequence share the fate of such onesidedness." That is to say, it would destroy itself or be destroyed, since political defeat would mean revolution.

Ruge never answered this argument. The reason was that at heart it was his own position. He differed from Rosencranz because of his realisation that the *existing* state was an expression

[1] *Neue Studien*, Vol. II, p. 52 (Leipzig, 1875).

of a definite political tendency although it pretended to be more than that. He knew that it was a clerical, romantic, feudal class state. His purpose was to make the state " a classless state," i.e. to make it conform with the Hegelian definition of a state. It is here that we must look for the real cause of the rift between Ruge and Marx. For Marx, the very nature of the state demanded that it be a class state. The only significant question was whose state it should be. Every political party aims to acquire state power by fair means or foul in order to use it for class purposes. It reigns in the name of the entire community; it rules in behalf of the few. Every philosophy of politics is a class philosophy expressing class politics. Specific interest and needs are behind politics; political ideals are the instruments of those interests. The party is an organisation which attempts under the banner of these ideals to transform existence through action. It was in this spirit that Herwegh, one of the rebel poets of Germany at this time close to Marx, intoned his hymn to *die Partei*:

> *Partei ! Partei ! Wer sollte sie nicht nehmen,*
> *Die noch die Mutter aller Siege war !*
> *Wie mag ein Dichter solch ein Wort verfemen,*
> *Ein Wort, des alles Herrliche gebar ?*
> *Nur offen wie ein Mann : Für oder wider ?*
> *Und die Parole : Sklave oder frei ?*
> *Selbst Gotter stiegen vom Olymp hernieder*
> *Und kämpften auf der Zinne der Partei !*

II

FROM POLITICAL LIBERALISM TO SOCIAL DEMOCRACY

Although Marx and Ruge shared many common positions against the obscurantists of their day, important differences separated them almost from the outset. These remained latent until the final rift in 1844. Unfortunately the occasions of their disagreements were often attended by conflicts of moral judgment upon the private lives of mutual friends. This, together with the historians' love of personalia, has so obscured the theoretical relationship between them that most of the accounts of the break are merely a record of their suspected spites, jealousies and ambitions. Ruge's letters, it is true, emphasise these things and it cannot be denied that fundamental oppositions of temperament accentuated the differences between them.[1]

The objective issues, however, were there even if they were not clearly recognised by Ruge. Marx insisted upon dragging them forth. His criticism of Ruge's philosophy of politics makes manifest the differences between them and explains why Ruge could not see them. Ruge had no sense for social and economic affairs. They were in his eyes aspects of the dominant political relations which in turn expressed abstract ethical values. Consequently all criticism of his social position appeared to him as an expression either of bad logic or of bad character upon the part of his opponents. Since he had a fearful respect for Marx's logic, he was naturally inclined to interpret Marx's criticism of the abstract formulas of political democracy as actuated primarily by unworthy personal motives. In later life, however, he grasped the objective differences between liberal republican democracy and revolutionary social democracy but by that time he had gone over to the camp of reaction. I shall trace the differences between Marx and Ruge as they gradually manifested themselves. These differences extend even to the period of their collaboration as co-editors of the *Deutsch-Französische Jahrbücher.*

1. *Is Atheism a Religion ?*

Both Ruge and Marx had dissociated themselves from B. Bauer because he refused to draw any practical political implications from his sweeping religious negations. Ruge, however,

---

[1] Ruge's own interpretation of the break between Marx and himself is given in letters to his mother, to Feuerbach and to Fleishner dated the 19 and 20 of May, 1843. Ruge's letter to Duncker (August 29, 1844) contains an amusing, even if spiteful, characterisation of Marx which shows in what fearful respect Ruge held Marx's " grossen Belesenheit und selbst seiner . . . gewissenslosen Dialektik." A full account of the falling out between Ruge and Marx over the private morals of Herwegh and Heine is given by Mehring (*Nachlass*, Bd. 2, p. 13). Heine's own characterisation of Ruge suggests that the latter erred on the side of decorum and respectability:

" Ruge is a philistine who has disinterestedly surveyed himself in a mirror and confessed that—after all—Apollo Belvidere is even more beautiful. Ruge has freedom in his soul but not yet in his limbs. For no matter how enthusiastically he rants about the beauties of Hellenic nakedness, he cannot make up his mind to remove his barbarous modern trousers or even pull off his Christian-Germanic underdrawers of morality " (loc. cit.).

refused to accept even the atheism which Bauer preached. He was willing to call himself a republican but not an atheist. The arguments for atheism were arguments for a new religion. " Atheism is just as religious as was Jacob wrestling with God: the atheist is no freer than a Jew who eats pork or a Moham-medan who drinks wine." Atheism is a negative theology. It has its rituals no less than the orthodox faith, its own dogmas and orthodoxies. But man has a religious need which cannot be satisfied by negations. To say that *this* does not exist or *that* does not exist is not enough. For, first, we cannot logically prove that something does not exist. We can only show that the evi-dence is not sufficient to establish existence. And, secondly, man desires to accept something positive which will sustain him in the ordinary crises, sacrifices, and devotions of life. It is not a question of religion or irreligion, but of the *form* or *kind* of re-ligion. The religion of the spirit, the religion of freedom, the religion of humanity were the different names which Ruge gave in the course of his development to his positive affirmations. They marked his progress from the abandonment of the Hegelian philosophy of religion to the acceptance of Feuerbach's philo-sophy of religion.

Now Marx also referred throughout his attacks on Bauer to Bauer's religious atheism. But his reference is not to Bauer's arguments against the religion of revelation and authority but to Bauer's abstract, unhistorical philosophy of self-consciousness. What Bauer was doing was to substitute a supernatural philo-sophic idealism for a supernatural myth. For every time a man falls back upon abstractions which have no functional use and test in experience, he relapses into religion. It was the super-natural element in any belief which made it religious, not the mere practices of charity, devotion, sacrifice or what not which religious men perform. It is not what people do but the theory behind the doing which makes it religious. It is *theory* which makes of certain acts *sacraments*, and of certain accidents of birth and station, *grace*. To live a life of beauty or sympathy does not therefore make life a religion of beauty or a religion of sympathy unless these terms are used for something trans-cendental, for something which, having once arisen in human experience, is hypostasised and placed above the test of experience. If supernaturalism, in this sense, and religion are synonymous, then Ruge's own philosophy of freedom which was abstract, unhistorical and Hegelian to boot, is itself religious. True atheism is not another religion but a naturalistic philosophy. It is philosophical materialism as critical of the unhistorical abstractions of traditional atheism as of the historical idealism of religion. Marx was able to show that not only Bauer and Ruge but even Stirner, the arch-iconoclast, was religious, for all of them were dealing with abstractions that had no historical functional context. When Marx wrote that " religion is the opium of the people," the reference is to the *beliefs* of organised religion and the *practices* which followed from those beliefs. The beliefs considered by themselves would be mere fantasy: the practices, taken independently of the ideas behind them, would be meaningless.

2. *Tired Liberalism and Social Pessimism*

Marx opposed the supernaturalism of religion and philosophy not only because it was logically inconsistent and concealed its fundamental incoherence in a set of myths which it refused to submit to rational analysis, but because its social effects were disastrous upon those who took the doctrines they professed seriously. It produced either an irrational attitude towards social causation or a fatalistic resignation which paralysed action. Not that Marx was unaware that many of the religiously orthodox who accepted theological determinism were active in social affairs. His experience with the German pietists who persecuted him and his Young-Hegelian friends instead of leaving them to the wrath and mercy of God, was of itself sufficient to enforce the lesson. But he saw that religious fatalism was invoked to support the institutions which operated in the interests of the dominant groups in society and to console those who suffered from these institutions. Poverty, war, property, royalty, social obedience, were defended and strengthened by religious sanctions. They were regarded as institutions beyond the power of man consciously to alter. Whatever change was necessary would be produced by divine processes working themselves out with a " higher " wisdom to realise a " higher " good.

There was danger that a political liberalism which based itself upon a half-hearted supernaturalism would fall into a mood of resignation when its own " human " efforts proved unavailing. A succession of defeats, with which the pendulum of reaction had begun in the forties in Germany, produced disheartenment in liberal circles. Instead of studying the social forces which were giving rise to conditions incompatible with the existence of the *status quo*—social forces which could not be stemmed by the prolonged successes of reaction—the liberals often retreated to bitter pessimism. The soul of the Germans was held responsible for their miserable social conditions, their blatant patriotism, their truckling *Untertänigkeit*, for their callous philistinism and religious pietism. The correspondence exchanged between Ruge, Marx, Feuerbach and Bauer apropos of the launching of the *Deutsch-Französische Jahrbücher*, indicated how profoundly dispirited Ruge was at the obstacles which *der Geist der Freiheit* was meeting in its " boring from within " tactics in Germany. Some characteristic sentences from one of Ruge's letters to Marx read:

" And so it is. This generation was not born to be free. Thirty years of political degeneracy, of contemptible pressure which ruled and censored even the secret thoughts and feelings of human beings in accordance with the dictates of the secret police, have degraded Germany and set her back politically more than she ever was before. You say: a ship of fools which is at the mercy of the wind and waves cannot escape its fate and that fate is the revolution. But surely you will not add that this revolution will be the salvation of these fools. On the contrary your metaphor carries with it the idea of destruction. But I do not even grant you the destruction. . . . Oh! this German future! Where are its seeds sown? Perhaps in the shameful history which we have until now lived through? Or in the despair of those who have some idea of freedom and historical honour? Or perhaps in the scorn which other peoples have poured upon us. . . . Read how free men speak, read how much sensitiveness they still attribute to us—to us who possess none at all; and then pity Prussia, pity Germany. . . . Our people has no future; what sense is there in our calling ? (Briefwechsel von 1843, Marx-Engels, *Gesamtausgabe*, I, 1, p. 560.)

Marx's letters reveal a totally different spirit. He does not deny the depths of servility and brutality to which Germany has sunk. But he goes on to explain the principle and system which has produced it. He does not deny that the intellectual integrity of the retainers of feudalism—the priests, officials, professors, and journalists—has been corrupted, and that the will of sincere lovers of freedom has been paralysed by despair or disgust. But he insists that the development of social forces will either compel the reaction to become even more reactionary—which would be suicide—or will inject a critical leaven into the very culture of reaction itself. We must not lose sight of the fact, he argues, that man is a feeling animal before he is a thinking animal and that no system of thought can fix the feelings of the entire population. At a certain point, even under the worst of oppressions, in order to preserve one's very existence, a feeling of self-respect, a desire for freedom, arises. The point at which it arises depends, not only upon the objective conditions but upon men like Marx and Ruge themselves. This feeling for the essential dignity of human personality, for social freedom, must be an essential element of any fundamental revolutionary movement. " Only this feeling," wrote Marx, " which with the disappearance of the Greeks disappeared from the world, and with the coming of the Christians took flight to the blue mist of heaven—only this feeling can transform society (*Gesellschaft*) into a community (*Gemeinschaft*) of free men " (Ibid., p. 561). But although feeling and intelligence are necessary elements of a revolutionary movement and always the proximate causes of action, they are not the basic causes of the revolutionary movement. The basic cause must be sought in the objective tendencies of the environment which create the conditions and occasions of feeling. Gropingly, Marx suggests what these causes are (he was not yet a Marxian socialist in 1843). Not only the reactionary measures of the government but even more so the system of competition and commerce, of property and human exploitation. A feeling mankind which thinks, and a thinking mankind which feels, will now know where to find the instruments of social liberation. The longer it takes for the social forces within existing society to develop, the greater the number of thinking and feeling people there will be who will rally together, and "the more completely will that order (*Produkt*) come into the world which the present carries in its womb."

3. *The Class State* versus *the Social State*

All of the Young-Hegelians started their careers by singing hymns of praise to the Hegelian conception of the state. Marx was no exception. There was something inherently plausible in conceiving the state to be an expression of the common interests of society, of the common needs and ideals. The plausibility, Marx discovered, was due to the human *wish* that it be so. And the tendency was to transform the wish into a fact. Hegel had done it. The Hegelians of the right and centre had done it. And even some of the left Hegelians imagined that the facts of state power could be made to correspond with the ideal of state power merely by intellectual decree. It was only when Marx became the editor of the *Rheinische Zeitung* and was obliged to comment on the day by day activities of the government that his views on the nature of the state changed. He gradually came to see that political equality was a *condition*, not the *guarantee*, of social equality, and that without social equality all talk about the community of interests and the divinity of the state was so much empty rhetoric. Where there was no social equality, the state was an *instrument in use* in society but was not itself an expression of the whole of society.

The significant occasion upon which this was brought home to Marx was the debate held in the Rhenish Provincial Assembly on the wood-theft laws (*Holzdiebstahlgesetz*). The legislators were intent upon putting teeth into the law which made appropriation of dead wood from the forests a crime. The small land-proprietor was amply protected by the fact that he did not have much to protect and was himself in the neighbourhood. The large land-proprietor could not have his wardens adequately defend his woods unless wood-stealing was declared a penal offence and enforced. A great to-do was made in the Landtag about protecting the large land-owners as well as the small, since, as citizens of the community, they were both entitled to equal rights of protection. Marx seized this principle and hurled it at the heads of the representatives, barbed with the following question: what protection was the state giving to the poor, the paupered wood-stealers themselves, who were also citizens of the political community ? (*Gesamtausgabe*, I, 1, 283–4). The poor were not stealing wood in order to sell it. They merely made sporadic raids on private forests in their vicinity in order to gather fuel for their own cottages. The stringency of the winter and the relatively high price of wood had intensified the abuse. And, as a matter of fact, the poor had always enjoyed the immemorial right (forgotten conveniently by the historical school of law) of carting off dead wood. But now, on the pretext that sometimes injury was done to *living* trees, the poor were to be prohibited from taking *any* wood. The state had stepped forward to defend the property of one class of its citizens. But it did nothing to defend the welfare and the very lives of a still larger class—those who had no property. If it were, as it claimed, a classless state above privileged economic interest, its protecting zeal would extend to all sections of the population. But judging the state by the specific activity of its courts and legislatures, it certainly did not seem to be the incarnation of impartial reason which Marx in the first flush of his Hegelianism had regarded it.

This event marked the complete abandonment in Marx's thought of the Hegelian theory of the state. The state, Marx now declared, was rooted in a soil other than the self-development of the logical idea. Its voice was the voice of reason, but its hand was the hand of the privileged. " The organs of the state have now become the ears, eyes, arms, legs, with which the interest of the forest owners hears, spies, appraises, defends, seizes and runs" (*Gesamtausgabe*, I, 1, 287). The hypothesis was crystallised in Marx's mind that the moving force, ground and motive of the enactment of all law which affected the social relations of different classes was not an impartial theory of justice but class interest—a class interest which concealed its selfishness and greed, sometimes even from itself, with mouth-filling phrases about personal right and liberty. In concluding his discussion of the Laws on Wood-Stealing, Marx wrote: " Our whole exposition has shown how the Provincial Assembly has degraded (*herabwürdigt*) the executive power . . . the existence of the accused and the very idea of the state . . . *to material instruments of private interest* " (Ibid., p. 300).

4. *The Social Basis of the Class State*

Marx's philosophy of the state and society received further development in his discussion of the Jewish question (*Zur Judenfrage*). Why is it, he asks, that political emancipation of the Jew is a solution neither of the Jewish problem nor a solution of the social problems which arise from the so-called " Jewish " principles of commerce—principles which were, of course, the basis of the entire Christian world ? Marx's general answer is that in bourgeois society political emancipation bestows a formal and empty right to participate in the mechanism of government. It does not free anyone from a real disability, because, except for the ruling classes, there is a fundamental dualism between the social aspects of life and their political forms. To understand what Marx means here by the terms " political " and " social " and " dualism " it is necessary to approach his definitions genetically.

Feudal society was socially and politically a unit. The principle of political authority, invested in a few, arose from an authoritarian system of economic production, and found an organisational counterpart in religion, the family, and education. The class which was excluded from the processes of control in one field was excluded from active control of the others. Those who ruled in any field ruled in every field. A political change in this society could only be accomplished in virtue of prior social changes. After feudal property relationships were dissolved, the bourgeois property forms which replaced them pretended to be special and autonomous, free of organic connection with the rest of culture. The bourgeois property relations, far from " elevating property or labour to a genuine social element, rather completed its *separation* from the whole of the state, constituting them into *special* societies within society " (*Gesamtausgabe*, I, 1, 596–7). The political bourgeois revolution sanctified this anarchic organisation by pretending that through the myth of the general will the sphere of operation of private property was restricted only to private affairs, not public. In theory, no individual who did not own property would suffer because of the political activities of those who did own property. The bourgeois political revolution split society up, and every individual within it, into two. A man was a capitalist *and* a citizen; a worker *and* a citizen; a peasant *and* a citizen. Theoretically, and for the workers and peasants actually, there was no organic social relation which bound their citizenship and their vocational activity together. As a matter of fact, these last two classes were citizens only in name because the state power was always used to protect the owners of capital in their use of capital; and it was precisely in their use of capital under existing social relations that the source of contemporary social degradation was to be found. The more idealistic and democratic *in theory* the political life of a people is, the more firmly does the dualism between the citizen and the worker rivet *in practice* social inequalities upon it. " The fulfilment of the idealism of the state is at the same time the fulfilment of the materialism of bourgeois society. The overthrow of the (feudal) political yoke was at the same time the overthrow of the bonds which had held the egoistic spirit of bourgeois society confined " (Ibid., p. 597).

The organisation of feudal society extended some protection even to the serf. In bourgeois society all the organising relations or bonds between men are reduced to bare terms—elements— atoms. Man becomes the basis of society, not social man—but egoistic man. Egoistic man is responsible only to and for himself, not to and for others. Since everyone is legally and nominally alike, no one can complain. This conception of egoistic man, Marx properly points out, is the theoretical basis of the doctrine of the *natural rights* of man and of the recurrent slogans of *personal freedom*. But it has dangerous consequences. " The freedom of egoistic man and the recognition of that freedom is tantamount to the recognition of the unchecked (*zugellosen*) movement of the cultural and material elements which constitute the content of his life." Instead of being freed from religion, man receives religious freedom. Instead of being freed from property, he receives the freedom to hold property. Instead of being freed from the evils of competition, he receives the freedom to compete.

Real political emancipation, Marx contended, must be social. It must remove the dualism between the citizen and worker, citizen and peasant, citizen and professional, etc. It must make of freedom a social principle and in this way humanise, concretise and extend the sphere of politics. When this is done, all of culture becomes an organic whole. There are no dualisms or dichotomies to disturb it. Each still has his personal life, his unique personality; but it is the flower produced by social organisation, not the crushed by-product of uncontrolled social mechanism.

" Only when the real individual man has given up his abstract character as a citizen and has become *truly human* (*Gattungswesen*) in his empirical life, in his individual work, in his individual relations, only when man recognises and organises his ' forces propres ' as *social forces* and therefore no longer permits himself to be separated from them by political forms, only then has human emancipation been achieved " (Ibid., p. 599).

5. *Socialism and Politics*

Certain conclusions followed from this position which were incompatible with Ruge's liberal democracy. They were developed by Marx in the form of a critical gloss upon Ruge's article *Der König von Preussen und die Sozialreform*. Both appeared in the Paris *Vorwärts*, 1844. Ruge's article was written on the occasion of the weaver revolts in Silesia and concerned the government's belated attempt to adopt certain half-hearted measures to relieve widespread distress. Ruge was inclined to dismiss these revolts as having no social significance and demanded the organisation of a political party to achieve the ends which the weavers had failed to attain by their insurrection. Political activity within the framework of the existing state must be the sole instrument of social reform.

This implied that the state was quite distinct from the existing social institutions which it politically administered. It implied that within the basis of the existing political framework, fundamental social reforms could be carried out. It was against these views that Marx took the field. Socialism, he maintained, could not be brought about by political reform. The existing state was just the reverse face of existing social institutions. To destroy the latter, it was necessary to destroy the former. But it was the professed goal of political reformers not to destroy the existing state but to accept it and use it as an instrument of piecemeal and gradual reform. This is the logic—the fallacious logic, according to Marx—of all forms of state socialism. " The existence of the state and the existence of slavery are inseparable. The ancient state and ancient slavery—an open and classic contradiction—were no less essentially welded together than the modern state and the modern world of usury—a sanctimonious (*scheinheilige*) Christian contradiction " (*Gesamtausgabe*, Abt. I, Bd. 3, p. 15). No political attack of itself is sufficient to abolish those social forms of inequality which it is precisely the function of the state to enforce and defend. " Without a revolution socialism cannot be carried out " (p. 59).

According to Marx, in so far as the revolution abolishes the old society, it is social; in so far as it destroys the power of the old society, it is political. Every social revolution, then, must of necessity be a political revolution. But not every political revolution is a social revolution. This distinction is important: for it enables us to understand why Marx consistently opposed the insurrectionary tactics of extremists who staked all hope for social revolution not so much upon the organised revolutionary proletariat but upon a small group of professional revolutionists who would seize and hold the state power from above. A social revolution, Marx maintained, was not something to be achieved by a political *party*, but by a social class under the freely chosen leadership of a party. Whether or not this social revolution could be realised peacefully was a function of the specific situation. But there must be an ideological and material readiness to meet any form of opposition which might arise.

It was the way in which Marx fashioned the issue between himself and Ruge which brought home to Ruge a consciousness of where his own social loyalties really lay. Marx's theory of the state remained unintelligible because Ruge, still thinking in Hegelian categories, did not grasp its essentially historical character. Marx's theory of social action was emotionally abhorrent to him because it seemed to have the ring and hardness of the class struggle, to promise further bloodshed and to constitute a threat not only to the existing economic order but to its culture as well. Ruge failed to see that Marx's theories were really the ideal expression of the actual class struggles in Western Europe which were soon to reach incandescence in the revolutions of 1848. At the root of Ruge's failure was that variety of philosophical idealism which treats *abstractions* as if they were *powers*, which regards principles as valid in their own right without reference to their historical causes, accompaniments and consequences.

CHAPTER V

MAX STIRNER AND KARL MARX

IT IS NOT generally known that Karl Marx wrote a book on Max Stirner.[1] And those who do know are usually puzzled as to why the tough-minded precursor of Nietzsche should have been called Sankt Max or Der Heilige Max—the variant titles of this peculiar book. But a more fundamental question must be answered first. Why was it necessary to write a book—one which was never published—against Stirner at all? Only some indication of the *Zeitgeschichte* of the days in which it was composed can make quite intelligible in what way the critical discussion of Stirner marks an important stage in the intellectual development of Marx. And yet the most striking thing about this book is that the issues which Stirner raised and Marx met, like many others previously discussed, have a definite relevance to the conflict of ideas and attitudes in the contemporary world in Europe and America to-day. Indeed, we might even say that this is due to the fact that Stirner and Marx are here discussing the fundamental problems of any possible system of ethics or public morality.

Moses Hess, too, the father of "true or philosophical" socialism, wrote a brochure against Stirner; and at a certain period during the forties his followers wrote books and pamphlets against Marx and Engels defending the philosophy of altruism. The issues were the same in all of this discussion. As we may suspect, Stirner and Hess leaned over backwards in opposite directions. Both attributed to Marx the systematic defects of the other.

I

THE PHILOSOPHY OF MAX STIRNER

Max Stirner by his own confession came to fulfil the movement which was begun by Strauss, deepened by Bauer and

[1] This was part of the two-volume work which Marx planned for his *Deutsche Ideologie*.

transferred to a new plane by Feuerbach. Strauss' concept of the absolute community had been declared religious by Bauer while Bauer's own ideal of critical self-consciousness had been revealed as anachronistic theology by Marx and Feuerbach. Stirner taught that the Feuerbachian worship of man was just as superstitious as the theologies which Feuerbach had exploded. He went on to claim that just as " man " was a myth, so the ideal of moral obligation, which presumably was derived from the social nature of man, was also mythical. It was a fetish— a convenient fiction by which those in power disarmed the classes over whom they ruled. On the basis of a method shared by all the Young-Hegelians, Stirner's *Der Einzige und sein Eigenthum* seemed to be drawing conclusions utterly opposed to all the affirmations with which the philosophical rebels had startled the world. The logical consequences of his philosophy of anarchism seemed to smack more of Hobbes and Machiavelli than of the latter-day apostles of love and humanity. No wonder then that the revolutionary spirits of the decade turned fiercely upon him; while the conservatives gloatingly used his book as an object lesson to point out where the philosophy of revolution led. Stirner was unmoved by both. All *isms* were religious. The free spirit feared the anathemas of radicalism as little as the excommunications of conservatism. He was fortified by his slogan " *Ich Hab' Mein Sach' auf Nichts gestellt.*"

1. *Ideals as Illusions*

What is a moral ideal ? Stirner asks. Something which dominates or controls conduct. Whose conduct ? My conduct. What is a political or religious fetish ? Something which dominates my conduct until I have realised why and how it has been constructed. What is the difference, then, between a religious fetish and an ethical ideal ? None, answers Stirner, except that we are usually more conscious of the fetishistic character of the first than of the second. Consider all the ideals which the Young-Hegelians have discarded as empty abstractions—God, the state, the nation, the church, respectability. Why, asks Stirner, should they be rejected, refuted and denounced ? Because instead of serving man's interests they have been used to serve the interests of the ruling group which has propagated these ideals most widely: because they correspond to nothing which *I* can objectively experience; because, upon analysis, they turn out to be meaningless abstractions: and finally, because they stand in the way of the free assertion of my unique personality, imposing rules or claims which are irrelevant to my own best interests in any particular situation.

But now, Stirner goes on, let us look at what our Young-Hegelian friends offer us in their stead. Humanity, justice, truth, love, communism, etc. They are admirable and enthusiastic slogans. But what do they mean ? Why should I die for humanity or communism any more than for God and Country ? After all, what is humanity ? It does not seem to be particularly concerned about me. And when I act in its behalf I discover I am acting for the benefit of my neighbour. But my neighbour is only another me. Why should I act for his " me " instead of " mine " ? And if at basis we are one, then the best way of serving humanity is to serve myself. Humanity !—Feuerbach's Man !—what a grotesque abstraction ! If it includes everything men have done, why should it be worshipped, since it includes the low and despicable as well as the good, whatever that may be ? If it is equivalent to what individual men at the present age are, then their conflicts prove that it is not one thing but many, that it is a word which we use to cover up our weakness and disarm others; if it is equivalent to what may be developed in the future, then it is not even in existence—all the more an abstraction. Humanity, the Cause, the Common Good ! " Man, your head is haunted ! " exclaims Stirner in impatience. " You have wheels in your head ! You imagine great things, and depict to yourself a whole world of gods that has an existence for you, a spirit realm to which you suppose yourself to be called, an ideal that beckons to you. You have a fixed idea ! "[1]

Nor is it any different with such ideals as truth or justice. If the sabbath is made for man and not man for the sabbath, the same holds for the truth. The truth must be used, not worshipped. And if it is used by man, it cannot be always used

[1] *Der Einzige und sein Eigenthum*, p. 45. All references to Stirner's writings are to the English translation (Modern Library edition), translated under the title *The Ego and His Own*.

irrespective of consequences. Why should I die for the truth ? What is there sacred about it ? If love of truth is set up as a rule to regulate human behaviour why am I bound to keep it, especially if I have seen to it that others will ? The truth is a matter of the best policy and like all things expedient depends in several ways upon me, not vice versa. " As long as you believe in the truth, you do not believe in yourself, and you are a— servant, a—religious man. You alone are the truth, or rather you are more than the truth " (pp. 372–3). Stirner, by this, does not mean that truth does not exist, and that it is impossible to give a meaning to the term humanity but merely that when they are taken as ideals for human behaviour, the individual always reserves the right of discarding them. They are not objectively imposed from without. They are only the instruments of personal purposes. " The divine is God's concern; the human, man's. My concern is neither the divine nor the human, not the true, or the good or the just or the free but simply and solely what is mine. And it is not a general one, but is—unique as I am unique " (p. 5).

2. *Social, All-too-Social*

For the Young-Hegelians the positive upshot of classical German philosophy had been its discovery of the social nature of consciousness. What Kant, Fichte and Hegel had stated in terms of transcendental idealism, they sought to express more empirically in terms of history and psychology. The locus of all individual rights and obligations was declared to be social. Stirner, who had rejected the constructions of idealist philosophers on the ground that he could find within his head only his own consciousness and no transempirical ego, felt that the emphasis upon the social nature of the mind, as well as the evaluation of all ideas in relation to the social whole, constituted a serious threat to individual freedom and the autonomy of personality. There was already in existence a religion of the community, an ethics of love and a politics of socialism based upon Feuerbach's analysis of the social nature of man. " Society from which we have everything is a new master, a new spook, a new ' supreme being ' which takes us into its service and allegiance " (p. 131).

In a society of egoists an appeal to society is a method of acquiring disinterestedness. It furnishes a criterion with which the egoist can judge himself. But Stirner protests that it is the egoist who is here judging himself with the eyes of others. And this gives him not disinterestedness but insight into the interests of others. Why is your idea better than mine, your taste superior to mine ? The most I can grant, says Stirner, is that they are different. And we ourselves are different. The Declaration of the Rights of Man does not state a fact but an aspiration. Men are equal only as this ego, that ego, and another ego. But the my of *my* ego is unique and incomparably unequal. The other egos, and the relationships between them which compose the state, are only objects of my ego. My social duties to them are self-legislated. They flow from my will and my power. There is no tyranny so ruthless and insensitive as that of " sacred " society.

" People is the name of the body, State of the spirit, of that ruling person that has hitherto suppressed me. Some have wanted to transfigure peoples and States by broadening them out into ' mankind ' and ' general reason '; but servitude would only become still more intense with this widening, and philanthropists and humanitarians are as absolute masters as politicians and diplomats " (p. 253).

3. *Immoralism*
The inevitable consequence of interpreting ethical rules as means to personal fulfilment is, in Stirner's eyes, the radical revision of the existing ethical code. There may be no connection between the fact that Stirner was a teacher at a boarding school for young women and his attack upon the moral conventions. But he preached with great zest that the first of the traditional virtues to be discarded as hostile to genuine personal freedom was sexual inhibition. The doctrine of self-renunciation had no justification in experience. Whoever makes of chastity an absolute virtue has become the victim of religious dementia. No metaphysics of the spirit can serve as a premise for the mortification of the flesh. Peace of mind must be sought not by arbitrary suppression of desires but by their judicious organisation. Of the two evils—the dry-rot of conventional virtue and

the exuberance of animal appetites—the second is the lesser evil; it is the healthier and the more poetic. Apostrophising the heaven bound spirits of the young, Stirner exclaims: " The habit of renunciation cools the heat of your desire, and the roses of your youth are growing pale in the chlorosis of your salvation (*Bleisucht deiner Seligkeit*). The soul is saved, the body may perish. O Lais ! O Ninon ! how well you did scorn this pale virtue. One gay grisette for a thousand virgins grown grey in virtue " (p. 65).

Stirner did not stop there. To the horror of the respectable citizens of Germany and to the consternation of his former friends, the Berlin café revolutionists and humanitarians, he challenged the absolute basis of moral edicts against polygamy, against blasphemous desecration, even against incest. " Take notice how a ' moral man ' behaves, who to-day often thinks he is through with God and throws off Christianity as a bygone thing. If you ask him whether he has ever doubted that the copulation of brother and sister is incest, that monogamy is the truth of marriage, that filial piety is a sacred duty, then a moral shudder will come over him . . . " (p. 48). The moral shudder, for Stirner, is the sign that true spiritual emancipation has not yet been won, that the mind has yet to win its way to a realisation that morality exists for man not man for morality. In justice to Stirner it should be remembered that his protest is not against the things people do but against the reasons advanced for doing them. On the basis of Stirner's philosophy one can lead an exemplary life, in the traditional sense, provided one knows what it is he is doing and why.

Despite his avowals of complete ethical antinomianism, Stirner does seek to formulate his moral code. It turns out to be a variant of Hobbes' doctrine. All social life appears to be a conflict of right against right. What is a right ? Stirner asks. It is a claim which some power stands ready to enforce. That power may be mine; it may be my neighbour's; it may be physical; it may be mental. But without the power to enforce a right, what is called a right is only a claim, a desire, an expression of what I want. The fact that I have an interest in anything is sufficient to justify my claim, but it justifies it for *me* not for my neighbour; just as my neighbour's claims and desires are justified for him by the fact that he wants them. But when what I want conflicts with what my neighbour wants (and it must be remembered that for Stirner every social command is only an expression of what someone other than myself wants) what makes either one of these conflicting claims a right? The possession and exercise of the power necessary to take what I want, to enforce my claim.

" The conflict over the ' right of property ' wavers in vehement commotion. The Communists affirm that ' the earth belongs rightfully to him who tills it, and its products to those who bring them out! I think it belongs to him who knows how to take it, or who does not let it be taken from him, does not let himself be deprived of it. If he appropriates it, then not only the earth, but the right to it too, belongs to him. This is egoistic right: i.e. it is the right for me, therefore it is right. . . . The tiger that assails me is in the right, and I who strike him down am also in the right. I defend against him not my right but myself " (p. 199).

Human freedom for Stirner is not merely freedom from restraints and persecutions, but freedom to action. The free man is not one who only knows (we may know why we are unfree without thereby attaining freedom); the free man is the one who does. To do implies to be able to do, to have the power to do. Stirner logically concludes that " my freedom becomes complete only when it is my might." Freedom cannot be given; it must be taken: and it must continually be defended even if in doing so we deprive others of their freedom.

4. *The Cult of the Ego*

If Feuerbach is the negation of traditional theology, Stirner, as one of his contemporaries remarked, is the negation of traditional ethics.[1] Feuerbach taught that Man had created God in his own image; Stirner that the individual ego had created Man in his own image. One had dissolved the subject (God) into all of its predicates; the other had dissolved the predicate (Society) into the personal pronouns—I, me, myself. Nor was Stirner

[1] Cf. *Gegenwart*, 1851, Vol. VI, pp. 311–12.

any clearer about the meaning of the " I " than was Feuerbach about the essence of " Man."

Stirner's peculiar doctrine of individualism arose not only from a confusion of the various senses of human freedom but was rooted in the ambiguities of the conventional hedonistic psychology of his day. He assumed as a fact that human beings in all actions desire their own interests. He assumed further that one's own interests are necessarily exclusive. The facts, however, compelled him to admit that sometimes human beings—either through ignorance or training—will as their own interests other people's good. He adopted two different positions to account for this. Sometimes he argues as if one's own interests were served by the satisfaction derived from serving others, even if serving others involves sacrifice, suffering or death. This was the familiar hedonistic argument for the proposition that all people are egoists. Granting it for a moment, Stirner's exhortation to the individual to be an egoist would be completely pointless, for his definition makes the gratification of any desire— our own good, or that of our neighbour's—an illustration of egoism. If a man who martyrs himself is an egoist because he thereby satisfies the desire to serve his cause, and if a man who betrays his cause is an egoist because he satisfies the desire to get money, then the word egoism loses any distinctive meaning. As it always must when it is used to qualify the cause of action instead of the object of action !

But more often Stirner admits that he does not believe that both of these men are egoists. He holds that the man who sacrifices his life for a cause is a "damned fool." He does not know his own best interests. He is still superstitious. *Es spukt in seinem Kopf.* Here Stirner shifts to a normative position. He tells man what he *ought* to pursue. And he now defines the real ego in terms of those selected pursuits—i.e., those things which Stirner himself thought desirable. From the indubitable proposition " I am I," he goes on to the proposition " My real I is a certain kind of selfish, exclusive enjoyment." The self or ego, then, is not the empirical self as it is revealed in ordinary experience—a mixture of strength, weakness, selfishness and unselfishness—but an ideal self which is constructed on the basis of certain psychological tendencies and used as a norm of judgment on the part of the individual. But here, as Stirner's critics were quick to point out, he finds himself transfixed by his own logic. Is the egoistic self to be worshipped as an absolute ideal ? Is our ordinary empirical self, which is not steely selfish, not to feel free to pursue something else ? How does this egoistic ideal then differ from any other *idée fixe* ? Does it not become, in Stirner's own terms, a superstitious worship of one possible good under all circumstances, and therefore religious ? And if it is not an absolute goal, if the individual can choose to be not an egoist, then the validity of what he chooses does not depend upon the choosing but on the consequences of what is chosen. This prepares the way for a scientific ethics, the possibility of which Stirner had denied.

II

MARX'S CRITICISM OF STIRNER

As has already been indicated, Stirner's *Der Einzige und sein Eigenthum* exploded like a bombshell among the ranks of his former comrades-in-arms. Their bitterness is revealed in the hurried denunciations and refutations they drew up. Bauer hastened to answer Stirner, Feuerbach responded feebly in a review, Hess and his friends frothed at the mouth in a whole series of writings, while Marx hacked away at the roots of Stirner's position. The criticisms of Marx are in a sense a running commentary upon Stirner's book; for the most part they are unintelligible unless read together with Stirner's text. The unprejudiced reader who peruses them independently may regard Marx's comments as a series of critical expectorations. They seem to betray, on first impression, a revolting intellectual snobbery and a desire to score upon Stirner for reasons other than the purposes of argument. A closer study will show, however, that although there is present an indisputable personal tone, Stirner's arguments are squarely met. In fact, Marx, as distinct from all other of Stirner's erstwhile friends, gauged the positive merit of Stirner's work as well as the negative.[1] We shall begin by

1 Engels had already written to Marx in the course of a letter expressing his criticism of Stirner (November 19, 1844): " But what is true in his principle, we, too, must accept. And what is true is that before we can be active in any cause we must make it our own, egoistic cause—and that in this sense, quite aside

pointing out those phases of Stirner's thought which were in consonance with Marx's own attitudes and which were recognised as such by Marx.

1. *The Positive Aspects of Stirner's Work*

(*a*) A good deal of Stirner's argument was directed against the contemporary vogue of sentimental and idealistic philanthropy which sought to solve the social problem by appealing to man's pity and sense of fair play. In Marx's eyes, there was more honesty in Stirner's contention that we have a right to consider ourselves than in the exhortations of a sickly altruism to consider only others. Further, there was a greater strength in Stirner's position as well as honesty, for it preached an implicit class war doctrine. The Hobbesian *bellum omnium contra omnes* could not have any literal meaning in a highly industrial society; its actual application meant the war of one class against others. The conflicts *within* classes are gradually subordinated to conflicts *between* classes. In revealing the hollowness of slogans which appealed to humanity, country, or abstract freedom, Stirner prepared the way for a realistic analysis of the issues these phrases were used to conceal. In opposing empty abstractions, Stirner went so far that the only " real " thing for him became the immediate and sensuously concrete. This nominalism constituted a serious limitation in his analysis but the realistic impact of his criticism of the empty and abstract appeals to reason, justice and humanity served as an effective antidote to the vapid sentimentalism of books like Bettina von Arnim's *Dies Buch gehört dem Könige*, which appealed to the king to add to his good works the alleviation of social distress.

(*b*) Stirner's repudiation of inherent natural rights cleared the ground for the revolutionist's attacks upon the absolute right of property. Although Stirner had no insight into the origins of private property in the means of production or into the social basis of private right, his attack upon the sacredness of property placed the whole discussion as to the nature, function

from any material expectations, we are communists in virtue of our egoism, that out of egoism we want to be human beings and not merely individuals " (*Gesamtausgabe*, Abt. III, Bd. 1, pp. 6–7).

and limits of private property on an empirical plane. The discussion now could proceed by distinguishing between the kinds of private property, their historical conditions and development, the relation between property and the power it gave over others' personalities, the minimum of private property necessary for the assertion of one's own personality, etc. Here, too, Stirner's solutions were too simple. The substance of his philosophy of property was that a man had a right to as much property as he could hold. The belief in the sacredness of property was a powerful ideological means of " holding on " to one's property, especially when that belief had been implanted into the heads of those who had no property. That, Stirner claimed, was the secret of the idealistic philosophy of law. It was intimately connected with his attack upon the absolutistic state as a fiction imposed upon the community for the benefit of the few who ruled. Marx could agree with Stirner's criticism of the doctrine of natural rights without subscribing either to Stirner's arguments or to the egomania he put in its place.

(c) The most significant of all of Stirner's views was his emphasis upon the fact that formal freedom was an empty abstraction. Freedom is a freedom *to do*. Where one is nominally free to do what one pleases but lacks the material means wherewithal to do it, he is unfree. A man is free to run, hop, skip or walk only when he has a pair of sound legs. A man is free to choose his vocation only when he has the means to train himself. Stirner's claims that genuine freedom implied material power came as a very welcome note in view of the influence which the ideals of *formal* political democracy had upon the liberal bourgeois elements in Germany. Political democracy, which aims at free competition, could never of itself bring about social democracy. " Competition," Stirner correctly saw and said, " suffers from the unfavourable circumstance that the means for competing are not at everyone's command, because they are not taken from personality, but from accident. Most are without means, and for this reason without goods " (p. 276). Man is a bundle of interests and his freedom lies in the expression of those interests—interests to work, love, play, etc. A revolution which stops short at political forms can never guarantee the free expression of any interest except the interest to talk.

This is important enough. But it is noteworthy that whenever the freedom to talk becomes effective in its influence on other interests, it is curtailed. " Liberty of the press is only permission of the press, and the State never will, or can, voluntarily permit me to grind it to nothingness by the press " (p. 297). Stirner, however, was no adherent of social democracy. In fact, he regarded it as the means by which the weak oppress the strong. He admitted that its concept of freedom was more consistent than that of political democracy; but he protested that it there-fore prevented the super-egoist from gratifying his own liberty by denying liberty to others.

2. *The Ego as an Abstraction*

Marx begins his criticism of Stirner by going to the roots of Stirner's philosophy. That philosophy, he claims, is as idealistic as the philosophy of the " ghostly dualists " whom Stirner had attacked. Stirner had merely rejected their specific ideals such as the quest for God, freedom, immortality and humanity. But he had retained their method—a method which disregarded the temporal and social locus of ideals and which sought to find one absolute ideal as the outcome of abstract logical or psycho-logical analysis. What had Stirner actually done ? He had replaced the abstractions of religion and speculative philosophy —God and Man—with an even more monstrous abstraction, the ego.[1] After all, why were the ideals of patriotism, church, family, rejected by Stirner as empty abstractions ? Because they were an inverted and disguised expression of certain objective social relations. They pretended to be something they were not. Men could not literally live for God or country. But is it any different, Marx asks, with the ego ? Is a life in the interests of the ego any more valid ? What is the self ? Is it not an abstrac-tion from a whole complex of social relationships, of selves in relation ? Strip a man of his social dependencies. Do we find his ego to be a fleshy cushion into which his friendships, his vocation, his love, his political relationships are stuck like so many pins ? Or is it not truer to say that if a man is so stripped, he is destroyed—at least his uniqueness is destroyed. Personality

[1] *Gesamtausgabe*, Abt. I, Bd. 5, pp. 174, 265, 396 ff.

is a differentiation within a social continuum. It is not the pre-condition of social life but its most precious effect. Different social systems will give us different personalities and a different ideal of personality. The very attempt to understand personality involves, if not a reduction of the peculiar and unique to the general social framework of tradition, at least an attempt to discover its significance in the light of such reference. To worship the " pure ego " is to worship something which never was or can be. It is to lapse into the same idealistic error as Bruno Bauer against whom Stirner had so fiercely polemicised.

3. *Stirner's Subjectivism*

Stirner was not content with asserting an ethical subjectivism. His abstract conception of the self as a condition of social life, instead of as a result of social life, leads him to epistemological subjectivism as well. From the proposition: ' nothing is good or bad, but thinking makes it so ' he goes on to derive the proposition that ' nothing exists but thinking makes it so.' Having proved that the ideas of state, emperor, country, etc., do not correspond to what they claim to represent, that they are devoid of all supernatural sanctions, that they involve a slave-conception of the self—having proved all this—Stirner stops short. As if he had thereby deprived the institutional equivalents of these ideas of their power ! The state does not cease being an enemy—a force to be reckoned with—after it has been pointed out that if there were no subjects there would be no state. Not all relations are internal to the terms they relate. Of course, Marx argues, my own personal existence is implied in the consciousness of having an enemy intent upon putting an end to me. That I have an enemy implies that I exist. But the realisation that my enemy and myself are correlative concepts, coupled with the refusal on my part to acknowledge that I have an enemy, does not rob my enemy of his danger to me. I am not through with the state when I understand that state piety has been artificially induced in me by education. It still remains a power which recognises me even if I do not recognise it.

Marx's point here can be driven home by citing an amusing incident from the life of Edgar Bauer who shared Stirner's subjectivism but not his egoism. Edgar Bauer had been brought before the Prussian courts for denouncing the Prussian State. After sentence had been pronounced, he was asked if he had anything to say. He calmly replied that the decision was logically null and void. The existence of the state implied the existence of subjects. The state had no jurisdiction on any but its own subjects. But he, Edgar Bauer, refused to recognise the state. It had no validity for him. It therefore did not exist for him. The dialectic was perfect but what it did not prove was that the state had no power over him. The iron bars and stone walls of his cells were proof of that power. It was rumoured, however, that Bauer convinced himself on the basis of his solipsism that this was a mistake, and that the prison—cells, bars, and all—had been posited by his deeper Self-consciousness.

Stirner's philosophical weakness, Marx claimed, derived from the fact that he, too, thought that a dialectical sentence of coventry upon the state would conjure its power away. To refuse to admit the sovereignty of the state as Stirner and his anarchistic followers did, is futile unless this is the beginning of a concrete struggle against the state institutions. But Stirner and those who share his ideas cannot effectively struggle against the state because they do not realise what the real source of its corporate abstractions is. " Stirner forgets that he has only destroyed the fantastic and ghostly form which the notion of ' fatherland,' etc., assumes in the skull of ' the adolescent ' (*Junglings*) but that he has not even touched upon these ideas in so far as they express real relations " (*Gesamtausgabe*, I, 5, 107). Those real relations are to be found in the economic, socio-historical foundations of the age. By his inability to view the development of the ego and its abstractions as the historical expression of a complex of social institutions, Stirner falls far behind Hegel. The doctrine of objective mind remains closed to subjectivist theory.

4. *Stirner's Social Nominalism*

Marx devotes considerable effort to show that Stirner's reduction of the objective social and industrial relations under which men live, to states of consciousness in the mind of the individual, is inconsistent, confused, and inadequate as an explanation of the social process. It makes a causal explanation of social phenomena and, therefore, intelligent social action, impossible. Marx begins by proving that Stirner cannot even talk of the individual's state of mind without reference to the entire social complex in which he lives. What an individual is cannot evidently be discovered in a single state of mind, nor in the fact that it is a state of mind. There must be a succession of states of mind. What unites this succession ? What controls the order of succession ? What determines its objective content ? The controlling importance of the external social world, Marx charges, is concealed by Stirner in his use of the objective pronouns " it " and " one." " It is found to be by the self," raises a problem as to why and how it is. " One knows that it . . ." implies a norm for the social group, an objective " one." The dynamic changes of things are converted by Stirner into changes within consciousness. The historical problems are ignored. " For Stirner," writes Marx, " the life of the individual consists in the differences between his mental states. The physical and social changes which precede the individual and create his changed consciousness, do not concern him in the least. Consequently for Stirner, the child, the youth, and the full-grown adult always find the world completely finished and given in the same way as they (at any moment) find themselves. Nothing is done to explain how there possibly can be something there."

But there is something there which demands explanation. Not only what the individual sees but how he sees it, can be understood largely in terms of something which is not a state of mind at all. Consciousness has an historical axis. The primitives actually do not " see " the same thing as the more developed races even though their biological structure may be the same. It is precisely because of the different character of their social environment that they see differently. What one is attentive to, the other overlooks; what is significant here, is indifferent there. Stirner's social nominalism, therefore, not only is incapable of explaining what the individual consciousness finds but cannot explain the significant modes of the activity of consciousness proper—its wishing, fearing and appraising.

Stirner, Marx charges, is erecting the contemporary order of things and consciousness into the historically invariant. Stirner's standpoint is religious because whatever history it does treat of, turns out to be a history of ideas. The world, as it existed before Stirner came on the scene, is explained, by a double inconsistency, as the result of man's mistaken religious ideas. In this criticism, Marx already indicates the germ of his new philosophy of history:

" The standpoint with which one satisfies himself in such histories of the spirit is itself religious, for in it one is content to stop short with Religion, to conceive Religion as a cause of itself. This is done instead of explaining religion in terms of material conditions; showing how certain determinate industrial and commercial relations are necessarily bound up with certain social forms, how these are themselves bound up with certain forms of the state and therewith with a certain form of religious consciousness. Had Stirner acquainted himself with the real history of the Middle Ages he would have discovered why the ideas of the Christians in the mediæval world took the exact form they did, and how it came about that these ideas later developed into others. He would have found that ' *Christianity* ' *had no history at all* and that all the different forms in which it was held at different times were not ' self-determinations ' and progressive realisations of the ' religious spirit ' but that they were effected by completely empirical causes quite removed from any influence of the religious spirit " (*Gesamtausgabe*, Abt. I, Bd. 5, pp. 134–5).

5. *Egoistic Anarchism as Self-Defeating*

Marx never lost an opportunity to attack the fundamental premise of all varieties of anarchism, viz., the abstract conception of the self and human freedom which made it impossible for the consistent anarchist to accept the principles of organisation and authority. The trouble with Stirner, the most noteworthy of them all, was that he drew an easy but oversharp dichotomy between the I and the external world. Where he thinks of the *I* as a mind or spirit, he writes like an idealist.

Where he thinks of the *I* as a body, as a creature of desires, he writes like a materialist. His *I* corresponds to nothing empirically real in social intercourse but is a pure conceptual product of two philosophical categories—disembodied idealism and naïve, gross materialism. As a matter of fact no individual begins his career by feeling himself in opposition to his environment. He only distinguishes himself from it comparatively late in life. Self-consciousness is the last mental trait to be acquired. The opposition therefore between the claims of the self and the claims of others is always specific, conditioned by certain historical and psychological factors. Although it is the source of all moral rules, it is not itself a morality. Neither love-your-neighbour nor love-yourself can serve as an intelligent maxim. For it is clear that sometimes we do not love our neighbours for the sake of our neighbour's neighbours, and sometimes in loving oneself we may be serving others, to wit, our family or class.

" The Communists," says Marx, " do not preach morality. That is what Stirner is doing. They do not desire to turn the ' private individual ' into a professional ' for-love-sacrificing creature.' . . . But they alone have discovered that what have been called ' general interests ' in the whole course of history have really been the extension of the ' private interests ' of particular men. . . . The opposition between these two forms of interest is only apparent, for the general is continually being produced from the other, the private interest. General interests do not represent an independent power with an independent history. The apparent opposition between them is always being produced and destroyed. We are not here confronted with an Hegelian ' negative unity ' of the two sides of an opposition but by a materially conditioned destruction of a previously existing form of the individual " (*Gesamtausgabe*, I, 5, 227–8).

Marx's position may be clarified by an illustration familiar to all trade union organisers and a commonplace problem already in Marx's time. Suppose an individual refuses to join a trade union organisation on the ground that his freedom to produce, to take advantage of his monopoly of skill, would be lost. The general interest of the group of workers conflicts with the private interest of the individual in question. The individual as he finds himself at any definite moment can choose to throw in his lot with his fellow-workers at an immediate material loss or run the risk of even a greater loss and restriction of freedom which comes from the absence of union organisation. The question, however, is not only one of material interests. It is that, and something more. Every individual regards certain values of loyalty, sympathy, co-operation, as goods, too. They are part of that structure of values which defines the self. By throwing in his lot with his fellow-workers his whole personality is fulfilled in a way which would be impossible if he were to stand aside and alone. The general interest of the group demands a temporary sacrifice of the pecuniary interests of the individual to the end that the very character of the individual be so transformed that this pecuniary sacrifice appear as natural and uncompelled. When he identifies himself with the group, then the group will more naturally regard and effectively protect his individual differences than he himself can. The absence of group support, in time, deprives the individual of an opportunity to capitalise his specific abilities, since in an open competitive market their value tends to sink. His private interest, which includes the non-economic as well as the economic, lies with the group, unless he is prepared to play a lone hand against all. The conflict of interests, here, is real and whatever harmony is achieved involves genuine sacrifice. But the common activity which harmony between fellow-workers makes possible tends to create the institutional guarantees and mechanisms by which the advantages of the specific capacities of all may be made available for all.

If this be true for the relation between the individual and the group, why, it may be asked, is it not true for the relation between the class and society as a whole. If there is no necessary struggle between the individual and the class, why is there a necessary struggle between classes ? For Marx the answer lies in the analysis of the relations between classes in the mechanism of economic production. The opposition between the individual worker and his class, when it exists, is temporary and clearly subordinate to what they have in common. The individual is not destroyed but strengthened by the collective security gained by his class. But the opposition between class and class is more fundamental than that which unites them, for the strength of one can only be achieved in virtue of the weakness of the other. In a capitalistic profit economy—more so than in any other— the continued well-being of those who rule is contingent upon the continued exploitation of those who toil. In a sense, for Marx there is no " one society " even though those who rule speak ostensibly in its name. The working classes—whenever there is a serious conflict of interests with other classes—are regarded as existing outside of society.

In concluding this phase of his criticism of Stirner, Marx points out that Stirner's apotheosis of self-interest, historically regarded, is as far from serving the interests of the worker's self as the most otherworldly altruism. It is through the emphasis upon the self-interest of his class that the individual worker best realises his own. Any gain he achieves by betraying his class impoverishes his own personality and leaves his class worse off than before. Until classes are abolished social loyalty is class loyalty. In taking this position Marx's own value judgments appear sharp and clear.

6. *The Petty-Bourgeois Roots of Anarchism*

The hidden strength of Stirner's argument lay in its peculiar natural law doctrine. The Hobbesian morality is an instrument to enable the individual to get and keep what is his own. Giving each man his own is, in a way, Stirner's definition of justice. But what is a man's own ? A man's own is his *Eigenthum*—his property, any object of his desire. In preaching a moral philosophy upon the basis of egoism, Stirner is really coming to the defence of the petty-bourgeois proprietor who sees what he produces, interprets the whole process of production on the basis of its local character, and regards both the development of large industry and the organisation of workmen as a conspiracy to deprive him of the legitimate fruits of his labour. Despite its Bohemian flavour, Stirner's thought reveals that painstaking and touchy sensitiveness to what belongs solely and exclusively to the individual which is generally associated with the peasant proprietor or shopkeeper. Says Marx, " He offers us an additional proof of how the most trivial sentiments of the petty-bourgeois can borrow the wings of a high flown ideology " (*Gesamtausgabe*, I, 5, 236).

The two key concepts of Stirner's which Marx selects for analysis are the allied terms—" one's own " and " one's interest." Marx has no difficulty in showing that one's own is a highly artificial abstraction from communal effort and production. No man working together with others, dependent upon the funded store of social knowledge and material can make a claim for what is exclusively his own. Even when working alone he finds that much more than his own " unaided " efforts have gone into the production of the specific goods he creates, e.g., the techniques, traditions, language, and science without which he could do nothing. Marx is not interested in denying that there are certain principles of individual desert which should be applied in certain historical periods to the varying capacities and achievements of individual men. But his primary purpose is to show that the nature of the social productive process is such that it makes the absolute slogan " each is to receive the full product of his toil " inapplicable. Whatever is produced is a collective product. It is only the collectivity of labour, as Marx later showed in *Capital*, which can claim exclusive right to what is produced.

Marx's criticism of Stirner's concept of self-interest, even though it is left undeveloped, is even more profound. He quite properly traces Stirner's use of the term to an uncritical acceptance of Bentham's psychology.[1] For Bentham, interests are psychologically invariable. The motives to human conduct can be sought in these fixed and inflexible interests. They are part of the psycho-physical organism. In appealing to them, Stirner seems to be preserving the appearance of naturalism and yet applying unchangeable criteria of the good and bad. Marx denies that interests are the primary subjects of psychological study. They are socially conditioned not psychologically primitive. They cannot be discovered merely by studying minds or bodies, immediate desires or thought. These are all mediated by a highly

[1] Marx's criticism of Bentham and utilitarianism still possesses *actualité* to-day. Cf. translation of some relevant passages in Appendix III.

complex social environment which gives a definite cast to man's psychological drives.

The fixation of interests through division of labour and class relationships confronts one much more directly than the fixation of interests through (immediate) " desires " and " thought." Stirner can no longer argue from the universality of the interest of self-preservation to any specific mode of selfish social behaviour. The interests of self-preservation determine, perhaps, the great susceptibility of the human being to the social stimuli and habits which he naturally acquires. But in any case the explanation of the specific interests for which men struggle must be sought not in their minds and hearts but in the society and classes in which they live.

CHAPTER VI

MOSES HESS AND KARL MARX

No ACCOUNT of the intellectual development of Marx would be complete unless it considered Marx's relationship to an influential group of German radical thinkers who called themselves " true " or " philosophical " socialists. So important and dangerous did Marx regard their views that for years both he and Engels carried on a fierce polemic against them in the radical periodicals of the time. This was brought to a climax and finish in the special section of the *Communist Manifesto* devoted to " *der deutsche oder der wahre Sozialismus* " (IIIc) in which after a short summary and refutation of their views, Marx accused the " true " socialists of being allies of the feudal reaction.

The understanding of the situation is complicated by the fact that the leading figures of " true socialism " stood closer to Marx and Engels than any other radical German group in the forties. We know that Moses Hess, the chief theoretician of the movement, converted Engels to communism, and Zlocisti, Hess's biographer, claims that Hess was not without influence on Marx, too. More interesting is the fact that Hess collaborated with Marx in writing *Die Deutsche Ideologie* (1845); part of the manuscript is in his handwriting. Hess was also an ally of Marx in his struggles against Bruno Bauer, Ruge, Stirner, and Feuerbach. After the first critical writings of Marx and Engels against " true socialism " appeared, Hess avowed himself convinced by their arguments, forswore his past literary habits and plunged into a study of political economy (Letter to Marx, July 28, 1846). His essay—" Die Folgen der Revolution des Proletariats " (1847)— published before the *Communist Manifesto* was written, is Marxian in tone and analysis, save on some organisational issues. Yet the *Communist Manifesto* published early in 1848 unmistakably concentrates its fire on Hess, making allowances neither for the actual development of Hess's views nor for his revolutionary integrity.

Another factor which has made it difficult for some to understand Marx's criticism is the general acknowledgment that, personally, Moses Hess was a man of singular purity of character. He was sensitive to every form of injustice, passionate in his devotion to principles, and almost saintly in his every-day behaviour. He was unable to hate even those who had harmed him. Although subjected to a lifelong poverty, even more grinding than that of Marx, he never wavered in his allegiance to revolutionary ideals. He was very active in the First International where he joined forces with Marx against Bakunin. Early in life he broke away from his orthodox Jewish home and married a prostitute—" in order to atone for the evil society had done "—with whom he lived in happy marriage until his death. His friends nicknamed him " the communist rabbi."

Both the vehemence and justice of Marx's denunciation of the " true socialists " have been challenged by students of the period. Koigen,[1] Hammacher,[2] and Zlocisti,[3] have maintained that Marx himself was at one time a " true socialist " (about Engels' " philosophical socialism " there is no question at all), and that historically there is no more justification for believing Hess to be a precursor of Marxism than for accepting Marx's characterisation of him.

Mehring,[4] Bernstein,[5] and G. Mayer,[6] do not maintain that Marx was a " true socialist " but they are unequivocal in stating that Marx and Engels did less than justice to " true socialism " in general and to Hess in particular. Riazanov takes a middle

[1] Koigen's *Zur Vorgeschichte des modernen philosophischen Sozialismus in Deutschland*, Berne, 1901, p. 149.

[2] Hammacher's *Zur Würdigung des wahren Sozialismus*, in Grunberg's *Archiv für die Geschichte des Sozialismus und der Arbeiterbewegung*, Vol. I, pp. 89 ff.

[3] Zlocisti's *Moses Hess, der Vorkämpfer des Sozialismus und Zionismus*, Berlin, 1921, pp. 232 ff. The whole of Chapter IX should be read in this connection. Zlocisti's biography of Hess is frankly partial towards its subject, but it contains a very lively account of Hess's social and intellectual *milieu*. His discussion of the relation between Marx and Hess is vitiated by a stubborn misunderstanding of Marx on salient points. For example he is capable of writing the following: " Although Hess placed himself decisively in the Marxian camp, one thing distinguished him from the ' leader ' [Marx] viz., activity. For in the last analysis the Marxian conception excluded in *a priori fashion every organisation directed to the achievement of specific goals*. Everything develops out of the relations of production according to rigidly determined laws. It is this development alone which undermines itself by its own laws; so that capitalism collapses of itself " (p. 255).

[4] *Aus dem literarischen Nachlass Marx-Engels*, Vol. II, pp. 348, 390–2.

[5] " It is objectively unjustifiable to describe Hess's writings as ' foul and enervating literature ' " (Marx's characterisation of " true socialism " in the *Communist Manifesto*) quoted by Zlocisti, op. cit., p. 260.

[6] *Friedrich Engels, Eine Biographie*, Vol. I, pp. 106 ff. (1920).

ground[1]; but Lukács defends Marx in every particular and even asserts that far from being a " true socialist," Marx was not even a genuine Feuerbachian.[2]

For our purpose it is immaterial whether Marx was a " true socialist " or whether Hess was a forerunner of Marx. That they shared a great many positions together is indicated by their common derivation from Hegel and Feuerbach on the one hand, and their common struggles against Bauer's oppositional tendencies on the other. More important are the differences which manifested themselves between them. Even if it should turn out that Marx was a " true socialist " and that the views he argued against were those that he himself had earlier embraced, it would still be necessary, in tracing Marx's intellectual biography, to consider his criticism of " true socialism " as self-criticism.

I

THE PHILOSOPHY OF MOSES HESS

" *In Frankreich vertritt das Proletariat, in Deutschland die Geistesaristokratie den Humanismus.*"—HESS.

" True socialism," was a pseudo-political tendency among a certain group of literary men, publicists and philosophers in Germany, all of whom had been influenced by Feuerbach. It was not a system of thought. In a sense, every " true socialist " had his own philosophy. Hess, Grün, Lüning, Kriege, Heinzen, each developed his position in his own way so that no general exposition can be an adequate account of all the " true socialists." If one must choose a representative of this tendency, there is no choice but to turn to Moses Hess. He was the recognised leader of the group. By virtue of his unremitting activity in behalf of revolutionary ideals, he had already won the title

---

[1] Riazanov: " *Up to a point*, the severe criticism of German or " true " socialism contained in the *Manifesto* is a self-criticism . . . of Marx's own philosophical development " (explanatory notes to *Communist Manifesto*, Eng. trans., p. 213. Italics mine. To what point is however not indicated).

[2] Lukács: *Moses Hess und die Probleme in der idealistischen Dialektik*, Leipzig, 1926 (Sonderabdruck), p. 27 ff. At the time the above was originally written, Cornu's study on *Moses Hess et la Gauche Hegelienne*, Paris, 1934, had not yet appeared.

of the "father of German communism." Unfortunately, the
philosophy of Hess is not a unified doctrine. It is futile to look
for system or consistency in it. Hess was by turns a Spinozist,
an Hegelian, a Feuerbachian, a Marxist, a natural science
monist, and a combination of them all. It will therefore be
necessary to select for exposition only those of his views which
Hess held in the forties and which were in large measure shared
by his "true socialist" comrades. Marx's criticism will then be
more intelligible.

1. *The Social Status of the German Intellectual*

It was Heine who first proclaimed that the Germans had
succeeded in doing only in thought what others had already
done in fact. This was a pointed way of saying that although
the Germans were lagging behind other western nations in their
social and political development, their philosophical theory
from Kant to Hegel had already given an adequate ideological
expression of the needs and ideals of bourgeois society. In
Germany proper, however, the bourgeoisie had not yet come to
power and the class relationships were obscured by a host of
traditional, religious, sectional and political factors. The country
was predominantly agricultural; the semi-feudal estates provided a food supply sufficient not only for the domestic market
but for export. Political power was largely concentrated in the
hands of the nobility. This power had been challenged by
Napoleon in two ways. First, by a direct attempt to introduce
democratic and constitutional customs in those parts of Germany which he had conquered; and second, by the indirect
effects of the imposition of the Continental system, which by
barring English manufacturers from Germany, called into
existence a German industrial class (cf. Engels, "Der Status
Quo in Deutschland," Marx-Engels, *Gesamtausgabe*, Abt. I,
Bd. 6, p. 231 ff.). With Napoleon's defeat the first danger was
removed—except for the *promise* of a constitution which the
Prussian King had made in order to spur his subjects on against
the invader. But the second danger remained. The German
bourgeoisie which had grown strong enough to dominate the
domestic market during the Napoleonic wars, continued to
grow. Manufacturing, mining, and shipping were developed on

a wider scale. The bourgeoisie demanded a tariff-union (*Zollverein*) for all the thirty-nine German states, and got it. It demanded a protective tariff for Prussia, and got that, too. At every step, however, it encountered the opposition of the landed feudal interests whose wealth and power had been adversely affected, first, by the Napoleonic wars which had closed the French and English markets, second, by the English Corn Laws, enacted after the restoration of peace, and third, by overseas competition in agricultural and grazing products. The struggle between the rising bourgeoisie and the nobility was mediated by the monarchy which tolerated the bourgeoisie because it increased the national wealth and supplied new sources of revenue. Politically, however, the monarchy favoured the landed nobility because it feared that the development of industry would force the surrender of absolutism and accelerate the national unification of Germany. Meanwhile, the consequences of the agrarian reforms of Stein had increased the number of independent peasant-proprietors who, together with the local hand-workers, small tradesmen, etc., constituted a class of petty-bourgeoisie. Its interests were as much opposed to the large landlords as to the industrial capitalist. A small, inarticulate and newly created class of proletarians, which accompanied the growth of industry, suffered an intensive exploitation that often takes place when a country is first opened to manufacture.

In this confused social and political scene, government was possible only with the help of a great bureaucracy of officials who administered the complicated laws and regulations which grew out of the conflicts of so many different interests. In the course of time the bureaucracy began to consider itself an independent class with independent interests. But since by training and origin it was feudal in outlook, it was unsympathetic to the bourgeoisie. With growing resentment the latter found that the red tape, and the bribery necessary to break it, were interfering with normal industrial expansion and adding to the cost of production. Its economic interests demanded the overthrow of the absolute monarchy, but it was itself so strongly infected with the semi-feudal *Staat-und-Ständes-philosophie* that it preferred to truckle to the nobility and bureaucracy rather than to risk an open fight. Its only possible allies were the proletariat and a part of the petty bourgeoisie. The first was too weak, and the second—in Germany—more royalist than the king. And so the German bourgeoisie hoped to win its much needed reforms not by open class struggle but by (1) involving the nobility in the net of its investment schemes, (2) by making the government dependent upon it for its finances, and (3) by petitioning the king and his bureaucracy for a liberal constitution in the name of " social progress," " humanitarianism," and " philosophy."

It is against this background that the " true socialism " of the radical German intellectuals must be understood. They were acquainted with the great French socialist writers without having acquired a clear insight into the class stratification of their own country or a consciousness of the specific needs of the proletariat as a class.[1] As a group the intellectuals could only function either by direct or indirect service with the bureaucracy—which meant going over to outright reaction— or by expressing the demands of an opposition class. In the thirties, the Young-Germans and the Young-Hegelians had frankly adopted the point of view of the German bourgeoisie and had agitated for all the constitutional rights which England and France were enjoying. But with the disintegration of these schools of thought and with the dissemination of French socialist ideas, the German intellectuals lost their enthusiasm for the bourgeoisie. Instead of continuing with them in a common struggle against the absolutist monarchy, they turned all their weapons against bourgeois culture and politics, criticising the social consequences of industrial production. In their most advanced phase they spoke in the name of the proletariat, but the only proletarians they knew were the ones talked about by the French socialist writers. Or what was even more confusing, they sometimes proclaimed that "*Das Proletariat ist die Mensch-heit* " (the proletariat is humanity), so that it would appear, as Marx once caustically observed, that in struggling to abolish classes, the communists were striving to destroy humanity.

[1] " To these *true socialists* belong not only those who call themselves socialists *par excellence* but also the greater part of those literary men in Germany who have accepted the party name of communists. These last are, if that is possible, even worse than the true socialists " (Engels, loc. cit.).

In fact, whatever revolutionary consciousness developed among the German intellectuals took place quite independently of the development of the German proletariat. Hess was not only unacquainted with the German working classes, he was even unaware of the existence of communistic groups among the German workers in Paris. "When I came to Paris," he writes, " I was no more aware of the existence of communistic groups of German journeymen than they were of me " (*Sozialist-ische Aufsätze*, ed. by Zlocisti, p. 122). And Engels in one of his letters to Marx, writing of the great interest in communism which he and Hess had succeeded in awakening by public meetings, admits that they were winning converts among all classes except the proletariat.

" All of Elberfeld and Barmen, from the money aristocracy to the *épicerie*, was represented. Only the proletariat was not there. . . . Things are going fine. Everyone is talking about communism, and we are winning new followers every day. Wuppertaler communism is *une verité*, yes, almost a force. . . . The dumbest, most indolent and philistine of people who are interested in nothing in the world are beginning to become enthusiastic [*schwärmen*] about communism " (*Gesamtausgabe*, Abt. III, Bd. 2, p. 14).

Engels, himself, had already perceived the limitations of a theory of communism which took its point of departure from abstract ethical principles without relating them to the concrete struggles of the working class. In the preface to his *Condition of the English Working Class* (1845), he admits that one of the aims of his book is to put an end to all communist " *Phantas-tereien und Schwärmereien pro et contra* " and to provide a factual analysis of the economic realities which were shaping the social destinies of the proletariat and determining the conditions of their emancipation. The majority of the radical German intellectuals, however, were insensitive to the exist-ence and importance of social class divisions. Imbued with the ideals of a *perfect* society, they were unable to join the bureau-cracy which administered *present* society. They also refused to make themselves a vehicle for the specific temporal demands of the bourgeoisie or proletariat. The only standpoint from which they passed criticism upon society was an allegedly classless ethics whose values expressed not the immediate need of this or that class but the *essential* needs of the whole of society. They felt themselves to be the prophets of the good society whose organisation could be deduced from the " true nature " of man. They were concerned with the sufferings of the proletariat and the disparity which existed between their present life and their life as it ought to be. But they had no conception of what constituted the proletariat. The proletariat was identified with an abstract category of distress. The " true socialists " sympathised with the proletariat as they would sympathise with the cause of any underdog. They claimed to be socialists as much for the sake of the *ultimate* welfare of the nobility and bourgeoisie as for the sake of those whom these classes oppressed.

It should now be clear why such a position tended to strengthen the belief that it was possible to find an objective social philosophy which was valid for all classes of society.

2. *Communism as Humanism*

The philosophy of Hess was born of a desire to find fundamental principles of social organisation which would make possible the elimination of all conflict between man and man, and class and class. Early in his career, as a follower of Spinoza and Hegel, he believed that valid principles of social order could be derived only from a knowledge of the metaphysical structure of existence. The good life is a life based upon the insight into the unity and necessity of all things. Virtue arises from the *knowledge* of our status and function in the all-embracing totality called by both Spinoza and Hegel, God. Two difficulties, however, compelled Hess to modify his original Spinozism. First, its contemplative outlook upon life conflicted with his *consciousness* that a great many things had to be done, that problems were pressing for a solution which could not be found by viewing them *sub specie aeternitatis*. Secondly, a consistent Spinozism and Hegelianism seemed to imply that in the complete vision of the order and connection of things, everything was blessed with necessity, and that evil was non-existent. This would call into question the very reality of the social problems of evil and oppression which irked Hess's sensitive nature and which had furnished the starting point of his whole philosophical enquiry. The practical upshot of this philosophical ethics was to identify religion with morality and to make the problems of daily life which confronted him, unimportant and unreal.

Hess's task was now to find a philosophy which would justify the autonomy of moral *activity*. Like most of the Young-Hegelians, he turned to Fichte. The active personality of Fichte, his early enthusiasm for the French Revolution, and his apparent social and political liberalism had initiated a kind of Fichte-Renaissance among the Young-Hegelians. Since it was from him that Hegel had taken over and developed the dialectical method, the Young-Hegelians could with good philosophical grace couple their allegiance to the hero of the *Atheismusstreit* with their school loyalty to Hegel, the philosopher of the restoration. About the same time that Hess was writing his pieces in the *Rheinische Zeitung* and his essay, "Philosophie der Tat," Köppen, the close friend of Marx, published an article on "Fichte und die Revolution" in which he declared: "Now that the impulse to free political development has again come to life in us Germans . . . the voice of the purest, most determined, and strongest character among German philosophers will be better understood and will find a readier reception than ever before."[1] Hess, however, was more interested in grafting Fichte's metaphysics of activity upon Spinoza's doctrine of substance (something which Hegel had already done) than in Fichte's explicit political doctrines. "Not being but action is first and last . . . Now is the time for the philosophy of spirit to become a philosophy of activity. Not only thinking but the whole of human activity must be lifted to a plane on which all oppositions disappear . . . Fichte in this respect has already gone further than the most recent philosopher" ("Philosophie der Tat," *Sozialistische Aufsätze*, pp. 37, 50).

In invoking the Fichtean principle of activity to supplement the Spinozistic doctrine of Substance, Hess was expressing in an esoteric way the conflict which he had already described in more popular fashion as the conflict between religion and morality.

---

[1] *Anecdota*. . . . Vol. I, 1843, p. 154; for more complete documentation of Fichtean tendency among the Young-Hegelians, *see* Speier, "Die Geschichte-philosophie Lassales," in *Archiv für Sozialwissenschaft*, Vol. LXI, pp. 118 ff.; as well as for a convincing interpretation of Lassalle as a "wahre Sozialist" (p. 360).

The religious outlook, he contended, was essentially one of acceptance, an acceptance of the order of the universe—called indifferently God, Nature, Reason, or Spirit—of which human beings were a part, and whose mysterious and purposive ways could only be dimly apprehended by faith and intelligence. The standpoint of morality on the other hand, was one of assertion —an assertion of what ought to be and what is not, an imposition of a new order and not merely the recognition of an old. The root of religion was man's feelings; the source of morality was the practical necessities of life. So long as human beings strive after ideals of perfection, there can be no completely irreligious men; so long as they live in society, they cannot be completely immoral. Irreligion is simply a word for other people's religion; immorality, a term for behaviour different from our own. The essence of religion is *worship*; the essence of morality, *conscientiousness* ("Religion und Sittlichkeit," ibid., p. 28).

The conflict between religion and morality, Hess went on to say, can only be avoided if both observe a proper division of labour. Religion has no business in politics or with the concerns of the state. It is a private matter—an affair of the individual soul faced by the immensities of the cosmos. The field of politics belongs to ethics; its object is the general interests of mankind. "Let religion educate, edify, and elevate the *individual soul*. Let it support the weak and console the suffering. But in public life let man show himself not in his individual but in his general character. Public life—the state—demands not weak but strong, courageous and independent men."

But now Hess found himself confronted by even greater difficulties. If religion could not serve as a basis for social peace, how could ethics take its place? In affirming the Fichtean principle of activity, Hess was subscribing to the view that individuality is a brute metaphysical fact. Principles cannot act in time and be acted upon; only individuals can. In the social field, individuality expresses itself in the different personalities whose relationships constitute the social order. But, if virtue be no more than *conscientiousness*, if each individual is to fulfil the law of his own nature, what is the guarantee that social peace and freedom can be secured? Hess is asking how genuine social morality is possible. A social morality based upon convention or contractual promises between personalities breaks down as soon as an individual or a group becomes sufficiently powerful to violate the compact with impunity. A social morality based on authority or revelation is incompatible with the autonomy of moral action. Yet a social morality *must be grounded on some objective order*. It cannot be the order of nature. And at this point Hess turns to Feuerbach. Morality must be grounded on the " true " nature of the human species, on Man viewed not as a series of isolated individuals or as one abstract universal, Humanity, but as a living unity whose different parts have developed from a common source and are bound together by a feeling of natural kinship. But man cannot live as man— and here Hess improves on Feuerbach—unless he recognises that his human needs require new institutions; that all the social and political conflicts of the past and present have grown out of the root evils of private property; that money plays the same rôle in distorting man's practical life which religion plays in distorting his intellectual life. Having read Proudhon and the Utopian French socialists, Hess tries to link up their conclusions with Feuerbach's method:

" The essence of God, says Feuerbach, is the transcendent essence of man, and the real theory of the divine nature is the theory of human nature. Theology is *anthropology*. That is the truth, but it is not the *whole* truth. The nature of man, it must be added, is social, involving the co-operative activity of all individuals for the same ends and interests. The true theory of man, the true humanism is the theory of *human society*. In other words, *anthropology is socialism* " (loc. cit., pp. 115–16).

The logical corollary of this position was that the struggle for human freedom and social security must be waged not in the name of the proletariat, but in the name of humanity.

3. *Communism as the Ethics of Love*

The specific content with which Hess filled this abstract humanism is not hard to guess. It was a variant of the Feuerbachian ideal of love. Although the full realisation of communism depended upon the existence of certain social conditions (about whose nature Hess at this stage was rather vague), communism as an *ideal* was already implicit in every altruistic tendency which stirred within the human breast. The historical development of society, he held, may be legitimately viewed as a result of the conflict of two great passions—*egoism*, manifested in individual self-assertion against others, and *love*, as expressed in all action inspired by the consciousness of the essential identity of the individual with mankind. Egoism or selfishness is the final source of all social oppression and exploitation. Cruelty, fraud and robbery, feudalism, chattel and wage slavery, pauperism and prostitution are possible only because men draw a circle around themselves and their nearest of kin, and focus attention so strongly upon the field of their immediate vision that they become indifferent, and ultimately blind, to the interests and the very existence of those who live beyond the line. Social institutions are such as to place a premium upon selfish behaviour. And although this behaviour is hedged in by rules of law imposed by the state, these rules themselves represent the organised selfishness of dominant groups. Capitalism or " the system of free competition is the last word of egoism." It distorts and perverts every phase of culture—religion, art, education—by substituting for the ideals of the collectivity, private interest and private satisfaction as controlling factors.

Although the history of society has been the progressive replacement of the egoism of one group by the egoism of others, it is significant that all groups come to power by professing allegiance to theoretical principles of love and humanity, freedom and equality. The more altruistic their declaration, the more consistent—as the history of the English and French bourgeoisie illustrates—their egoism. The fact, however, that in order to move great masses into action, vehement lip-service to the ideals of *love* and *humanity* is necessary indicates that " the real nature of man " recognises that these ideals alone are ultimately valid and yearns for their fulfilment. But they can only be fulfilled when private property and the arbitrary power which its possession gives over other human beings, is abolished. " Communism is the law [*Lebensgesetz*] of love applied to social life." It is not enough to preach love to realise communism, as Feuerbach does; nor can it be brought about by preaching hate. Love must be organised into action; recognition of the identity of the real interest of all mankind must be carried over into every phase of personal and social life:

> " You have been told that you cannot serve two masters at once—God and Mammon. But we tell you that you cannot serve either one of them, if you think and feel like a *human* being. Love one another, unite in spirit, and your hearts will be filled with that blessedness which you have so vainly sought for *outside* of yourselves, in God. *Organise,* unite in the real world, and by your deeds and works you will possess all the wealth, which you have so vainly sought, in *money.* So long as you do not strive to develop your own nature, so long as you strive to be not *human* but *superhuman* and *inhuman* creatures, you will become inhuman, you will look down contemptuously upon human nature, whose real nature you do not recognise and treat ' the masses ' as if they were a wild beast. The beast which you see in the people is in yourself " (" Über die Not in unserer Gesellschaft und deren Abhilfe," *Sozialistische Aufsätze,* p. 149).

Hess left it unexplained how this belief in the essential unity of mankind could be reconciled with his characterisation of those who did not share his belief. Perhaps it is too much to expect this of one whose first interest was not in social analysis —but, like the old Hebrew prophets, in social justice.

If, anthropologically, communism was humanism, and ethically it was humanitarianism, it followed that the appeal to action would be framed not in terms of material interests but in terms of culture, creative activity, peace, honour, justice, and other ideal goods. The " true socialists " took the field against all those who pretended that the communist movement was exclusively, or even primarily, a movement of the proletariat, and who spoke as if its demands centred around the needs of the stomach. How could communists preach the ideal of classlessness and still appeal to *one* class against another ? How could the ideal values of communism be regarded as the concern *only* of the proletariat when they really flowed from the real nature of man ? Hess admitted, to be sure, that in France the movement was proletarian, but he explained this by saying that the French proletariat was communistic " not out of egoism but out of humanity." The proletariat becomes communistic out of love of mankind. But why should one, asks Hess, who out of love of mankind is already a communist, regard himself as a proletarian? And in fact there are communists who are not proletarians and there are proletarians who are not communists. All that one can say is that since the proletariat suffers most from the effects of organised egoism (which Hess identifies with capitalism), it is more likely than any other group to feel and understand the unity of mankind, and the necessity of establishing communism to realise it. Hess makes a point of correcting Lorenz von Stein, an Hegelian of the centre, whose book, *Der Sozialismus und Kommunismus des heutigen Frankreich* (1845) introduced, so to speak, the theories of French socialism to the German public. Despite his reactionary tendencies, Stein had made some surprisingly realistic analyses of the French revolutionary movement. He had grasped the importance of the class struggle in French history and had distinguished between the " proletariat " as an historical category bound up with capitalism and the " poor " and " unfortunate " to be found in any society.[1] Hess insists that Stein has given a misleading account of communism. " It is an error—and this error is due to the egoistic narrowness which cannot rise to a truly human outlook—yes, it is an error diligently spread by the reaction, and by Stein above all, that socialism develops only among the proletariat, and among the proletariat only as a question of fulfilling the needs of the stomach " (*Sozialistische Aufsätze*, p. 129).

Socialism is not a question of bread, although it may be that, too. It is in the first instance a question of man, of moral values, especially of human dignity. These values Hess formulates differently at different times. Sometimes it is simply *truth* which is the communist ideal ; only under communism will social parasitism and the civilisation of lies based on it disappear. Sometimes it is creative work in which effort and enjoyment will always be found together. Sometimes it is character or

[1] As far as the mooted question of Stein's influence on Marx is concerned, it is sufficient to point out that Stein prophesied that the existing proletariat would not develop in Germany. Responsibility for the existence of the proletariat is laid at the door of the *Weltgeist* (cf., op. cit., p. 29).

virtue, defined by Hess, as the "freedom to follow the law of one's own life" (which dangerously approaches the ideal of bourgeois freedom). But through the entire scale of ethical variations developed by Hess, there sounds one fundamental theme: the social revolution presupposes a *moral* revolution.

4. "True Socialism" as Reactionary Socialism

Had the "true socialists" restricted themselves to declarations of brotherly love, they probably would have been remembered only as another Utopian socialist sect. But they prided themselves upon having advanced beyond their master, Feuerbach. If thinking flowers in action, then political thinking must concern itself in the most intimate way with the contemporary issues of politics. As has already been indicated, the German bourgeoisie was struggling against the nobility and bureaucracy for the democratic rights already enjoyed by the bourgeoisie in France and England. The "true socialists," posted on French communist theory, knew that in a bourgeois democracy the proletariat was exploited even more openly than in an absolute monarchy, that the *formal* rights of Press, assemblage, trial by jury, etc., could not be effectively exercised where glaring social inequalities prevailed. Speaking, then, for the proletariat—for the future of humanity—the "true socialists" repudiated the demands of the bourgeoisie, attacked their spokesmen as hypocrites, and succeeded in confusing the intellectual strata of the petty-bourgeoisie who had regarded the change from an absolute monarchy to a constitutional republic as genuine social advance.

In this crusade against bourgeois liberalism the chief offender was not Moses Hess but Karl Grün and after him, Otto Lüning. But Hess was not without faults. He paraded an indifference to the political programme of the democrats and was quick to accuse them of compromise, insincerity and cowardice. Even communists were suspect if their origins were bourgeois. The badge of real ethical purity was proletarian. "Most communists," he wrote, "who stem from the bourgeoisie go no further than general phrases and attempts at compromise [between the old order and the new]; it is only the proletariat which carries things to a decisive *break* with the existing order" (*Rheinische Jahrbücher*, Vol. II, 1846, p. 65).

Hess maintained that the real cause of social distress was economic, and that to agitate for political reforms was therefore a waste of time. All governments, except revolutionary ones, were indifferent to the welfare of the proletariat. Addressing German liberals, he wrote:

" Has the King of Prussia shown less concern for the misery of the poorer classes than the French assembly for the French King? So convinced are we by reflection upon the facts and upon the real causes of social distress that this is not so, that all liberal political strivings appear to us as immaterial, even as downright disgusting " (*förmlich zum Ekel geworden sind*) (*Gesellschaftsspiegel*, Bd. 1, Heft 1, p. 2).

It was Karl Grün, however, the man upon whom Marx poured out the vials of his wrath, who formulated the anti-liberal attitude of " true socialism " most sharply. The promise of a constitution which the King of Prussia had made in 1815 was long overdue. At every opportunity the bourgeoisie reminded him, his counsellors, and his successor, of this unredeemed pledge. Every incident of domestic unrest was capitalised by bourgeois and liberal opinion to point out that constitutional safety-valves of popular resentment were better than none. The clamour for a constitution became particularly strong after the revolt of the Silesian weavers. It was in answer to this that Grün wrote:

" Who in Prussia wants a constitution? The liberals. Who are the liberals? People who sit within their four walls, and some *littérateurs* who either themselves own property or whose horizon is bounded by the wishes of the worthy factory owners. Does this handful of owners with their literary hacks constitute the people? No. Does the people desire a constitution? Not in its dreams. . . . Had the Silesian proletariat a consciousness . . . it would protest against a constitution. The proletariat has no consciousness . . . but we . . . act in its name. We protest "(*Rheinische Jahrbücher*, Vol. I, pp. 98–100).

Lüning was more interested in awakening the proletariat to its great mission of social salvation than in drawing it into supporting the political demands of the bourgeoisie. " There is only one way of making the proletariat conscious of its humanity, that is through the organisation of education."[1] And so the " true socialists," each in his own way, helped the reactionary nobility in its struggle to retain sole political supremacy in Germany.

5. *Communism and Nationalism*

Hess was the first socialist of his day to link up the question of nationalism with the theory of communism. Nationalism is of two varieties, just as internationalism is of two varieties. True nationalism, which may be defined as pride in the distinctive character of local culture, has been perverted into the false nationalism of modern states by the institution of private property. So long as competition and war between individuals prevail within communities, it is inevitable that the same principles be applied by the organised groups which constitute states in their relations with each other. The struggle between nations takes more gruesome forms—wars, massacres, etc.— than the struggle between individuals within the nation, because there is no consciousness of common ties of local culture to diminish the cruelty towards others called forth by a conflict over the means of life. Just as it is necessary to find a rule to regulate the distribution of goods within the community in order to give each one an opportunity to develop his personality, so it is necessary to find a rule which will apply between nations so that each nationality will be able to develop its distinctive culture. " The problem of the elimination of national hate is intimately bound up with the problem of egoistic competition. International war cannot cease until individual war, *competition,* ceases. All the problems, all the difficulties, all the contradictions which have arisen in this country flow out of this fundamental question." [2]

Commercial nationalism generally gives rise to a spurious renaissance of national culture. Everything becomes " national "

---

[1] *Dieses Buch gehört dem Volke*, a periodical, Vol. II, 1846, p. 102, quoted by Speier, loc. cit., p. 126.

[2] *Sozialistische Aufsätze*, p. 86. In his *Die europaische Triarchie* (1841), a work which brought him to public attention, Hess already proclaimed the necessity of a federated national unity of England, France, and Germany without interpreting nationalism as an expression of material egoistic interest.

and therefore the concern of the true patriot, e.g., " religion and a protective tariff for monopoly enterprises; freedom and cotton; mediæval ruins and modern industry; gravestones and railways." In this way national cultures, which are the bearers of unique value, become claimants to total and exclusive value. They no longer are content to live peacefully side by side, faithful to their own national genius and yet tolerant of others; they seek to impose their own culture upon others in the name of a militant and holy nationalism. They thereby destroy not only the unique value of other cultures but their own.

False nationalism breeds a false internationalism—cosmopolitanism. True internationalism recognises the necessity of distinct cultures and nations. " But only the individual is real," and nationality is the individuality of a people. It is no more possible for humanity to exist without particular peoples and nations than to exist without particular individuals.

Like most of his contemporaries Hess had a strong belief not only in the existence of national traits and character, but in their fixity. National traits may be an historical product, but *the kind* of development which is possible to each nation is determined by its essential nature. The German is essentially contemplative, the Frenchman passionate, and the Englishman practical. These traits will be found reflected in their revolutionary movements too. The German is a communist out of philosophy; the Frenchman, out of his strong feeling for justice; the Englishman, because of material interests. All three elements are necessary; but in the struggle for socialism, the Frenchman will give the signal for action.[1]

6. *Transition to Realism*

It would be a great injustice to Hess to close the exposition of his thought at this point. For his " true socialism " phase lasted only a few years. By 1847 Hess had already abandoned his appeal to humanity and the essential nature of man and had undertaken a study of political economy. His essay, " Die Folgen des Revolution des Proletariat," no longer speaks of ideal presuppositions of communism but of material conditions, not in terms

[1] For an amusing contrast between the French and German type of revolutionist, cf. *Sozialistische Aufsätze*, pp. 156–7.

of the development of the spirit of humanity but of the development of productive forces. In this essay of Hess will be found, with a clarity and precision quite foreign to his other writings, the theory of the concentration and centralisation of capital, the theory of increasing misery, the theory of overproduction to account for the periodicity of crises, the doctrine that the collapse of capitalism is inevitable, and the view that the development of revolutionary consciousness is a simple and direct outgrowth of economic distress—theories which were to receive classic formulation, together with a denunciation of " true socialism," a few months later, in the *Communist Manifesto*. The change in tone and subject matter is so striking that mere paraphrase cannot convey it. I quote therefore some characteristic passages:

" A revolution of the proletariat presupposes before all things the existence of a proletariat—presupposes a struggle, not merely about abstract principles but about concrete and tangible interests, presupposes that the very existence of the great majority of the workers is threatened, that these workers know who the enemy is they have to fight, and that they have the means in their own hands to achieve victory. . . . It remains to ask what must social relations be in order to produce uniform oppression of the workers as well as the instrument of their liberation ? . . . We have already indicated how free competition—in the last instance free-trade—makes wages equal. But before free competition can reach the highest phase of its development . . . a certain series of economic facts must precede it. . . . Machines must be discovered, instruments of production must be perfected and multiplied, work must be subdivided, more must be produced than consumed, business crises must arise as a result of overproduction and threaten to ruin an entire country in case the obstacles which remain in the way of industry are not removed. . . . Once social relations have reached this revolutionary height, nothing can stop the proletarian revolution. All measures to revive and develop private interest are at last exhausted. . . . It is large industry which, as we saw, in the last instance provides the means and conditions for the overthrow of the existing social order based upon private industry, private trade, and private property. It is large industry which creates a revolutionary class and unifies it against the ruling bourgeoisie. It is large industry which makes the proletariat subjectively conscious of the necessity of shaking off its yoke in that it gives the proletariat a consciousness of its position. . . . What fetters production to-day? The business crises? How do crises arise? Through overproduction. Why is more produced than can be consumed? Have, then, all the members of society more than enough of what they need? By no means, most of them lack the barest necessities of existence, not to speak of everything else which man needs for the development of his natural dispositions and capacities. . . . Why, then, this overproduction, this distress in the midst of plenty? Well we have seen: the more progress private industry makes, the more capital accumulates in private hands, the more those who are propertyless are compelled to sell their personal labour-power [*Arbeitskräfte*] in order to secure the necessary means of life. The worker, however, who is compelled to sell himself or his labour-power, becomes a commodity. Its value obeys the same economic laws as other commodities."[1]

It remains to ask where Hess derived these views, especially since, in some of his later writings, the echoes of his earlier doctrines are still to be heard. There can be no question but that Hess read Ricardo and the Ricardian socialists in the light of Marx's views as expressed in the *Anti-Proudhon*. It is a legitimate inference that these views were developed for Hess by Marx in their last period of collaboration. As we proceed to Marx's criticism of Hess, it is necessary to bear constantly in mind that for all his dislike of the personal characters of Marx and Engels, after 1847 Hess regarded himself as a Marxist.

II
MARX'S CRITICISM OF " TRUE SOCIALISM "

Marx's criticism of " true socialism " was motivated primarily by his opposition to the political tactics of the " true socialists,"

[1] *Sozialistische Aufsätze*, pp. 215–16.

the ultra-revolutionary strategy which controlled it, and the philosophical rationalisations they offered in its support. We shall not concern ourselves here with the special historical circumstances of the political struggles but with the principles with which Marx approached them—principles which have a scope and validity much wider than the particular *milieu* in which they originally arose. The philosophical constructions of the " true socialists " have shown a greater vitality than their politics. Like most of the theories Marx contended against, they have turned up again and again in different historical situations, tricked out in new phrases and flounces, for all the world fresh and unravished by criticism. Their systematic exposition and analysis may serve to illustrate the Marxian criticism of the *type* of view they illustrate. In any concrete case the specific meaning of these doctrines depends upon the historical context in which they function, but the general logic of the argument can be considered in relative independence of the particular historical situation.

1. *Intransigent Theory and Reactionary Practice*

Despite widespread opinion to the contrary, Marx and Engels were never doctrinaires. Clear about their principles, they never sought to force them upon a movement if such action threatened to disrupt or paralyse the forces which had been assembled for a common action. " Every step towards a real movement," Marx once wrote, " is more important than a dozen programmes." More important not because principles are unimportant—for without correct principles action is blind—but because principles which were not taken up by mass movements and linked to immediate interests are ineffectual. Behind this view was a deeper conception of what a principle is. On many occasions Marx and Engels maintained against those who talked nothing but principles that " communism is not a doctrine but a movement. It starts not from principles but from *facts* " (*Gesamtausgabe*, I, 6, 294). What they meant was simply that social and political principles express the real situations in which men find themselves and the needs of those situations. To transfer principles which express the felt needs of masses of people from one historical situation to another, in which class forces and relations are quite different, is to make abstractions of these principles. No matter how revolutionary those principles may originally have been, once they become abstractions imported from without *into* a different situation, they invariably help reaction rather than hinder it. They constitute a form of religious fixation.

This was the case with the " true socialists," many of whom were so radical that for years they were the comrades-in-arms of Marx and Engels. The revolutionary socialism of the French proletariat had developed in the course of the struggle of the French workers against the bourgeoisie which had been firmly entrenched in power since 1830. In Germany, however, the bourgeoisie, far from having attained power, was objectively the most dangerous foe of the existing government. The ultra-revolutionary " true socialists," however, had read the literature of French socialism to some purpose. They attacked the German bourgeoisie with the greatest vigour, and in the name of socialism opposed all the liberal reforms as half-measures designed to strengthen the position of the bourgeoisie at the cost of the working class. In Marx's eyes they were obstructing a real mass movement against the semi-feudal Prussian régime and lending objective aid and comfort to the reactionaries. The reactionary Press actually used their denunciations of the bourgeoisie as evidence that the workers themselves were opposed to " immoral " liberalism.

Marx and Engels did not, of course, believe that the bourgeoisie should not be criticised and their theoretical hypocrisies exposed. But they held that the chief emphasis of the criticism should fall upon the reactionary *status quo* in Germany, and that the criticism of the bourgeoisie should be of such a nature that none but those who were more radical than the bourgeoisie could use it.

" Our attack upon the bourgeoisie," wrote Engels, " distinguishes itself as much from that of the true socialists as it does from that of the reactionary nobility, e.g., of the French legitimists or of Young England. The German *status quo* cannot exploit our attack because it is directed even more strongly against it than against the bourgeoisie. If the bourgeoisie is, so to speak, our *natural* enemy whose overthrow will bring our party to power, the German *status quo* is much more our enemy because it stands between us and the bourgeoisie and prevents us from coming to grips with the bourgeoisie. That is why we do not in the least exclude ourselves from the oppositional mass movement against the German *status quo*. We constitute only its most advanced faction—a faction which through its unconcealed *arrière-pensée* against the bourgeoisie assumes a definite position " (*Gesamtausgabe*, I, 6, 234).

In the course of their criticism of the " true socialists," Marx and Engels repeatedly emphasise the dangers of the over-simple classifications which the " true socialists " made of class forces and oppositions in Germany. As opposed to the " true socialists " who saw only three classes struggling for power—the landed nobility, the industrialists, and the workers—they stress the greater complexity and diversity of social stratifica-tions. They make not only the distinctions indicated above but many others just as relevant to the formulation of realistic political policy. They recognise the social importance, because of the special interests involved, of the landlords who have heavy holdings in industry, of the free peasant, of the peasants still in feudal ties, of the officialdom, of the petty bourgeoisie, of the handworker. They demonstrate that the demands of the bourgeoisie, if granted, carry with them the possibility of a *partial* and *temporary* fulfilment of the immediate needs of all groups except the feudal landlords and bureaucratic official-dom (Ibid., p. 243). The bourgeoisie in the struggle for democracy against reaction must be supported even by communists. Any other attitude, no matter how principled it may appear and no matter how sincere its proponents, is political madness which aids reaction.

2. *Socialism by Education or Socialism by Struggle*

It was not only against the politics of the " true socialists " that Marx and Engels took the field. They objected to the way they expressed the ideals of socialism and the methods they stressed as necessary for its realisation. The "true socialists" believed that socialism could be achieved by educational enlightenment and the dissemination of culture. Socialism was presented as a cultural demand with only a casual reference to the economic facts which made that demand both possible and reasonable. The driving forces for the organisation of socialists were to be humanitarian, æsthetic and moral. Starting from the proposition that "the true (or ideal) man is an harmonious creature," they deduced the organisational schemes of socialism—as well as its right and might—from a knowledge of human nature. According to this Platonic conception, social systems were to be judged by their capacity to further the realisation of self-harmony for the great masses. Capitalism, of course, is condemned out of hand as a barbaric throwback compared to which even feudalism is a human and sensible social order. What are called the economic necessities of society and the needs of economic development can only be understood as indicating the ethical direction of social activity. A conscious and clearly formulated ethical philosophy is, therefore, of primary importance for the revolutionary movement.

The ethical ideals of socialism, supported on the fixed basis of true human nature, are to penetrate the masses by organised educational effort. "There is only one way," to recall the well-known sentence of Lüning, "to make the proletariat conscious of their humanity, that is, through the organisation of education."

All the fundamental assumptions behind this position were challenged by Marx and Engels—the assumptions concerning human nature, the nature of morality, the character and efficacy of education. A great many of the criticisms directed against the "true socialists" on these points were intended for Feuerbach and conversely. We shall therefore postpone detailed consideration of Marx's views until we discuss his relation to Feuerbach. But here a brief indication of their drift and impact can be given.

First of all, Marx and Engels insist that the human nature to which the "true socialists" appeal as the guide to social organisation is an historical variable. It does not explain society but society explains its specific expressions. To understand human nature, then, at any definite time we must understand the nature of the society in which human beings live. When we do this we find that human nature is not something homogeneous to which we can appeal for justification of any concrete social proposal. Class divisions, interests, and values enter as refracting and polarising influences upon it. Failure to understand this leads to an identification of the special psychological type which prevails in a given society with the concept of " man as such " —a familiar phrase in the writings of the " true socialists " and other Feuerbachians. Politically, this failure to make the necessary differentiations leads to the attempt to think in terms of the " public," " the community," " the nation," and blurs the clash of interests in a vague formula interpretable in opposite ways. Whether aware of it or not, the lucubrations of the " true socialists " which they addressed to all classes really celebrated the virtues of the progressive-peace-and-comfort-loving citizen. In the *Communist Manifesto,* Marx accuses " true socialism " " of proclaiming the German nation to be the normal nation and the German philistine to be the normal mind " (*Gesamtausgabe,* I, 6, 552).

Secondly, the arguments which Marx urged against Stirner's abstract morality he turns against the " true socialists." Where Stirner had glorified selfishness, Hess and his followers had preached unselfishness. Marx points out that selfishness and unselfishness are in themselves neither virtues nor vices. The social context and content of psychological impulses give them their moral quality. The concrete *needs* of the working class must be the point of departure for its morality. Conventionally, this may appear to be selfishness, but it is only through its self-assertion as a class that a decent life can be won for the individual members of the class, and, ultimately, for all individuals. Where the concrete needs are not sufficiently stressed the invocation to selflessness, to humanity, weakens the immediate struggles of the class, leads to concern over the enemy's " soul " and to despair about one's own. Marx comments very bitterly on the religion of self-abasement implied in Kriege's words:

" We have more important things to do than to worry about our miserable selves: we belong to humanity."[1]

---

[1] *Wir haben noch etwas mehr zu tun als für unser lumpiges Selbst zu sorgen: wir gehören der Menschheit.*"

" With this infamous and disgusting servility towards a
' self ' which is distinguished and separated from ' humanity '
—and which is therefore nothing more than a metaphysical
and even religious fiction—with this certainly ' miserable '
slavish degradation, this religion, like all others, ends. Such
a doctrine which preaches crawling and self-contempt is perfectly fitted for brave—*monks*, but never for energetic men
especially in times of struggle " (*Gesamtausgabe*, I, 6, 18).

It was not the fact that the " true socialists " spoke in the
name of morality which led Marx to oppose them but the *nature*
of the morality they professed—a morality which was timeless
and placeless, that dealt in injunctions which were never specific,
and which turned men's attention away from the determining
social forces of human behaviour.

Thirdly, when the " true socialists " spoke of the necessity
of organising the education of the working class they seemed to
imply that socialism as a fully formed theoretical doctrine was
to be carried into the working class from without almost in the
same way in which the apostles brought Christianity to the
women and slaves of Rome. Again, it was not their stress on
education but on the kind of education which was at fault.
And the kind of education they advocated followed from the
kind of socialism they believed in. Since the realisation of
socialism was conceived to be the task of all enlightened people
and not particularly the special task of the working classes,
there was no provision for linking up socialist teachings with
their daily life and struggles. Since the appeal was to the " good
sense," " reason " and " conscience " of humanity, it " condemned the destructive tendencies of communism and proclaimed its impartial detachment towards all class struggles "
(Marx). Since the social question was first and last an ethical
question, the " socialist " education of the " true socialist "
dwelt not upon the objective tendencies of social development,
which Marx and Engels taught were the basis of revolutionary
programme and practice, but upon the miserable and inhuman
consequences of capitalist production. It turned the attention of
the German workers and petty bourgeoisie not to the mechanisms
of social institutions but to the individuals who were most

prominently identified with them. It dealt with the individual motives of the kings of politics and finance; it encouraged the hopes that their humanity would triumph over their greed for profit and power.

Already in his controversy with Bruno Bauer, Marx had settled with this kind of education, but whereas Bauer was engaged in propaganda for social enlightenment in general, Hess and his friends were convinced that socialism as a specific form of social enlightenment could be effectively propagated in this way. Marx and Engels had the greatest respect for the French Utopians from whom the " true socialists " borrowed many of their arguments. But what was already a mistaken point of view in France was doubly mistaken when reasserted in a different country a generation later. Since " true socialism " was not only a political movement but a literary one as well, Marx and Engels were compelled to follow it into *belles-lettres* to expose the mis-education wrapped up in its fragrant metaphors.[1] Engels' criticism of Karl Beck's *Lieder vom armen Mann* may serve as illustration of the themes the "true socialist" poets selected, how they developed them, and the point of view from which the critical analysis was made.

In his poems Beck sang about the cares and trials of " the poor man," " the little man " and called the rich men—the Rothschilds of the day—to account for existing social misery. But there was no inkling of the real source of the trouble in any of his writings. Pitiful appeals alternated with empty threats to those whom Beck, together with the other " true socialists," held personally responsible for the course of German economic life. Apropos of Beck's opening poem " An das Haus Rothschild " Engels writes:

" Right off in his *ouverture*, he reveals his petty-bourgeois illusions that gold ' rules according to Rothschild's caprice '; an illusion which carries with it a whole series of fantastic misconceptions about the power of the House of Rothschild.

" The poet does not threaten the destruction of the real power of Rothschild, the social foundation upon which it rests; he merely desires that it be applied in a human way.

[1] Marx in *Die deutsche Ideologie* and Engels in a series of articles in the *Deutsche Brusseler Zeitung*, entitled " German Socialism in Verse and Prose."

He complains that bankers are not socialistic philanthropists, dreamers or purveyors of human happiness, but just bankers. Beck celebrates the cowardly petty-bourgeois *misère*, sings of the ' poor man,' the *pauvre honteux* with his miserable, pious and inconsequential wishes, of the ' little man ' in all his forms, but not of the proud, threatening and revolutionary proletariat. The reproaches and threats with which Beck overwhelms the House of Rothschild . . . rest upon childish illusions concerning the power of the Rothschilds, upon an entire lack of knowledge of the connection between this power and the existing situation, and a complete misconception of the means which the Rothschilds had to use to become and remain a power " (*Gesamtausgabe*, I, 6, 33).

Socialist education for Marx and Engels had to be based upon a knowledge of the fundamental economic tendencies which determined the social existence and conditions of life of the proletariat. Otherwise the proletariat was likely to be infected by all sorts of utopian illusions peddled by " well-wishing " representatives of other classes. But more important, such education must be acquired in the struggles and battles of the class war. The class struggle is not a doctrine, but the school in which doctrines arise are tested and used or discarded. The working class not only becomes conscious of itself in these struggles, but it changes and re-educates itself by its revolutionary practice.

3. *Nature, All-Too-Peaceful Nature*

The ethical ideals of the " true socialists " flowed from their conception of a peaceful and harmoniously developed human nature. The model for this human nature was physical nature, especially in its peaceful modes. A diluted and vulgarised Spinozism was propagated as the chief philosophical support of this ethical and social theory. The organic bonds by which the totality of existence was held together in a mystic unity could serve, once they are recognised, as the ties of social life. The *feeling* of natural kinship between man and the world without, experienced when we recall the physical conditions of our origin and of our achievements, establishes its existence. That kinship is a metaphysical fact which holds, since men are part of nature, for human relationships, too. A false education has obscured this feeling and clouded our consciousness with artificial distinctions. We need only reflect, however, upon those qualities which have always been regarded as social virtues to see that they presuppose a fundamental unity between man and man, and man and nature.

All sorts of arguments were adduced by the " true socialists " to win support for this sugary natural piety. Even formal logic was laid under toll. For did it not teach that differences between species could only be made on the basis of a *common* genus ? And that any distinction between man and nature therefore presupposed their fundamental unity ? Was not this the central theme of Hegel's expositions of the socially organised Absolute ? Was it not the abiding spiritual insight of Christianity which stressed the brotherhood of man under the fatherhood of God or Nature ? " See the lilies in the field ! " And does not science bring daily proof that man cannot set himself up against nature or seek peace by flight to a supernatural realm ? " Has not man arisen," asked the " true socialists " in the *Rheinischen Jahrbücher*, " out of a primal world, is he not a creature of nature like all others ? Is he not built out of the *same* stuff and endowed with the *same* general powers and qualities which animate *all* things ? "

Marx's response to this mysticism reduces itself to two simple points. First, he denies that nature is as peaceful as the " true socialists " seem to think and protests against the tendency to make of the term " unnatural " an ethical category. Strictly speaking, nature is what it is discovered to be and nothing can be dismissed as unnatural. Secondly, whatever the facts of nature may be which make social life possible, it is a mistake to regard man and man's consciousness from the point of view of what they have in common with everything else. When this is done we get a false conception of man and his mind, with all the important things left out; human beings are considered to be natural bodies, and the self-consciousness of man is transformed into " the self-consciousness of nature." This constitutes respectively the first steps towards mechanical materialism or absolute idealism. The "true socialists" take them both, and the *mélange* of materialistic Hegelianism and idealistic Spinozism is the philosophical result.

(a) That nature is not as peaceful as the kind-hearted " true socialists " believed, Marx has little difficulty in proving. In the face of the manifest facts of natural cruelty or rather the indifference of nature to peace or war, the illusions of the " true socialists " can be explained only as the pathetic fallacy of reading their ideals of what society *should* be into natural processes. " See the lilies in the fields ! " " Yes," comments Marx sarcastically, " see the lilies in the field, how they are chewed by the goats, transplanted by ' men ' to the lapels of their coats, and how they snap together under the unchaste love-making of the cow-girl and donkey boy " (*Gesamtausgabe*, I, 5, 456). The psychological motivation of the apotheosis of natural peace and of the " true socialist " lament that no human society in the past ever modelled itself on the laws of nature, Marx explains as follows:

" Ideas were smuggled into nature which the ' true socialist' wished to see realised in human society. Just as earlier the individual man became the mirror of nature, so now the whole of society. From the ideas smuggled into nature conclusions were drawn bearing upon human society. Since the authors did not concern themselves with the historical development of society and satisfied themselves with this barren analogy, it is not hard to understand why society was not always a faithful picture of nature " (Ibid., p. 459).

This is a significant passage because Marx has been accused of precisely the same intellectual procedure—reading his wishes into the natural world and then adducing the world, as so conceived, as evidence in behalf of his dreams. It is unlikely that any man as critical-minded as Marx would fall a victim to a type of thinking which he so often condemned. Marx's emphasis upon the changing historical patterns of society and his stress upon the transformative effect of struggle show how little he shared the illusions of the " true socialists."

" We would gladly believe that ' all social virtues . . . are derived from the feeling of natural human kinship and unity.' It is well to remember, however, that on the basis of this

' natural kinship ' feudalism, slavery and the social inequality of all epochs, rested. In passing, let us also note that this ' natural human kinship ' is an historical product which is constantly being transformed in daily activity. It is always something quite natural no matter how inhuman and unnatural it appears before the tribunal not only of ' man ' but of a subsequent revolutionary generation " (Ibid., p. 464).

(*b*) The attribution of what is true of part of nature to the whole of nature, as well as the inferences from one part to another, usually reduces itself to the logical fallacy of the undifferentiated middle-term. Everything that happens to man is in one sense a natural fact but it does not warrant drawing conclusions about Nature as a whole, or about other natural facts, unless an analogous structure is observable. Social phenomena, for example, may suggest approaching certain natural occurrences with definite categories just as the division of labour observable in human societies may help us discover something about the organisation of a colony of bees or ants. But such hypotheses are at best weak and conjectural, and even when they seem to be confirmed, closer examination will generally show significant differences between the behaviour patterns of men and those of any other living or non-living things. All materialistic and idealistic reductions of the totalities of experience to one set of categories whether it be of matter or mind ultimately rest upon the systematic neglect of difference, novelty and uniqueness. What Marx wrote of the " true socialists " in this connection is just as valid against numerous schools of idealism and materialism which have succeeded them. I give only a fragment of his interesting analysis. Speaking of the shift from the term nature in one meaning to nature in another, he writes :

" This whole prologue is a model of naïve philosophical mystification. The true socialist takes his point of departure from the idea that the split between life and happiness must cease. In order to find a proof for this proposition he calls nature to his aid and tries to make it appear that such splits do not exist within it. From this he concludes that since man is likewise a natural body and possesses the general characteristics of bodies, this split ought not to exist for him. With much greater justification could Hobbes derive his *bellum omnium contra omnes* from nature, and Hegel upon whose constructions the true-socialist stands, see in nature the lewd (*liederliche*) moments of the absolute Idea and even refer to the animals as the concrete anxiety of God. After having mystified nature, our true socialist mystifies human consciousness in that he makes it into a 'mirror' of mystified nature. Of course, as soon as ideas which are nothing more than the conceptual form of pious wishes concerning the human relationships of *nature*, are smuggled into the expressions of consciousness, then it follows forthwith that consciousness is only a mirror in which nature sees itself. And just as it was previously established by considering the qualities of man as a natural body, so here by considering his qualities as a merely passive mirror (*blosser, passiver Spiegel*) in which nature comes to consciousness, it is proved that the splits which were read out of nature must be eliminated from the human sphere. . . . ' Man possesses self-consciousness.' That is the first fact which is expressed. The drives and powers of the particular natural creature are transformed into the drives and power of ' Nature.' They then naturally ' appear ' in this creature *particularised*. This mystification was necessary in order to establish later the union of these drives and powers of ' nature ' in man's self-consciousness. Herewith the self-consciousness of man was easily transformed into the self-consciousness of nature in him. This mystification undergoes the appearance of being dispersed by the subsequent fact that man takes his revenge upon nature, and because nature finds *its* self-consciousness in him, he seeks his self-consciousness in it—a procedure through which he finds no more in nature than what he has put into it by the above described mystification " (*Gesamtausgabe*, I, 5, 456–7).

4. *Was Marx a " True Socialist " ?*

We now turn to the comparatively unimportant question whether Marx himself was ever a " true socialist "—a question around which many scholarly disputes have been waged. As distinct from Engels he never called himself a " true socialist."

And if " true socialism " be defined politically, he was never within hailing distance of the doctrine. But neither was Engels. Marx on many occasions employed phrases which appeared in the writings of the " true socialists." He did this, however, not only in the forties but throughout his life. For example, in the statutes of the First International, which he wrote, we read that the purposes of the International are : " to acknowledge truth, justice and morality on the basis of conduct . . . towards all men, without regard to colour, creed or nationality " (cf. Stekloff, *The First International*, p. 446). The use of such phrases was permissible, Marx explains in a letter to Engels, because the substance of the doctrine is not obscured by them and some people find their way to a revolutionary position through them. *Suaviter in modo, fortiter in re*, was the principle which guided him when he came into conflict with working-class views which were similar to his own. Where he recognised, however, a fundamental difference in point of view, Marx was loath to compromise even on terminology, for fear of obscuring issues. That is why he called himself and his party communist, when the *Manifesto* was written. And when there was a possibility that enemy groups might masquerade with the same phrases that the socialists of the time used, he scrupulously insisted upon the necessary qualifications.

For Marx the essence of " true socialism " was its abstract, classless morality. Neither in his Left-Hegelian nor materialistic phase, then, can he properly be regarded as having been a " true socialist." His opposition to the " true socialists " would not have been so intense if he had not observed the way in which extreme reactionaries were making use of their slogans. *Der Rheinischer Beobachter*, for example, a Catholic government sheet, was almost calling itself communist and using the phrases of the " true socialists " in criticising bourgeois hypocrisy. And those whom Marx in the *Manifesto* calls feudal or Tory-socialists were trying to capitalise upon the impressions which the literature of " true socialism " was making on the German public. Of this Tory-socialism, Marx wrote : " They waved the beggar's wallet in their hand as a flag in order to get the people behind them. But as often as this took place, the people caught sight of the old feudal coat of arms upon their behinds and dispersed

with loud and scornful laughter " (*Gesamtausgabe*, I, 6, 546).
It was Marx's consciousness of the fact that the feudal socialists
were waving the doctrinal flags of the " true socialists " which
gave his words the sharp bite they had whenever he discusses
" true socialism." That many of the things he said of Hess were
unjustified, Marx's subsequent attitude towards him reveals
clearly. But politically, Marx felt it was his revolutionary duty
to oppose with all energy those who blocked the possibility of
making any gains by the working class, no matter how small, in
its struggle for liberation. He did not spare his friends any more
than he spared himself. And although he was furious at stupidity,
it was not out of intellectual *hauteur* but out of a realisation
that if correct theories have practical consequences, mistaken
theories have no less practical consequences. There were many
things that he did not see; but he always saw the implications
of doctrines, programmes, and sometimes even the choice of
words, for the class struggle. It is in this sense that the following
passage which treats of the terminological sentimentalities of
the " true socialists " must be understood:

> " In the real world there exist, on the one side, owners of
> private property and on the other, a propertyless communist
> proletariat. This opposition becomes sharper day by day and is
> heading for a crisis. Consequently, if the theoretical represen-
> tatives of the proletariat desire to accomplish anything by
> their literary activity, they must above all get rid of all phrases
> which weaken the intensity of this opposition, all phrases
> which glide over the opposition and which offer the bourgeoisie
> an opportunity, impelled by its sentimental quest for security,
> to approach the proletariat. All of these bad characteristics we
> find in the slogans of the true socialists. . . . We are well aware
> that the communist movement cannot be corrupted by a pair
> of German phrasemongers. But it is necessary in a country
> like Germany where philosophical phrases have for centuries
> had a certain power, and where the absence of the sharp class
> oppositions which prevail among other nations makes the
> communist consciousness less militant and decisive—to
> oppose all phrase-making which waters down and weakens still
> further the consciousness of the total opposition of communism
> to the existing world order " (*Gesamtausgabe*, I, 5, 453).

CHAPTER VII

LUDWIG FEUERBACH AND KARL MARX

THE SIGNIFICANCE of the life and thought of Ludwig Feuerbach (1804–72) is only now emerging in contemporary philosophy. The rise of Marxism, the development of what is called *Existenzialphilosophie* in Germany (Heidegger, Jaspers), the renaissance of Hegelianism, and the increasing interest in the philosophy and psychology of religion have gradually brought Feuerbach into the field of vision of philosophic consciousness. It would be more accurate to say that he is being restored to his place, for as lonely and modest a figure as he was, during one brief decade the whole of German philosophy and culture stood within his shadow. If Hegel was the anointed king of German thought in the period from 1820 to 1840, then Feuerbach was the philosophical archrebel from the time of the publication of his *Das Wesen des Christenthums* to the eve of the revolution of 1848 in which he took a minor part. There is some truth in the contention of a recent monograph on Hegel that Feuerbach's philosophy represented the historical antithesis of absolute idealism—an antithesis which was prepared by the structure of the Hegelian system itself. " Feuerbach was Hegel's fate."[1] Historically considered, their thought represents essential, and yet essentially opposed, phases in the same movement of ideas.

The most important single factor in the rediscovery of Feuerbach has been the unintermittent interest of Marxists in the thought of a man whom both Marx and Engels, in the formative period of their philosophy, enthusiastically acclaimed as their intellectual leader. Although they later regarded their dependence upon Feuerbach in their early struggles to liberate themselves from the toils of the Hegelian system as " an unendurable debt of honour," Marx and Engels accepted some of the basic principles of Feuerbach's thought as the foundation stones of their own philosophy of dialectical materialism. The obvious

---

[1] Glockner, H., *Die Voraussetzungen der Hegelschen Philosophie*, Stuttgart, p. xviii, " Feuerbach belongs to Hegel as much as the beaker of hemlock to Socrates."

influence of Feuerbach on Marx has led Marxists to evaluate Feuerbach exclusively from this point of view. As legitimate as this approach is for certain purposes, it has tended to obscure the historic position of Feuerbach as an independent thinker in the history of philosophy. And not alone in the history of philosophy. Feuerbach's psychology of religion, despite the acute criticisms which Marx passed upon it, still remains the most comprehensive and persuasive hypothesis available for the study of comparative religion.[1]

In this chapter I shall present the central ideas of Feuerbach's philosophy as they developed from the time he broke away from Hegel to the year 1850 (after that date Feuerbach relapses into positions which he had criticised earlier). Only then will it be possible to evaluate his influence upon Marx, and Marx's criticism of him, without doing injustice to Feuerbach's merits as a philosopher in his own right.

In one of his numerous self-characterisations, Feuerbach classifies his works under various heads—historical, philosophical, religious, psychological. He immediately adds, however, that " despite the differences among my writings, strictly speaking all of them have only one end, one will, one thought, one theme. This theme is always religion and theology and whatever is connected with them."[2] Feuerbach defined the religious phenomenon as such, as the projection and hypostasis of some element of human experience into an object of worship. He attempted to show that the whole of traditional philosophy represented the same arbitrary isolation of a local and limited feature of experience from its context in social life, and its subsequent erection into an absolute principle whose validity was independent of all space, time and society. Traditional philosophy, then, was religion, too, both in its essential nature and in its processes of construction. The difference for Feuerbach was merely that in religion the hypostasis found its expression in concrete objects of sense and imagination while in philosophy the hypostasis was abstract and conceptual. Hegel also held that philosophy and religion were the same in content and differed only in form, but

<hr>

[1] Cf. R. H. Lowie, " L. Feuerbach—A Pioneer of Modern Thought," *Liberal Review*, Vol. II, No. 2.

[2] *Sämmtliche Werke*[2], Bd. 8, p. 6. Hereafter *S.W.*[1] refers to the first edition, *S.W.*[2] the second edition, of Feuerbach's works.

whereas for Hegel both had as their object *knowledge*, for Feuerbach both were essentially *emotional* attitudes reflecting man's needs and lacks. The detailed arguments by which Feuerbach reaches these positions we shall examine below, but this identification of religion and philosophy must be borne in mind in order to understand the oft-quoted aphorism of Feuerbach's " My philosophy is no philosophy." His rejection of philosophy is a rejection of traditional philosophy just as his rejection of religion is a rejection of traditional religion. And just as he substitutes a new religion for the old, so he develops a new philosophy.

The motivation of Feuerbach's philosophy, then, must be sought in the motivation of Feuerbach's religion—both in its critical and positive aspects. He himself, in protesting against the easy dismissal of his doctrines as atheism, reveals in words as clear as day that his fundamental interest in the problems of religion and philosophy is social and political.

" It is a question to-day, you say, no longer of the existence or the non-existence of God but of the existence or non-existence of man; not whether God is a creature whose nature is the same as ours but whether we human beings are to be equal among ourselves; not whether and how we can partake of the body of the Lord by eating bread but whether we have enough bread for our own bodies ; not whether we render unto God what is God's and unto Cæsar what is Cæsar's but whether we finally render unto man what is man's; not whether we are Christians or heathens, theists or atheists, but whether we are or can become men, healthy in soul and body, free, active and full of vitality. *Concedo*, gentlemen ! That is what I want, too. He who says no more of me than that I am an atheist, says and knows *nothing* of me. The question as to the existence or non-existence of God, the opposition between theism and atheism belongs to the sixteenth and seventeenth centuries but not to the nineteenth. I deny (*negiere*) God. But that means for me that I deny the negation of man. In place of the illusory, fantastic, heavenly position of man which in actual life necessarily leads to the degradation of man, I substitute the tangible, actual, and consequently also the political and social position of mankind. The question concerning the existence or non-existence of God is for me nothing but the question concerning the existence or non-existence of man " (*Sämmtliche Werke*, 1846, Preface to Vol. I, pp. xiv–xv).

Feuerbach never concretised his conception of " man," and it was at this point that Marx's criticism of Feuerbach's abstractions was to take hold. But the upshot of Feuerbach's philosophy was clear. Corresponding to his vague, grandiose language which celebrated the powers and virtues of man, we find a vague sentimental humanitarianism whose political expression was strong in eloquence but feeble in detailed analysis of the specific social problems which arose in bourgeois society. Under the circumstances, it is natural, then, that the best pages in Feuerbach are those devoted to the criticism of the dehumanisation of man. He had a complete grasp of the psychological processes by which man forgot the human origin of his own creations; but possessed little insight into the social agencies which had reinforced and traditionalised these psychological processes.

I
FEUERBACH'S METHOD

Few philosophers have been as keenly aware of their points of connection and division with philosophic tradition as Feuerbach. Towards the end of his career, spurred by the professional philosophers' neglect of his life-work, he stressed the essential difference between his approach and theirs, and took pride in referring to himself as the philosopher of the common man. But, like all reflective thought, his philosophy was far removed from the attitude of the common man who is too absorbed in daily routine even to rise to a standpoint which can be dignified as philosophical. It would be truer to say that Feuerbach attempted to do justice to the nature of *common experience*—a common experience born of practical activity and accessible to all human beings with the possible exception of professional philosophers. As early as 1839 in a communication addressed to Reidel, he characterised his philosophical method as follows:

" The practical tendency (in the higher sense of the terms) of my literary activity is expressed in its very method. The method consists in this: that it aims to achieve a continuous unification of the noble with the apparently common, of the distant with the *near-at-hand*, of the *abstract* with the *concrete*, of the *speculative* with the *empirical*, of *philosophy* with *life*. . . . In speculative philosophy I miss the element of empiricism and in empiricism the element of speculation. My method therefore is to unite both not as two different materials but as different principles, i.e. empirical *activity* and speculative *activity*. And for me the mediating link between these real, not abstract, opposites is *scepticism* or *criticism* of what is *only* speculative as well as of what is *only* empirical " (*Sämmt-liche Werke*[1], Bd. 2, pp. 174–6).

On other occasions, he speaks of his philosophy as scientific. So-called metaphysical laws are valid only if they can be established as laws of natural science.[1] Whoever goes out of the realm of science and employs methods which are not continuous with those which have been fruitful in the natural sciences, relapses into obscurantism, and will soon be lost among the impenetrable verbal clouds of traditional philosophy. As we shall later see, Feuerbach's conception of science and scientific method was very crude and gave rise to philosophical excesses every whit as monstrous as the idealistic nightmares he combated. But he was aware that a new path had to be opened up with the instruments of science, not with the guesses of the higher intuition or with the logical formulæ of the schools. For more than a quarter of a century Feuerbach flaunted his unorthodox point of view—quite loath to call it a philosophy—before a public which, when it did not ignore him, misunderstood him. He complains in a letter to Bolin:

" They still do not see that I have no other philosophy than an inescapable one, a philosophy which a man cannot discard without ceasing to be human; that this philosophy has nothing in common with traditional philosophical thought, including that of Kant; that its basis is natural science to which alone

[1] " Mir gilt kein Gesetz der Metaphysik das ich nicht als Naturgesetz nachweisen kann " (*Briefwechsel mit Kapp*, 1840, p. 84).

belongs past, present and future, while philosophy, at least the kind which appropriates the name, can only claim that past which contains the *peracti labores* or rather the *errores* of mankind " (*Ludwig Feuerbach in seinem Briefwechsel und Nachlass*, ed. by Karl Grün, Leipzig, 1874, Vol. II, p. 191).

The very difference underscored by Feuerbach as existing between his method and that of traditional philosophy makes it difficult to describe the former in terms of the latter. Nor are Feuerbach's frequent invocations to science of any help. For he was not interested in science but in man. " God was my first thought; Reason my second; Man my third and last " (*S.W.*[1], Bd. 2, p. 410). His unending quest was to uncover the human in the supernatural, the sensible in the intelligible, the psychological in the logical, and at least as far as programme was concerned, the social in the scientific. That man created God in his own image does not detract, according to Feuerbach, from the value or validity of God. It is only when man is unconscious of his own creations, when he cannot isolate the passions and desires which move him to creation, that he falls into error. Feuerbach's method, then, is in the widest sense an anthropological one. It is an attempt to reveal the nature of man in whatever man does. The nature of man, however, is to be found in man's emotions, more specifically in his emotional needs, lacks and drives. Instead of Descartes' " Cogito ergo sum," Feuerbach proclaimed a " Sentio ergo sum." Sensory experience was the criterion of existence, not logic or reason, no matter how divine. Indeed a reason which did not depart from and return to some sense-experience—whatever may have been its intervening career—was not reasonable. It could have no relevance to man or human affairs. " The subject of divinity is Reason, but the subject of Reason is man." To all philosophical and religious problems, Feuerbach therefore adopted a critical, genetic method of inquiry, probing for the psychological roots out of which flowered the whole of human culture. In developing his method Feuerbach followed neither a consistent nor a progressive line. Until his *Wesen der Christenthums* was published, in which he applied his critical-genetic method to religion, more particularly Christianity, Feuerbach achieved methodological self-consciousness largely through polemic. To grasp the significance of his method, it is necessary to follow Feuerbach through his early critiques of (*a*) the rationalism of Hegel, (*b*) the mysticism of Schelling, and (*c*) metaphysical or absolute materialism which, before the emergence of scientific materialism, was the stubborn and solitary opponent of idealism of every variety.

(*a*) *Critique of Hegel*

To Feuerbach, as to the rest of the Young-Hegelians, Hegel was the revered Father Parmenides of philosophy upon whom hands were laid only after prolonged wrestling with his central ideas. His *Zur Kritik der Hegelschen Philosophie* (1839) was written in a manner which carefully distinguished it from attacks made against Hegel from the evangelical right that came in increasing frequency after the publication of Strauss' *Leben Jesu*. The fundamental points of criticism still have a surprising freshness to them. These reduce to two: that the Hegelian method of deducing existence from essence, the ideal from the real, established nothing which it did not already assume at the outset; and that Hegel could only sustain the appearance of observing this method by systematically distorting the character of sense perception, by hustling it, so to speak, out of the world of space and time and material organisms into a timeless realm of meaning. Feuerbach, himself, in this essay, as well as in all subsequent ones, never developed a coherent and unambiguous theory of sense-perception. Sometimes he regards sense-perception as giving the checks, signs, and conditions of knowledge; sometimes he speaks of it as if it were a form of immediate knowledge independently of any thought process. His main concern is to argue, against Hegel, that sense-perception was the primary medium through which the intractabilities of nature manifested themselves. Whatever its character, it was a necessary element in all knowledge, the metaphysical bone upon which the all-devouring logical method of Hegel had come to grief. The central passages on which Feuerbach concentrates his critical fire are the treatment of the category of Being in Hegel's *Wissenschaft der Logik* and the discussion of sense-perception and certainty in the *Phänomenologie des Geists*.

To win his methodological right to differ with Hegel's method, Feuerbach begins his criticism by regarding Hegel's philosophy as an *historical* fact. For all its claim to universality, richness of content, and *strenge Wissenschaftlichkeit*, the Hegelian philosophy arose at a certain determinate period and was preceded by a definite philosophical tradition which set some of its main problems. Like all philosophies it appeared in a particular time with a particular presupposition (*S.W.*[1], 2, 92). It must therefore surrender, as Hegel himself pointed out in relation to other philosophies, all claims to absolute truth. If every philosophy is a child of its time, then its truth is relative to that time. *Veritas filia temporis.* And since as an expression in time, it must make presuppositions, these presuppositions can be examined in the light of others.

Hegel, like most system makers who have built for eternity, asserted that his philosophy was presuppositionless. He begins his Logic with Pure Being. He does not begin with any special beginning. He begins with that which, according to him, must be the beginning of all beginnings. Closer examination, however, shows that Hegel's beginning is not as innocent as it looks. It is determined by the development of post-Kantian philosophy, particularly that of Fichte, with its quest for a first principle which contains implicitly within itself the contents of heaven and earth. Such a first principle would enable the philosopher to justify the existence of the world, together with its apparent evils, under the form of an immanent logical necessity. Hegel improved upon the method of Fichte and Schelling by stressing the moment of differentiation in the concept of the Absolute Idea (totality). By introducing the rich variety of experienced content into the dialectic process in which the categories burgeon out of each other by a self-generating movement, he appears to do justice to the empirically given. But, holds Feuerbach, he does not accomplish this by strict logical deduction. He either surreptitiously smuggles historical fact into the logic as he goes along, or begs at the outset, with the help of the shiny but deceptive category of Pure Being, the whole outcome of his philosophy.

Hegel does not establish the fact, according to Feuerbach, that the Absolute Idea—a meaningful organic totality perpetually renewing itself outside of time—is the inescapable consequence of his beginning. The Absolute Idea is his real beginning, his real presupposition. Hegel, of course, would have admitted this and maintained that since the universe is an organic totality, with everything involving everything else, in the nature of the case the starting point of inquiry already contained the end, and the end must always lead back to the beginning. Systematic thought must of necessity describe a logical circle and return to its original position. Feuerbach's point, however, is that the notion of the universe as an organic totality is not tentatively adopted by Hegel, and its existence established by the fact that no matter where we start in experience we must end with the Absolute Idea—the only form of circularity which is not vicious —but that the Absolute Idea in Hegel is an assumption dogmatically begged to begin with and not submitted to the controls of experience. The crux of Feuerbach's criticism may be stated as follows : If it is assumed that the universe is an organic totality through and through (which is implied in the meaning of the Absolute Idea) then no proof of the existence of *particular* organic connections, ingeniously worked out by Hegel, can be valid evidence of the original assumption which involves that assumption at some point in the proof. And if we do not assume that the universe *must* be through and through organic but set to work to see by detailed concrete investigation how much of it actually is, we will find many organic wholes islanded in a sea of ever changing particulars. We will not find, what according to Hegel we must find, that they make a great circle each of whose circumference points is itself a circle, i.e. a system of systems.

Hegel, says Feuerbach, knew what he wanted to prove before he began his logical demonstrations. Nothing objectionable in that. But what he wanted to prove he regarded as true even before he began—which is another matter entirely.

" That the beginning is made with Being is a mere formality, for it is not the true beginning, the true first; a beginning might just as well have been made with the Absolute Idea, for to Hegel himself even before he wrote his Logic, i.e. presented his logical ideas in a scientific form, the Absolute Idea was a certainty, an immediate truth. The Absolute Idea—the Idea of the Absolute—carries in itself the indisputable certainty of its absolute truth. It posits itself in advance as the truth. What it posits as " the Other " (to itself) already posits in its very essence the truth of the Absolute Idea again. The proof is consequently purely formal " (*S.W.*[1], Bd. 2, p. 209).

For Feuerbach philosophy must begin not with abstractions but with something which in the first instance is not even philosophical—with life, in all its concrete wants and needs. And of all abstractions that of Pure Being, as understood by Hegel, is obviously the most unsatisfactory. For it has no meaning. All being, says Feuerbach, is *determinate* being—being of a definite form or kind. To say that Pure Being is what all determinate being has in common is darkly to call attention to the fact that there are many different things in the world. The unity which underlies this difference is either a unity of discourse or at best a definite hypothetically formulated connection requiring empirical evidence for its support.

The specific form of being which Hegel must neglect in order to give his pan-logism a semblance of plausibility is sense-perception—that which is given as the *this, here* and *now*. In the *Phänomenologie* Hegel attempts to show that these terms represent universals not particulars. His analysis consists in interpreting *this, here*, and *now* in propositions like "*This* is a house "; " *Here* is a tree " ; " It is *now* night "—as if they were universals unable to express the specificity, uniqueness and individuality which we intend to communicate when we employ them. It is impossible according to Hegel to denote anything—even by pointing. All words—all symbols—*connote* meanings which can never be exhausted in any particular application or set of applications.

The certainties and immediacies which seem to be given in sense-perception are delusive. " The *this*," Hegel says, " reveals itself as a mediated simplicity or as universality . . . speech is truer (than sense-perception) ; in it we immediately refute our own intent. Since the universal is the truth of sense-certainty and since speech can only express this truth, then in so far as we desire to refer to a sensory fact (*sinnliches Sein*), it is impossible to say what we mean." Granted Hegel's argument, then sense-perception becomes a meaningless shadow irrelevant to knowledge, an obscuring veil through which reason must penetrate to discover the truth. Things turn out to be congeries of universals completely knowable and completely logical. The only problem which remains is to account for the existence of sense-perception and its *appearance* of reality.

Feuerbach argues at great length that Hegel's attempt to banish sensory experience from the field of knowledge is nothing more than a *tour de force*. The particularity of existence impresses itself upon man by compelling him to take note of it in his behaviour—in his every movement. And without a sensory experience, which is intimately involved in the knowing process, there could be no recognition of the differences between things. Hegel is only able to show that sensory experience, " the other " of thought, is itself a mode of intellectual apprehension because he contrasts it not with the genuine " other " of thought but with the *thought* of the other-than-thought (*nicht dem Anderssein des Gedankens, sondern mit dem Gedanken von dem Anderssein des Gedankens*). The other-than-thought, sense-perception, becomes a species of the same logical genus as thought, and in a few sentences Hegel celebrates his verbal victory over sensory experience. But how does it stand with the brute facts of immediacy as we actually experience them ?

" ' The here is for example the tree. I turn around, and this truth therewith disappears.' Of course, this is so in the *Phänomenologie* where one can shift positions at the cost of a word. But in the reality in which I must turn my clumsy body around, the here proves itself even behind my back to be a very real existence. The tree *limits* my back; it *forces* me from the place which it occupies. Hegel has not refuted the here which presents itself as an object of sense-perception distinct from an object of pure thought, but only the logical here, the logical now. He has refuted the concept of thisness, of hæceitas. He has demonstrated the unreality of particularised existence when it is *fixed* in consciousness as a (theoretical) reality. His *Phänomenologie* is nothing else but a phenomenological Logic " (*S.W.*[1], Bd. 2, p. 214).

In denying that a thing is composed of a set of universals, Feuerbach seems to swing over to the opposite point of view according to which no universals are constitutive elements of things. All reality is individual; logical relations are only abstract forms of speech which serve our convenience in identifying and organising individual things. Here we have the first intimations of Feuerbach's nominalism, a doctrine which, as we shall show later on, he never defended consistently. Parodying Hegel's argument on the nature of *this* and *that*, he writes, " My brother is called John, Adolf, but in addition to him there are innumerable others who are called John, Adolf. Shall I conclude from this that my John is no reality, that only in Johnness (*Johann-heit*) is truth ? For sense-perception all words are names, *Nomina propria*, in themselves quite indifferent to perception which sees in them only signs to be used in order to achieve its ends in the shortest way " (Ibid., p. 212).

That systematic knowledge cannot be developed on the basis of sense-perception alone, Feuerbach of course does not deny. He admits that even science, which he holds up as an illustration of the fact that sense-perception can be an important element in systematic knowledge, must recognise an inescapable opposition (*unvermeidlicher Bruch*) between objects of sense-perception and scientific objects (Ibid., p. 211 footnote).[1] But in science as distinct from philosophy this opposition between sense-perception and thought (in modern terminology, sense data and hypothesis) is not unmediated. That is to say, scientific thought even though it must transcend sense-perception takes its point of departure from it and returns to it somewhere in the process of scientific proof. Science is not opposed to ordinary experience. It does not deal with another order of being but is an effective human method of controlling experience. Philosophy, however, as a result of its failure to derive its problems from practical life, regards sense-perception, when it regards it at all, as an obscuring element hostile to thought. Philosophers, as Feuerbach trenchantly observes, have too often been like people who " have torn their eyes out of their heads in order to think

---

[1] In a later essay he actually defines the task of science, as consisting in " making a scientific object of that which is not an object " (i.e., of what is given in sense-experience), p. 234.

more clearly." This systematic dispraise of sense-experience has led either (1) to a rationalising of the whole universe in which the brutely given has appeared as a phase of Reason or (2) to the erection of a sharp dualism in which public and objective truths of reason have been contrasted with the uncertain opinion about the world of sense or (3) to the dismissal of the whole world of sensory experience as an illusion and to the conception of " reality " exclusively in logical, physical or spiritual terms. In opposing Hegel, therefore, Feuerbach was opposing the whole tradition of classical European philosophy. He was well aware of this. " The same objection applies to the Hegelian philosophy which applies to the whole of modern philosophy from Descartes and Spinoza down—the objection to its unmediated break with sense-perception, to its immediate presupposition of philosophy" (*S.W.*[1], Bd. 2, p. 211).

Feuerbach's later criticism of Hegel does not concern itself with the immanent difficulties of his philosophy. His criticism is expressed in a series of brilliant apothegms in which with profound insight he characterises absolute idealism from the outside. In his *Vorläufige Thesen zur Reform der Philosophie*, Feuerbach proclaims the secret of absolute idealism to be the secret of theology. The Absolute Idea, manifesting itself in all reality and appearance, is God. The process by which the Absolute Idea dirempts itself and plunges into matter in order to reaffirm itself on a higher plane of Reason is a philosophic myth expressing the mystery of the spirit become flesh. The doctrine that every existent is an object of knowledge for the Absolute Mind, merely reasserts in a more sophisticated form the belief that Nature was created by God, that material creatures are the products of an immaterial essence. The identification of the real with the rational and the rational with the desirable is a celebration in polyphonic prose of the goodness of God and all his works. With an unerring hand, Feuerbach traces the Neo-Platonic elements in the Hegelian philosophy, maintaining that absolute idealism is a kind of reborn Alexandrianism, that Hegel is not the Christian Aristotle but the German Proclus. Hegel, for all his erudition and insights, is the last of the great Christian apologists. He forged new weapons and ransacked an armoury of old ones in order to defend not the Christian way of life—which was renounced by Christians themselves after the fall of Rome—but Christian thought and tradition which sanctified the basic dualism of society. In words which Marx was later to repeat with but slight variation, Feuerbach proclaimed: " *The Hegelian philosophy is the last refuge, the last rational support of theology.* Just as once upon a time the Catholic theologians were *de facto* Aristotelians in order to combat Protestantism, to-day the protestant theologians are *de jure* Hegelians in order to combat ' atheism ' " (*S.W.*[1], Bd. 2, p. 262).

(b) *Critique of Schelling*

In 1843, soon after Schelling had been called to Berlin to undo the work of Hegel, Karl Marx addressed a communication to Feuerbach asking him to write a definitive criticism of Schelling for the *Deutsch-Französischer Jahrbücher*. In this letter Marx referred to Feuerbach as the philosophical antipodes of Schelling, as the mature imaginative genius of whom Schelling was the anticipatory caricature.[1] The justification for linking Schelling and Feuerbach together as contrasting expressions of a generic philosophic tendency will be more apparent when we discuss Feuerbach's psychology of religion. In his reply to Marx, Feuerbach refused to honour Schelling with an extended critique. He maintained that Schelling was openly lending himself to the uses of reaction and exploiting his early reputation in order to palm off the most outrageous obscurantist apologia for revealed religion under the title of *Die Philosophie der Offenbarung*. " Ach ! " he writes to Marx, " one need only open his lectures to fall unconscious before the corpse-like odour of Duns-Scotist scholasticism and Jacob Boehme's theosophy." Prior to Schelling's début at Berlin, Feuerbach had already sharply criticised his mysticism, especially his vague conception of an Absolute in which thought and being were identified, so that when thought was conceived as a species of imagination, the world turned out to be the product of divine imagining. The early advance Schelling made over Kant and Fichte was to return to nature not as the construction of the self but as something independent of, and yet related to, the self. He never

[1] *Gesamtausgabe*, Abt. I, Bd. 1, Zweiter Halbband, p. 316.

freed himself, however, from idealism because, in order to relate nature and self and avoid open metaphysical dualism, he interpreted nature as *another* self. Nor was Schelling faithful, according to Feuerbach, to the positive principles of idealism which interpreted mind and the self as a *rational* activity. " Nature is only the visible organism of our understanding," says Schelling. But the understanding for Schelling is *imaginative* perception. The distinctions and determinations within nature, whose discovery is the task of science, on his view have no objective status: they dissolve, reform, glide into fluid colourful outlines like the figures in a dream. " Philosophy becomes *beautiful,* poetic, gracious (*gemüthlich*), romantic but at the same time transcendent, superstitious, *absolutely* uncritical" (*S.W.*[1], Bd. 2, p. 220). Philosophy becomes outright mythology. No wonder, Feuerbach adds, that Schelling's philosophy of identity falls helplessly into the arms of the mysticism of the Görlitzer shoemaker (Boehme).

What was still more objectionable to Feuerbach, Schelling endowed the primal creative force of the world not only with an imagination but with a Christian imagination. And in a piece devoted to an examination of the relation between " Christianity and Philosophy," Feuerbach protests against making philosophy the hand-maiden of religion. His critical shafts here were obviously directed against right-wing Hegelians, who were trying to dissociate Hegel from his irreligious disciples, as well as against Schelling, who was assuring everyone who would listen to him at Munich that Hegel's philosophy was anti-Christian and that only his own philosophy of revelation could do justice to Christian mythology.

Orthodox Hegelians were defending themselves against the attacks of the religious fundamentalists by repeating after their master that the *content* of philosophy and religion was the same. Only the form under which the content was conceived was different. Philosophy dealt in ideas; religion in sensuous symbols. Feuerbach points out that this runs counter to one of Hegel's important metaphysical dicta—the inseparability of form and matter. The content of religion is really its form—the fantastic and compensatory projection of the human wish. This becomes clearer when we remember that as far as the content of belief is concerned, there is no such thing as religion in general. There are only specific religions. The task of the philosophical apologist of Christianity, therefore, is to deduce not the existence of *God* by definition, analogy, or logical reasoning but the existence and passion of Christ, and justify dogmas like the immaculate conception, the hierarchy of devils and angels. " God as such is not the essential specific content and object of the Christian religion— it is Christ " ($S.W.$[1], Bd. 2, p. 179). It is obvious that this deduction can only be accomplished by fantasy and myth. But once philosophy reaches for such instruments to establish conclusions it commits suicide. The conclusion which Feuerbach reaches is in line with the tenor of a still earlier work in which he argues that strictly speaking there is no more justification in speaking of a Christian philosophy than there is in speaking of Christian medicine or Christian mathematics.

Religion, for Feuerbach, is rooted in feeling and expresses itself in judgments which are overt or disguised wishes. These wishes reflect man's impotence in the world, his ignorance of its laws, and his desire to control events in harmony with his emotions. The inevitable consequence of all religion, Feuerbach holds, is belief in miracles. This means the abdication of philosophy. In religion, " feeling (*das Gemuth*) elevates itself into a God . . . it cannot abide anything which contradicts it; *its* wishes alone are the only valid laws. The law of the heart in contradiction to the real laws of the world finds its outward expression in the miracle. The miracle is therefore the *natural*, and for that very reason, the essential conception which religion has of the world " ($S.W.$[1], Bd. 2, p. 180).

Opposed to miracle in religion and to the fantasy in which religious desires clothe themselves are science and philosophy. These make reason central because it is the only surety of objectivity. They alone are capable of distinguishing between the true and the false. Absolute objectivity is for ever beyond human ken since knowledge, like all human activity, presupposes human organs of perception reacting selectively upon the world. But the difference between the inescapable anthropomorphism of science and philosophy and that of religion is that the first is controlled and the second is not. The relationships between man and the world which religion purports to find are nothing more than a peculiar inversion of psychological and social relationships between human beings. They tell us nothing about the external, physical world. The relationships between man and the world established by science tell us something about man, too, about his powers and capacities which make it possible for him to know and to feel—but they also give us objective knowledge of that which is related to man. This is all the objectivity human beings can ever achieve, but it is adequate for their needs and sufficient for science. Feuerbach reminds those who seek an objectivity which is independent of any actual or possible relation to the human processes of discovering it, that: "Every object, of course, can be apprehended and known by man only in virtue of its relations to man—even in science. What an object is does not lie hidden *outside* of or *behind* its relations—a notion admirably refuted already by Hegel " (*S.W.*[1], Bd. 2, p. 182).

The point of this contrast between Feuerbach and Schelling is to show that although Feuerbach, together with one variety of mystics, stresses feeling or affective experience as a necessary element in the knowledge process, he does not contrast feeling with reason, nor hold it up as a superior organ of intellectual vision capable of giving true conclusions about the world not vouchsafed by science. Whatever unity exists in the world must be discovered by the methods of science, not by intuition, imaginative synthesis, or any other surrogate for analysis and experiment. When Feuerbach uses the term feeling or emotion (as distinct from sensation) he always uses it as an empirical psychologist. It is a rather primitive empirical psychology, to be sure, but one capable of being improved upon. In passing, it should be pointed out that this difference between feeling as a concept of empirical psychology and feeling as a mode of knowledge of the One, God, Universe, or what-not, distinguishes Feuerbach's thought from that of Schleiermacher who in his definition of religion as consisting in " the feeling of absolute dependence " seems to suggest Feuerbach's position expressed in *Das Wesen der Religion*. The difference between the two concepts of dependence is that Schleiermacher's " feeling of dependence " has a religious-mystical character, a sense of finitude embraced by the shoreless infinite, and consequently represents the first step towards a theology: Feuerbach's " feeling of

dependence," as he himself says, is " no theological, Schleier-
machian, misty, indeterminate, abstract feeling . . . it is the
sense of the dependent feeling, dependent seeing, in short from
all sides and senses dependent knowing man " ($S.W.^2$, Bd. 8,
p. 55).[1]

(c) Critique of Absolute Materialism

One of the most paradoxical features of the development of
Feuerbach's thought is his apparent return to a philosophical
position which he had abandoned with great decisiveness during
a period when he was working his way towards a naturalistic
humanism. Feuerbach has been called many kinds of a materialist. And he undoubtedly subscribed to several different vari-
ants of the doctrine. But there was one type of materialism of
which he provided an almost classic refutation. Ironically enough
it is precisely with this type of materialism that he is tagged by
conventional historians of philosophy.

In an essay published in 1838, devoted to a criticism of Dorguth's *Kritik des Idealismus*, a year before his final break with
Hegel, Feuerbach makes a penetrating attack upon the doctrine
of absolute or metaphysical materialism upheld by Dorguth.
Although in this essay Feuerbach uses the term idealist to
characterise his own position, he employs it in a very special
sense. An idealist is anyone who refuses to accept the dogma
that everything in the world is material and that all intellectual
activity can be exhaustively explained in physical categories.
He grants without qualification all the scientific facts that
traditional materialists have adduced to demonstrate the
dependence of mind on body such as the correlation of specific
organs of the body with specific powers and aptitudes, but he
contests the philosophical construction which has been placed
on the facts. In attacking extreme materialism he is careful to
distinguish his own view from the current spiritualistic idealism
of German thought which taught that the body is a creation of
some non-empirical self. " Without body," he writes, " no mind;
he who has no body has neither mind nor an idea of mind, for
the mind is not a fact, not an immediate existence. . . . Minds

---

[1] For an elaboration of this, *see* S. Rawidowicz, *L. Feuerbach's Philosophie
Ursprung und Schicksal* (Berlin, 1931, pp. 188 ff.).

without bodies are mindless fantastic creations " (*S.W.*[1], Bd. 2, p. 149). But it does not follow from this that the activity of mind which we call thought, and in virtue of which we are able to distinguish between body and mind, is itself material and explicable merely as an activity of the brain. " Brain activity is only the condition, and not the positive but the negative condition, of thought." *Without* a brain we cannot think; we do not think *because* of it.

Feuerbach's arguments against absolute materialism (the phrase is his) are three. They are (*i*) the position is unintelligible in its own terms and involves a confusion of categories, (*ii*) it fails to explain the possibility and actuality of interaction between man's mind and body, and between man and his environment, and (*iii*) it is incompatible with the logic of scientific method, unable to do justice to the rôle of hypotheses or account for the existence of error.

(*i*) By trying to erect a rigidly materialist philosophy on the basis of a limited scientific knowledge, materialists were guilty of reaching conclusions which would make the existence of anything else but matter—including their own thinking—impossible. This always happens when instead of saying that a thing is *also x*, we say it is *only x*; in this case when we go from the proposition " Thinking is *also* a brain activity " to the proposition, " Thinking is *only* a brain activity."

> " At the very outset we must object to the proposition ' thought is an activity of the brain '—a proposition which is fundamental to his [Dorguth's] writing and which does not mean that thinking is *also* a brain activity but that it is *only* a brain activity, the essence of thought, thought *in puris naturalibus* . . . I say, we must object that this proposition appears to us, if not exactly brainless, completely meaningless on the simple ground that so long as the brain is not itself mind (*Verstand*), the activity of the mind must as such be a senseless activity. Consequently to characterise thought as a brain activity is to characterise the activity of thought as senseless " (*S.W.*[1], Bd. 2, p. 139).

To say that thought is a material activity is as senseless as to say that gravitation has a taste or smell, for according to

Feuerbach a proposition has meaning only when the predicate is of the same generic kind (*Gattung*) as the subject. Thought must be understood in terms of its own activity, its own products, before it can be controlled by a study of its conditions. It is the study of ideas which is relevant to the study of mind and not, in the first instance, the study of the body. The clue to our mentality is *what* we think, and not the structure of our brain, although without that brain we could not think at all. Without a recognition of the relative autonomy of thought which, for all its dependence on things, has an irreducible quality or nature, the very distinction between " matter " and " the idea of matter " could not be made. " Wo nur Materie ist, da ist kein Begriff der Materie " (Ibid., p. 147). Thought is not the proper subject matter of physiology but of philosophy and psychology. " To call thinking a function of the brain is to say nothing about *what* thinking is. . . . Such a characterisation does not characterise. . . . Thought must be something *more* than, something quite *different* from, a mere activity of the brain. An activity can be understood only out of what it does, in terms of its object and products. What it does, that it *is*. The product of thinking is thought. Therefore it is only in terms of thought that the nature of thinking can be understood " (Ibid., p. 140).

Feuerbach gives his dialectic one final twist. If thought is a product of the brain in the same way that bile is of the liver, then why does it not enjoy the same tangible, material status of the brain ? If it is unreal then it is an unreal product and there is nothing but brain, no thought; if it is real, then we can no more apply the distinction of true and false to ideas than we can to the brain. They are what they are. But take Fichte, the arch-opponent of materialism. How would the absolute materialists explain his thought ? As a function of the structure of his skull, composition of his blood, specific organisation of his brain, etc. Very well. To explain his thought as a necessary product of his brain is to hold that his *ideas* must be explained in terms of his brain—that they have the same inescapable objective reality of his brain. But how, then, can these ideas be judged and declared *false,* as all materialists do so declare them, and must, because, according to Fichte's ideas, materialism *itself* is false ?

(*ii*) Absolute materialism if it is to express itself in any mean-ingful terms must deny not the existence of thought but its efficacy. But if the efficacy of thought is denied then its very activity must be denied, for there is no point to the activity of thought, nor even any evidence of its existence, where it has no effects. These effects are often the best leads to thought, for it is in behalf of them that thought is initiated. In fact, Feuerbach argues, the effects of thought can be such that it may lead to the destruction of the very body whose evanescent shadow thought is supposed to be. Consider suicide—in which thought runs counter to the most fundamental drive of the human body. Man's thought is a necessary element, even if not the only one, in all such tragic activity. Animals do not take their own lives, although like men they are subject to the laws of physics and chemistry. Or consider, adds Feuerbach, such things as inven-tions in which material becomes transformed to realise an ante-cedent idea or thought. Or every act of self-sacrifice in which human beings, dominated by ideals, change the course of their life. " Explain to me," Feuerbach addresses the materialist, " the death of the sage or the hero who stakes his head upon his ideas. Explain to me the power of ideas upon the organism if the idea is nothing but an excrescence of the organism ? " (*S.W.*[1], Bd. 2, p. 146.)

(*iii*) Rejecting the reality of ideas, the materialists must fall back upon sense-experience as such to convey knowledge. Sense-experience which is always of the present can say nothing about the future. Materialists, therefore, are unable to anticipate experience, nor would they be able, if they were true to their own philosophy, to understand any scientific fact including the *nature* of sense-experience. Science can render experience because it is an anticipation of experience. The very life of science consists in its hypotheses which often run counter to what is apparently given to the senses. " With our senses we read the book of nature, but we do not understand it with them " (p. 151). If we understood with our senses, we would have no use of hypo-theses or theories. We could never err. Nor would we ever " know " more than was immediately under our nose. In his criticism of materialism on this score, Feuerbach identifies idealism with the belief in the power of ideas to disclose the truth of things. He holds up the Copernican system, whose conclusions violated the testimony of the senses, as an illustration of a glorious victory which idealism has won over empiricism, reason over the senses (p. 141). Paraphrasing a passage in Galileo's *Dialogus de Systemate Mundi* in which the latter expresses his admiration for Copernicus because, despite the apparent deliverances of experience, he chose to trust his reason rather than his senses, Feuerbach apostrophises the shade of Copernicus as follows: " O ! Nicholas Copernicus, be happy that thou hast not fallen upon our times, upon this age of spiritual degradation, of historicism, of empiricism, of positivism. Hadst thou come forward now with such a daring, heroic a priorism, thou wouldst at the very least have had to atone in a madhouse for thy idealistic chimera " (p. 144).

Feuerbach enjoins the materialists to take Copernicus as an object lesson of " *the* truth that every discoverer, every inventor, even of the simplest machine, was an idealist because he did not shrink back before the hindrances of matter, was not frightened by the contradictions of prevailing experience, or lose faith in the reality of his ideas." Experience, which Feuerbach admits is always indispensable, can only check, complete and supplement what thought discovers, but *the act of discovery* itself is an a priori one. The act of discovery—no matter how modest—is an act of genius. And an act of genius " is nothing but the *anticipation of experience*, the possibility of synthetic judgments a priori " (p. 144).

By an a priori, Feuerbach does not mean something known to be true independently of experience nor that which is the condition of all experience. In Leibnizian fashion he tends to identify the a priori with the power of understanding itself. " The understanding is a priori, i.e., *a se*. To pass judgment upon objects of experience independently of experience is nonsense (*Unsinn*): if ever a philosopher pretended to have or transmit a priori knowledge in this sense, he was a fool. . . . But the idea of sense phenomena, but the understanding— yes, gentlemen—that is a priori, the only a priori there is " (p. 151). To concretise his distinction between sense and reason —which he is careful to point out are not separate in the thought process—Feuerbach takes reading as an illustration. In order to study Plato, I must read him. To read him, I must be able to see. Without eyes, I cannot see—and in so far as I cannot find out about Plato's ideas in any other way I cannot think. But my eyes are not the organ of understanding but an organ of vision through which the signs (*Zeichen*) are understood. The words themselves are neither things nor ideas. " Seeing the letters is not yet reading and reading is not yet understanding " (p. 150). To read intelligently is not an affair of the eyes but of the mind. And this is true not merely of books but of the world at large. Sense images, Feuerbach repeats again and again, are signs used by thought,[1] necessary stimuli (*Anreizung*) to discovery of the truth but not truths themselves.

As we shall see later on, this is a far cry from the Feuerbach of later years, when he swallows whole the physiological interpretation of thought not only as an explanation of personality but of history as well. He never answered the difficulties he himself raised to that type of physiological empiricism which, in his own words, " forgetting the limits of physiology tried to kill the spirit with the anatomist's scalpel." But it is interesting to observe that, save for one brief review of Moleschott's work in 1850, Feuerbach never ceased distinguishing himself from traditional materialists, and on many occasions repeated,[2] with no great regard for consistency, the realistic undertones of his original criticism of nominalistic materialism. Nature for him always retained an intelligible pattern even when he was not sure whether its intelligibility was an object of the understanding or an object of sensation. In the writing we have just considered, he maintained that " only what is intelligible (*Verstandesgemäss*) is an object of understanding " and reposes his assurance that the " idealism " of science can render the intelligibility of nature by explicit reference to "the great thought of Spinoza" expressed in the Seventh Proposition of Book Two of the *Ethica*: " Ordo et connexio idearum (*d.i.—der Seelen*) idem est ac ordo et connexio rerum (*d.i.—der Körper*)." Feuerbach professes to find a confirmation of this maxim in the progress of science including comparative anatomy and physiology (*S.W.*[1], Bd. 2, p. 146).

---

[1] " Wo keine Bilder sind, ist kein Reiz zum Denken " (*S.W.*[1], Bd. 2, p. 149).

[2] Cf. especially *S.W.*[1], Bd. 2, pp. 322–3.

II

FEUERBACH'S PSYCHOLOGY OF RELIGION

If Feuerbach's general philosophy had to wait almost a century for proper recognition, his interpretation of religion evoked an appreciation which was almost immediate. Even the theological opponents of Feuerbach—or rather those whose vision and honesty transcended the limits of their sect—paid tribute to the psychological keenness of his analysis, despite the abomination in which they held his conclusions. The enthusiasm with which Marx and Engels greeted the publication of Feuerbach's *Das Wesen des Christenthums*[1] (1841) has been documented in a well-known passage in Engels' *L. Feuerbach*.[2] Strauss himself, who was as critical of his successors as he was of his predecessors and whose own critique of Christianity had been made with the weapons of logic rather than of social psychology, recognised that Feuerbach's work in this field was definitive for his period. When Zeller attempted to answer Feuerbach, Strauss wrote: " The defence is feeble. One becomes infected [with Feuerbach's doctrine] through contact with it, and in the end has lost more than has been gained. To-day, and perhaps for some time to come, the field belongs to him. His theory is the truth for this age (*Ausgewählte Briefe*, p. 184).

Feuerbach somewhere calls his books letters to mankind. The theme of this, his most important letter, was " Know Thyself."[3] In fact the original title which Feuerbach selected for his *Essence of Christianity* was " Know Thyself "—since its main thesis was that traditional religions arose out of man's unconscious deification of himself. He did not proclaim the end of all religion, but, like Luther, attacked the old religion in behalf of a new.[4] He did aim, however, to dissolve all theology, not by proofs of the truth of atheism, which he often characterised as negative theology, but by a critical genetic account of the nature and function of religious experience.

[1] Translated into English by George Eliot from the second German edition, London, 1854. Unless otherwise indicated all translations will be given from this volume.

[2] Duncker Ausgabe, p. 24.

[3] Cf. *Nachlass*, I, 334, ed. by Grün.

[4] Bolin reports that Feuerbach once referred to himself as Luther II (cf. L. Feuerbach, *Sein Wirken und seine Zeitgenossen*, Stuttgart, 1891, p. 58).

Feuerbach's *Essence of Christianity* brought the religious development which began with Hegel's death to a halt, for he outflanked all factions engaged in bitter exegetical struggle by approaching religious phenomena not as a sectarian theologian but as a philosophical psychologist. The book contested no doctrines, pleaded for no heresy. It devoted itself to an analysis of the religious phenomenon as specifically illustrated by Christianity. He attempted to show that the secret of religion was man, and that its objects of worship and devotion were fetishistic expressions of human emotion. He presents what he calls a direct and an indirect proof of this. The first part contends that all the predicates and attributes of God or the divine nature are identical with the predicates of human nature, and that by a well-known Aristotelian dictum, divine nature and human nature are therefore essentially one. The second part undertakes to establish that any attempt to distinguish in a thoroughgoing way between *theological* and *anthropological* predicates resolves itself into an absurdity. In all religion there is a grain of truth although concealed in a mystical and inverted form; in theology —which attempts to rationalise not the truth of religion, but its mystic and inverted expression—we have not only " the negation of human sense and human understanding " but also " the negation of religion " (p. x).

Religious belief has two roots—a cognitive-theoretical and a practical-emotional. The first gives rise to a more or less systematic theology, the second to the specific experience called religious. Strauss' critique, we have already seen, was directed against the intellectual constructions of theology. Religious belief naturally expresses itself in pictures or myths. These pictures, however, contain more than the feelings and ideal aspirations which enliven them. They suggest meanings which act as stimuli to man's sense of logical coherence and æsthetic fitness. They are elaborated in rational form, become the subject matter of critical reflection and then are revealed as hopelessly contradictory. They can only be given a semblance of intelligibility by being regarded as imaginative creations of the communal mind. This in essentials was the negative aspect of Strauss' work. Strauss had declared his interpretation of religion to be " mythical," that is to say, religious ideas had their source, if not their justification, in the funded tradition of folk-lore and the more obvious traits of mass psychology. Bruno Bauer's advance over Strauss was to call attention to the evaluation of sources and to the presence of tendentious points of view in their composition. Feuerbach's advance over both flowed from his realisation that neither of these avenues of inquiry led to the central fact of religion. Against Strauss, Feuerbach argued that religion was not a product of *poetic fancy* but of *real need*; against B. Bauer he held that it was not a need of the *understanding* but of the *heart*. The affective life of man was the key to his religion. Religious belief, to be properly understood, must be approached in terms of analytic group psychology and anthropology. It is the emotional needs and habits of individuals which really make intelligible their acceptance of tradition, tendentious apologetic and edifying fairy-tales. And although specific religious emotion may be coloured by an existing religion with its rich tradition and elaborate rituals, the emotion itself cannot be derived from it.

Feuerbach digs below the theoretical superstructures of theology to uncover the nerve of the *process* by which they arise. Let us, he says, look at the pictures, myths, legends, sacred truths—however they be called—which are associated with religious feeling. After we have examined them closely and made a study of the lives of those who project them—what relation, asks Feuerbach, can we discover between the two ? Never mind, now, whether these pictures are coherent, whether what they purport to say is true or false. Granted that once we introduce a logical control of religious ideas—they collapse, that they turn out to be " a web of delusions and contradictions." But does religion itself collapse ? No, because it is rooted not in ideas but in emotion. Religion, after all, according to Feuerbach, has only *one* root. The alleged cognitive-theoretical root turns out to be merely a prominent limb. Like all other offshoots it must grow and die, and others will take its place. Consequently, Feuerbach inferred, religion is an absolute fact with a necessarily varying content. That is why he felt justified in calling atheism one man's religion, and communism another's. " What yesterday was still religion, is no longer such to-day; and what to-day is atheism, to-morrow will be religion " (p. 31).

The questions which we must put to religious beliefs belong to a different order from those concerned with their " truth." We must ask what is their *genesis* ? Why do *these* beliefs and pictures come to life in this culture and not others ? What rôle do they play in the l:ves of those who give them credence ?

The fact that religion is a distorted reflection of man's life makes it difficult but not impossible to get at its earthly kernel. It presents the same problem as the dream to which Feuerbach often compares it:

> " Religion is the dream of the human mind. But even in dreams we do not find ourselves in emptiness or in heaven, but on earth, in the realm of reality; we only see real things in the entrancing splendour of imagination and caprice, instead of in the simple daylight of reality and necessity. Hence I do nothing more to religion—and to speculative philosophy and theology also—than to open its eyes, or rather turn its gaze from the internal towards the external, i.e. I change the object as it is in the imagination into the object as it is in reality " (p. xi).

Feuerbach submits the various " mysteries " of the Christian religion—the mystery of the logos and divine image, the mystery of the trinity, of the incarnation, of God as an understanding, moral, and suffering being—to a close analysis in order to demonstrate how *human* relationships are idealised, purified of elements judged to be unworthy, and glorified into shining abstractions. The Christian Religion is not merely a mausoleum which houses " the departed spirit of man " but like all religions a *judgment* as well. " What man praises and approves that is God to him; what he blames, condemns is the non-divine " (p. 96). God incarnates himself out of love to man—and love is *divine* because it expresses the highest form of *human* emotion. " God has a son: God is a father "—he is conceived in terms of the profoundest human relationships. God *suffers* not for himself but for others, and this is a divine attribute in the eyes of men because to suffer, and if need be to die for others, is the noblest of human actions. God has a *personality*—is more than the philosopher's Substance, pure Spirit or Reason—because without it the qualities of mercy, forgiveness, hope, faith, etc., which are essential to the ideal *human* personality, could not be attributed to him. Only to a personal God can man pray—and the simplest act of prayer expresses the essence of religion. " Not the prayer before and after meals, the ritual of animal egoism, but the prayer pregnant with sorrow, the prayer of disconsolate love, the prayer which expresses the power of the heart that crushes man to the ground, the prayer which begins in despair and ends in rapture " (p. 121).

It would be bootless to present Feuerbach's analyses of the Christian sacraments in further detail or examine the plausibility of his interpretations. Some indication must be given, however, of the flexibility of Feuerbach's psycho-genetic method. Religion is a gratification of man's emotional life achieved by congenial imagery which grows out of man's desires. These desires, however, embody not only ideals but *wants*. The approach to religion and religious practices may be made not only in the light of what people *have* but what they *lack*, not only through the projection of their earthly beatitudes but also through their frustrations. Frustrations may be material, they may also be psychological and sexual. Feuerbach has little to say of the material frustrations of religion but some of his intimations are suggestive and later research vindicated them. " The more empty life is," he writes, " the fuller, the more concrete is God. The impoverishing of the real world, and the enriching of God, is one act. Only the poor man has a rich God " (p. 72). It was not until he published his *Theogony*—sixteen years after the *Essence of Christianity* appeared—that Feuerbach made an effort at empirical analysis of the *material* cultures of different religions. In fact this aspect of his psychology of religion remained for him, upon the whole, a matter of programme.

Feuerbach does, however, make a serious effort to trace the effect of *psychological* repressions upon religious ideology. In passages reminiscent of a fashionable contemporary psychology, he describes the vicarious satisfactions derived by the early Christians from the denial of their sensual tendencies:

" The monks made a vow of chastity to God ; they mortified the sexual passion in themselves, but therefore they had in Heaven, in the Virgin Mary, the image of woman—an image of love. They could all the more easily dispense with real woman, in proportion as an ideal woman was an object of love to them. The greater the importance they attached to the denial of sensuality, the greater the importance of the Heavenly Virgin for them: she was to them in the place of Christ, in the stead of God. The more the sensual tendencies are renounced, the more sensual is the God to whom they are sacrificed. For whatever is made an offering to God has an especial value attached to it; in it God is supposed to have especial pleasure. That which is the highest in the estimation of man, is naturally the highest in the estimation of his God— what pleases man, pleases God also. Wherever, therefore, the denial of the sensual delights is made a special offering, a sacrifice well-pleasing to God, there the highest value is attached to the senses, and the sensuality which has been renounced is unconsciously restored, in the fact that God takes the place of the material delights which have been renounced. The nun weds herself to God; she has a heavenly bridegroom, the monk a heavenly bride " (p. 26).

Having revealed that the secret of theology is anthropology, and that the absolute mind under all its different guises is nothing else than the finite human mind, Feuerbach sounds the tocsin for a new religion which would recognise and renounce the fetishistic tendencies of all traditional religions and accept as a fundamental truth the proposition that " the consciousness of God is nothing else than the consciousness of the species." But before we present Feuerbach's philosophy of religion, we must stop to ask a simple question which has probably long since arisen in the mind of the reader.

What was there in Feuerbach's approach to religion to fire the rebellious hearts of the time and to make the outstanding figures among the Young-Hegelians—Ruge, Hess, Marx, Engels—look to Feuerbach as their leader? It was his theory of the natural fetishism of human activity—a fetishism which could be applied to illumine almost every social institution. If the religious fact *par excellence* is the alienation of man from himself, the erection of a *product* of man's own emotional and intellectual activity into an objective norm claiming a priori validity, then it could be shown that the whole of society was pervaded by a religious principle. Wherever man was ruled by his own unconscious creation—*there* was a religious and social evil. For all the Young-Hegelians and not only for Marx—the critique of religion was the beginning of all critiques. The same formula was extended from religion to politics, to ethics, to economics. The dualism which the church introduced into the life of man under the form of distinctions between the sacred and profane, the lay and the secular, had their counterpart in the dualism of the state which separated the political function of the community from the social and economic, which pretended in theory that all citizens were equal before the law but in practice recognised all sorts of irrelevant class distinctions. The transcendence of God meant in ethical terms the hypostasis of principles which were once functionally justified into oppressive absolutes and the cramping of progressive social tendencies by outworn institutions. The simple truth that ethical commands are demands of man's own nature made it impossible to accept the theory that man existed as a means to the state. Ruge, hitching his radicalism to Feuerbach's humanism, wrote: " The necessary consequences of a criticism which makes man the principle of the intellectual and moral world is the abolition of this dichotomy between the life of the state and the life of man [leading to] the political-ising of all men, all form a part of the community, and the humanising of the state, each person is an end to the state " (*Werke*, Bd. 6, p. 63). With the end of religious heresy, all political and social heresy ceases. If *theoretical* humanism is the explanation of all religion in terms of man, *practical* humanism is the derivation and reorganisation of all social institutions guided by the knowledge of the nature of man (Ibid., p. 65). Practical humanism must in the first instance be economic humanism. It focuses attention upon " the earth and its goods, (human) existence and its conditions, real men . . . and their work. It condemns the theology, philosophy and politics which have shown themselves incapable of really aiding man, i.e. of liberalising his economic and moral position " (p. 92). But it was Marx who, under the spell of Feuerbach's humanism, most clearly points out the reason why even the most highly developed state—a democratic republican state—is the incarnation

of a religious principle. It countenances under a theory of
political equality, practices of social inequality. In *theory*,
differences between citizens in respect to birth, station, vocation,
education, and property are declared to be irrelevant. In *practice*,
the state recognises, tolerates and defends the effects which
these differences have upon the everyday life—the " real "
life of men. In the modern political community, therefore,
man lives in two worlds. One is the world of his everyday
interests and activities, in which he suffers under all sorts of
disabilities and special privileges; the other is the world of
holiday enjoyment of theoretical political equality. The more
his real world is out of joint, the more insistently do the representatives of the state power assure him that his will is as
sovereign as any other in the community. What he lacks in fact,
he achieves in fancy—the familiar Feuerbachian theme. " The
organs of the political state are religious," writes Marx, " in
virtue of the dualism between the life of bourgeois society and
political life—religious, in that man regards the transcendental
(*jenseitigen*) life of the state which is so foreign to his real individuality as his true life, religious in so far as religion is the
spirit of bourgeois society, the expression of the separation
and division of man from man" (*Gesamtausgabe*, Abt. I, Bd. 1,
Erste Halbband, p. 590).

Feuerbach's conception of the process by which religions
grow and die provides a direct thread from Hegel—whom
Feuerbach criticised because he hid his insights in metaphysical
myths—to Marx—by whom Feuerbach was criticised for not
developing and generalising his own fruitful principles. In Hegel
development takes place by the necessary self-alienation (*Selbst-
Entäusserung*) of the Idea which like God generates the world
out of itself by logical activity. In Feuerbach " the necessary
self-alienation of the Idea " is naturalised and becomes the
self-alienation of man, the unconscious projection of human
nature in objects of worship. In B. Bauer and A. Ruge, not
only religion but politics with its notion of an absolute and static
state is shown to be the unconscious projection of human nature.
In Marx the self-alienation of man is traced to the processes of
work and its influence upon the development of human nature.
The secret of the whole of contemporary society is declared to

be the fetishism of the social relations of production in general, and of *commodities* in particular.

III
FEUERBACH'S PHILOSOPHY OF RELIGION

Feuerbach's original intent was not to destroy religion, but to understand it. But his moralistic interests carried him much further. He attempted nothing else than the reconstruction of religion. His *Essence of Christianity* is therefore a medley of different themes. Analyses of the Christian sacraments are often interrupted by invocations to man, sermons on love, and digressions on the nature of the community.

Feuerbach always thought of himself as a profoundly religious man. His life, work, and confessions testify to the presence of a simple natural piety which underlay the philosophic doctrines he found congenial. In a charming self-portrait he describes the basic feelings around which his preferences were organised. He confesses to a love of the simply organised—from flowers and birds to men, and to a distaste of split-organisms, split-allegiances, mixtures and dualisms of every sort. Only the organism which remains within its own natural sphere, which does not deny its own nature by trying to be something else, can realise the integrity without which there is no genuine originality. " Down to the smallest detail, even my senses agree with this inner feeling for the undivided, for that which is at one with itself " (*S.W.*[1], Bd. 2, p. 177).

No one can be at peace with himself unless he is at peace with his neighbour. The undisturbed enjoyment of one's own natural capacities depends upon others not only in the obvious sense that we need one another to perform our social functions but in that the *norms* of what constitute happiness are derived from the nature of the human species. There is only one force which binds human beings together in such a way that their common nature is felt to be more important than their differences —one force which makes their very differences common through mutual tolerance and sympathy. And that is love. The fount, medium and goal of all self-conscious human religion is love.

" A loving heart is the beat of the species throbbing in the individual " (*Wesen des Christenthums*, p. 266).

In addition to singing panegyrics to love,[1] Feuerbach makes an heroic attempt to justify the social uses of love. It is true that *homo homini deus est*, but it is also true that there are all sorts of men. The religion of love strengthens the moral relations between men, for the real source of moral relationships, be they between child and parent, wife and husband, brothers and friends, is love. Any other unity is a cord of sand when it is not a cord of rope—such as economic interest with a human being dangling at one end. "Political unity," for example, "is a unity of force" (p. 264). Only when social relationships become moral relationships can the oppositions between the egoism of the self and the needs of the species be resolved. And since Feuerbach held that " all moral relations are *per se* religious " although not vice versa, he preached his humanistic religion of love as the most effective agency of moral improvement.

In attempting to convert his readers to the religion of love, Feuerbach does not hesitate to play hard and fast with terms and definitions. The irreligious man, he argues, the real atheist, is one who is not only devoid of a sense of the sacredness of human relationships but also one who has no genuine aim in life," some goal in which he can lose and find himself. And as if it were the most obvious thing in the world, he identifies the possession of a true goal with love. " He who has no aim, has no home, no sanctuary; aimlessness is the greatest unhappiness. . . . Only activity with a purpose . . . gives man a moral basis and support, i.e., character. Every man therefore must place before himself a God, i.e., an aim, a purpose. . . . He who has an aim, an aim which is in itself true and essential, has, *eo-ipso*, a religion,

---

[1] I quote a typical passage: " Love is the middle term, the substantial bond, the principle of reconciliation between the perfect and the imperfect, the sinless and sinful being, the universal and the individual, the divine and the human. Love is God himself and apart from it there is no God. Love makes man God, and God man. Love strengthens the weak, and weakens the strong, abases the high, and raises the lowly, idealises matter and materialises spirit. Love is the true unity of God and man, of spirit and nature. In love common nature is spirit, and the pre-eminent spirit is nature. Love is materialism; immaterial love is a chimera. In the longing of love after the distant object, the abstract idealist involuntarily confirms the truth of sensuousness. But love is also the idealism of nature, love is also spirit, *esprit*. Love alone makes the nightingale a songstress; love alone gives the plant its corolla. And what wonders does not love work in our social life .What faith, creed, opinion separates—love unites " (*Wesen*, p. 47).

if not in the narrow sense of common pietism . . . in the sense of reason, in the sense of the universal, the only true love" (p. 63).

Feuerbach concludes his *Essence of Christianity* on still another note. Previously he had pointed out in his criticism of religions of nature that although man is a product of nature he becomes *human* only through other men. Now he returns to nature with words whose Hegelian overtones are unmistakable. " Moral feelings can effect nothing without Nature; it must ally itself with the simplest natural means " (p. 273). The virtues which men achieve are possible only because of the virtues of the natural things by which they achieve them. This is dimly perceived even by Christianity in its ritual of purification by water in the baptismal rites, and still more in its conversion of eating and drinking into the mystery of the Lord's supper. The sublimity to which man can reach is dependent on the material support which nature gives him. Man needs other men to gratify his human needs but he also needs nature. Therefore Feuerbach enjoins upon him, " In thy gratitude towards man forget not gratitude towards holy Nature." We must never renounce or try to deny our dependence upon that which is the origin of all we are and all we may become. Those who destroy the continuity between man and nature, reintroduce it in a mystic and emasculated form through a conception of a supernatural God. Mysteries upon mysteries are created. To the religion of the common man Feuerbach adds the religion of the common thing. " It needs only that the ordinary course of things be interrupted in order to vindicate for common things an uncommon significance, *to life, as such, a religious import.* Therefore let bread be sacred for us, let wine be sacred, and also let water be sacred ! Amen." With this sentence Feuerbach completes his book.

The political implications of Feuerbach's philosophy of religion were drawn by men like Hess, Grün, Lüning, Kriege—who opposed Marx's emphasis upon the class struggle as inhuman— and by others who drolly attempted to solve the social problem by loving in the spirit and flesh as many members of the human race as would suffer their embraces. Both Marx and Engels credited Feuerbach with his good intentions but found themselves compelled to attack the *Liebesduselei* of the disciples.

Looking away from the excesses, confusions and verbalisms

of Feuerbach's philosophy of religion, there still remains a conception which has inspired humanistic movements from the days of Protagoras to those of Dewey. Its abiding sense lies in its reference to an undefined natural and social whole of which man is an organic part, and which without impinging on his individual freedom, lifts him to a consciousness of a common lot and destiny with other men. To it all are called and all may be chosen. It is the unexpressed " religion " of all who cherish the value of individual personality wherever it may be found. Its ideals transcend differences of race and creed, nation and class. In its light men may seek their own good without getting lost in low personal calculation; and from its fire spring all the great social equalitarian ideals which burn in the breasts of men.

IV

FEUERBACH'S PHILOSOPHY OF ANTHROPOMORPHISM

As we have already seen, Feuerbach's critique of Christianity was undertaken in behalf of a new religion and with the instruments of what Feuerbach regarded as a new philosophy. In a series of subsequent writings,[1] he attempted to make this philosophy explicit. He boldly declared that the time had come for a reform of philosophy and essayed the ambitious task of laying down the lines along which the reconstruction could be carried out. Like all other philosophers who have called for a fresh start, he abandoned the conventional labels with which the different schools were tagged. But this studied avoidance of a neutral technical vocabulary and his preference for the homely metaphors of everyday speech often clouded his meaning. The result is that just as soon as we look behind the surface limpidity of his literary style, we find ambiguities and apparent contradiction. None the less the general drift of Feuerbach's thought is sufficiently clear to enable us to make out at least the main outlines.

[1] *Vorläufige   Thesen zur Reform der Philosophie* (1842); *Grundsätze der Philosophie der Zukunft* (1843); *Wider den Dualismus den Leib und Seele, Fleisch und Geist* (1846).

Every new philosophy arises to satisfy a need. What kind of a need ? Either, answers Feuerbach, a purely intellectual need whose fulfilment constitutes a chapter merely in the *history of philosophy*, as e.g., Fichte's development of the Kantian doctrine; or a human need which is met by a movement that marks a turning point in the *history of mankind*. Since according to Feuerbach " the periods of man's history can only be distinguished by his religious conceptions," the downfall of traditional Christianity—presumably the work of the Hegelian and higher criticism of the previous decades—has ushered in a new era of world history, with new needs and interests.

What were the new needs and interests which demanded a new philosophy ? They were the needs for *political freedom* which Feuerbach called " the most essential drive (*Trieb*) of man to-day " and the newly awakened interests in making society human, i.e., organised by ethical principles based on the true nature of man. The new philosophy had for its aim the negative task of clearing the field of the old philosophic systems. When they were not technical conceits of the individual philosophers, these latter were declared to be thinly veiled apologetics for dualistic religion. The more positive task was the development of a philosophic doctrine which would unify all anti-dualistic tendencies in contemporary culture. The new philosophy would also work out a programme for human amelioration and supervise its execution.

When Feuerbach describes the new men whose needs of heart and brain the new philosophy would express, his account sounds like an idealised self-portrait. The new man is one whose faith has vanished before critical doubt, who has renounced the Bible and enthroned reason in its stead, who has replaced religion by politics, put earth in place of heaven, work in place of prayer, material want in place of hell. Such a man must take his eyes from the City of God and turn them upon the state in which he lives. Salvation will come piecemeal—as a reward for practical political effort. The improvement of the state which Feuerbach does not hesitate to call the " religion of politics " is a condition for the improvement of man because in its true form the state is " unlimited, infinite, completed, divine man. It is the absolute man " (*S.W.*², Bd. 2, p. 220).

What are the leading ideas of this new philosophy " of and for man " ?

1. *Man as the Measure of all Things*

Feuerbach consistently denied that his philosophy was either materialistic or idealistic. To adopt the materialistic standpoint, according to which man is a complicated machine, is, he explicitly states, to adopt the standpoint of pathology. To accept idealism is to believe in some form of magic. In his *Vorläufige Thesen* he goes still further. His philosophy is " the negation of rationalism as well as mysticism, pantheism as well as personalism, atheism as well as theism." It is the *unity* of all these partial standpoints and truths, understood from the point of view of active, limited, temporal, needy, suffering man. The attributes are all Feuerbach's. They are designed to call attention to the fact which makes all of previous philosophy simply a bad start, viz., that cognition is not the primary phenomenon of either life or consciousness but feeling, want and limitation. What man is depends, to be sure, upon nature. " Thinking derives from being; but being does not derive from thinking " (*S.W.*[1], Bd. 2, p. 263). But the nature of man expresses itself, consciously or unconsciously, in his conception of the nature of nature. Man is a creature of space and time. All existence is temporal and spatial and in so far as anything can be intelligibly spoken about it must in one way or another be exhibited in some temporal and spatial context. " Only existence in space and time is *existence*. The negation of space and time is only the negation of their limits not of their essence. A timeless sensation, a timeless will, a timeless thought, a timeless essence—are figments (*Undinge*)." The refusal to recognise the pervasiveness of spatial and temporal characteristics has fateful practical consequences—even for politics, so that it is possible to recognise not only the human psychological process by which certain concepts are converted into timeless and spaceless abstractions but to trace the practical motive and effect of the conversion. " Space and time are the primary criteria of practice. A people which excludes time from its metaphysics and hypostasises (*vergöttert*) external, i.e., *abstract* existence sundered from time, necessarily excludes time from its politics, too, and hypostasises

the unjust, irrational and anti-historical principle of stability "
(Ibid., p. 256).[1]

As a creature of space and time, man is a *limited* being, for
space and time are finite. Without limitation, no existence.
Man's limitations are experienced primarily as needs and wants.
The very fact of existence with its thousandfold interrelations
and dependencies carries with it the idea of something needing
something else—the crops the rain, the stream its bed, the stones
the field upon which they lie. Existence as such seems to be
defined in terms of man's experience of need in very much the
same fashion as a modern philosopher defines it in terms of
care or anxiety (Heidegger). " Where there are no limits, no
time, no need, there we find no quality, no energy, no spirit.
Only the needy creature is the necessary creature [*Nur das
notleidende Wesen ist das notwendige Wesen*]. Existence free
from want is superfluous existence [*Bedürfnisslose Existenz ist
überflussige Existenz*]. What is free from need in general has no
need to exist. It is immaterial to itself and to others whether
it is or it is not. A being that has no need is a being that has no
ground " (p. 257).

Feuerbach is not attributing to nature in its isolation, attributes of human consciousness or feeling. The point is that nature
is never experienced as something isolated. Whatever reality
may be in itself, we feel it, handle it, and know it as it is *for us*.
A distinction between things-as-they-appear-to-us and things-
as-they-are-in-themselves would be meaningful only if we could
see things as they do not appear to ourselves, say, if we could
see them as God sees them. But this is absurd. I might try to
imagine what things are like from a point of view which is not
human. But this is always illusory. No matter what the metaphor, allegory or imagery under which I try to conceive things,
I cannot escape from myself. When I speak of how things might
appear to God, I am simply writing Him large and askew in
letters of my own nature. That is part of what Feuerbach
meant in his oft-repeated phrase " man is the secret of religion."
In this sense, man is the secret not only of religion but of politics,

[1] Feuerbach seems to have glimpsed some of the difficulties in an absolute
temporalism and distinguishes between nature which endures and its forms which
arise and pass away. " Temporal genesis applies only to the forms of nature not
to its essence " (Ibid., p. 263).

history, and nature, too (p. 264). The only possible plane upon which the distinction between " being in itself " and " appearance " can be defended is on the social plane in terms of the contrast between how a thing appears *to me* and how it appears *to others*—the human species. My vision is corrected by what others see, and the only test of my sanity depends upon the reaction, under relevant conditions, of the rest of mankind to my reactions. " The agreement of others is therefore my criterion of the normalness, the universality, the truth of my thoughts " (*Essence of Christianity*, p. 157).

Despite Feuerbach's declaration of independence from all previous philosophy, it is not hard to recognise the Protagorean strain in his thought. Whatever the world is, it at least is what it looks like to man and his body. It is no less real nor more real than what it appears to those creatures who see with different eyes, touch with different " hands," hear with different ears— save that the whole comparison is fantastic, for we can never know how things appear to other organisms. Strictly speaking, there is no more place in Feuerbach for the concept of material substance than there is for the unknowable. The material substance of things is the unity of the qualities experienced by man; the unity of the mind which experiences the qualities is to be found in the continuity of interest and need.

Again and again Feuerbach insists that the starting point of philosophy cannot be philosophy but the actual life of man. The primary fact in the life of man is neither the external world nor his own mind, but the existence of the human community which by providing a community of meaning makes truth, knowledge and self-consciousness possible. This accounts for Feuerbach's refusal to recognise the existence of the external world as a problem to be solved by philosophers, and for what may be called his social theory of epistemology which enables him to avoid it. As far as the *individual* is concerned the question of whether his ideas correspond to a real world which causes them, or whether there is a real world existing independently of his consciousness, cannot arise. The *social facts* of his own experience and not his psychological sense data provide the answers to the question in so far as it is a question. The very sense perception which the individual sets out to check against the external world must first be established to have veridical character by comparison with the perceptions of *others*, of the species. " As certain as the other person is a creature existing independently of me, so is the tree, the stone, an entity independent of me. Upon this certainty, upon the truth of the *alter ego*, of human beings outside of me in the truth of love, life and practice, is the truth of my own senses based for me and not on the theoretical meaning of sense perception, not on the origin of ideas out of sensation, not on Locke or Condillac " (*S.W.*[1], Bd. 5, p. 207).

Knowledge is not prior to experience for Feuerbach but one of its results. Nor, according to his analysis, is the subject-object relation prior in knowledge. No abstract subject confronts an abstract object but both are distinctions recognised in the course of social activity. The reality of the *human* subject is dependent upon his activity within the reciprocal interchanges of social life. The activity of the subject is dependent upon the existence of something—the end, or the material, or the other human person—which, in relation to the subject, is an object. Subjects and objects do not come together to create human activity: they are ever changing distinctions within it.

2. *Metaphysics as Esoteric Psychology*

The history of philosophy may from one standpoint be viewed as a series of attempts to discover some basic reality underlying the apparent confusions of ordinary experience. Such quests begin by denying the validity or reliability of what lies at hand; they end by capitalising the elements of ordinary experience in distorted form—in a distorted form because the earthly and empirical kernel of the abstract philosophic construction is not recognised. This in brief is why Feuerbach calls metaphysics an esoteric psychology, in the bad sense. " Die Metaphysik ist die esoterische Psychologie " (*S.W.*[1], Bd. 2, p. 248). Consider, for example, what philosophers call pure quality or quality as such. All qualities experienced by us are determinate qualities of determinate things. Things are not first given as existences to which qualities are added. Qualities are given with things. But they are always the qualities of experienced things. The experience (*Empfindung*) is as much involved in the notion of colour as is extension. The metaphysics of quality cannot be dissociated from the forms, occasions, and relations of the experience of quality—from what traditional philosophers have dismissed as subjective psychology. Failure to observe this leads to an artificial separation of existence and quality, thus preparing the way for the inevitable attempts to deduce existence from quality or add quality to a qualityless something. " Metaphysics or logic is only then a real immanent science when it is *not* separated from subjective mind " (Ibid., p. 248).

Or consider Kant's supra-empirical noumenal Self, Fichte's Ego, Hegel's Absolute Mind, Schleiermacher's Emotion—or the Reason, Will, absolute Good and absolute Bad which philosophers have identified with Reality. The predicates which philosophers have assigned to these terms are nothing more than distortions of the qualities of their empirical analogues. Is the absolute Mind (*Geist*) of Hegel, for example, anything else than the finite mind, cut out of its living context, endowed with intensified powers, and distinguished from other minds only by indeterminate and negative characteristics ? Like the various conceptions of the Divine, the different conceptions of the Real are nothing but embalmed abstractions of human traits and qualities. And if theology, as distinct from religion, is the attempt to rationalise the distorted forms in which man's own nature and needs appear, is not the whole of traditional metaphysics a kind of subtler theology ?[1] The methodological fallacy behind all philosophical and theological constructions of this kind is the transformation of the finite and the determined—in short, the existent—into something infinite and indeterminate—the non-existent. The infinite, the intelligible infinite " is the *true* finite. True speculation or philosophy is nothing if it is not true and universal empiricism " (Ibid., p. 253).

3. *The Social Nature of Truth*

Every relativistic theory of knowledge confronts difficulties in explaining the nature and criteria of truth. For of all things,

[1] " Der ' absolute Geist ' ist der abgeschiedene Geist der Theologie welcher in der Hegelschen Philosophie noch als *Gespenst* umgeht " (*S.W.*[1], Bd. 2, p. 246).

the truth is what appears to ordinary experience as pre-eminently objective. How can a philosophy which stresses the necessary *human* orientation of judgment do justice to the facts of objectivity ? And if it cannot substantiate its claim to objective validity, upon what grounds can one believe this theory of truth rather than another ? Must there not be some canon of reason which transcends the self and all its needs, and to which the human mind must conform if it is to distinguish between the true and the false, the actual and the possible, the real and the fantastic ? Feuerbach does not deny that this canon of reason exists and that as individuals in quest of the truth we are subject to it. But he holds that the canons of reason are the characteristic modes of behaviour and thought of man, of the human species. Not only are the sights and sounds of things what they appear to be to *our* eyes and *our* ears, but the truths about them are the truths as they appear to *our* minds. No more than we can frame a perception which is not our own perception can we frame a truth which is not a human truth. The truths of reason do not exist in and for themselves. To believe that they do is a view which might well be called supernaturalism in logic. Logical truths are the results of the concrete nature and activities of man. " It is *man* who thinks, not the Self, not Reason. . . . When the old philosophy therefore says *only the reasonable is the true and real*, the new philosophy responds, *only the human is the true and real*, for only what is human can be reasonable. *Man is the measure of reason* " (*S. W.*[1], Bd. 2, p. 339).

By stressing the nature of the species as a control upon the experience of the individual, Feuerbach strives to retain his basic humanistic theory of truth and still account for the necessary distinction between the *subjective*, in the sense of the false, and the *objective*, as the true. Not *I, you*, or *anyone else* is the measure of the truth, but man, the species. Not what appears to *me, now*, is the real truth, but only what is established as a result of the traditions, communication and experience of mankind—in short, in its science, conceived as a critical human activity and not as a set of eternal truths waiting to be discovered by man. " The measure of the species is the absolute measure, law and criterion of man " (*Essence of Christianity*, p. 16).

To say that something is " true for me " on this theory means " true about me " and can be verified in the way any other proposition is verified. In fact for Feuerbach, what only one individual experiences can never be established as true; it requires the certification of others before it can be admitted as evidence.[1] If truth is human, evidence is social. It is social not only because ideas arise through communication, which presupposes some form of community, but because, as we shall see, any sensory experience entering as an ultimate constituent in proof must be common to all men.

" That is true in which another agrees with me—agreement is the first criterion of truth; but only because the species is the ultimate measure of truth. That which I think only according to the standard of my individuality is not binding on another, it can be conceived otherwise, it is an accidental, merely subjective, view. But that which I think according to the standard of the species I think as man in general only can think, and consequently as every individual must think if he thinks normally, in accordance with law, and therefore truly. That is true which agrees with the nature of the species, that is false which contradicts it. There is no other rule of truth " (*Essence of Christianity*, p. 157).

In developing his argument Feuerbach combines his principle of sensibility (sometimes grandiloquently referred to as " love " and " passion ")[2] with his social theory of evidence in a very interesting way. Without attempting to square it in the least with his familiar doctrine that sensation is the source of immediate, underived, *sonnenklar* truth, he maintains the view that the testimony of the senses has evidential value not at the beginning but only at the end of intellectual inquiry, not to the raw and crude eye but only to the educated eye. Unconsciously, he returns to a distinction which the idealists,

[1] " Was ich allein sehe, daran zweifle ich, was der andre auch sieht, dass erst ist gewiss " (*S.W.*[1], Bd. 2, p. 330).

[2] Sentences, for example, like " Only that exists which is an *object of passion*— be it real or possible " (*S.W.*[1], Bd. 2, p. 323) are illustrations of the motivation of Feuerbach's emphasis on sensibility rather than serious propositions of his philosophy. He uses them to combat abstract rationalism. After identifying existence and love, he writes, " Love is the true ontological proof of the existence of things outside of our heads " (p. 324).

whom he condemns, denominated as the distinction between the empirical self and the intelligible or noumenal self which manifested itself in the empirical self but was more than it. This distinction for Feuerbach is not a distinction between the empirical and the non-empirical but a distinction between the private and the common. Human beings experience both as individuals and as members of the human species. They have, so to speak, a private mode of sensing and a public one. Their private sensations are checked and criticised in the light of their common sensing. This common sensing is not only the criterion of the validity of individual sensing, but it is, at the same time, the *result* of the checks, and comparisons made. The presupposition of the possibility of agreement between human beings about the contents of their experience is not only a common world but a common nature. We discover that we have common sensations or, as Feuerbach admits when faced by the possibility that the same things appear differently to different people, common powers *to discriminate* between different qualities given in sensation. Only in so far as we are the same can we understand each other. " Human beings have only one, or only one common Reason, because they have only one, or common, nature, common organisation. They understand one another. They think, therefore, with the same words. They think the same because they feel the same, because there are general sensations, sensations in which all agree " (*Nachlass*, Bd. I, p. 393).

The common sensations, the sensations in which all agree, are not first in the order of genetic experience but last; they are not the starting points of human perception and knowledge but the upshot. In our casual observations of things of ordinary life we get *Vorstellungen* which, because they are affected by our imaginations and expectations, have an element of the fantastic and capricious in them. When we attend to our experiences and guard against accepting them at their face value, the sensations so derived—although genetically secondary—are, as evidence, truer than what precedes them. *Sinnlichkeit*, then, has two senses —the obviously given, which contains an admixture of different notions, apprehended by *Vorstellungen*, and the *Gegenstand*, which contains nothing save what is revealed through the common sensation, sometimes called by Feuerbach " the unfalsified, objective perception " (*unverfälschten, objektiven Anschauung*) (*S.W.*[1], Bd. 2, p. 332). Feuerbach, then, does not believe, as some critics have maintained, that his " new " philosophy is a justification of the unreflective and uncritical positivism of the plain man. The plain man is justified as opposed to the idealistic philosopher in holding on to his senses and relating his reason to them. But this is just a beginning. He must work his way up from uncritical and unconscious perception to intelligent and self-conscious perception. This is the task of science.

> " The sensible is not the immediate in the sense of speculative philosophy, in the sense in which it is the profane, obvious [*auf platter Hand Liegende*], thoughtless, self-sufficing— that which is self understood. The immediate sensible perception comes *later* than the representation and fantasy. . . . The task of philosophy, of science in general, consists *not* in getting away from the *sensible, real* things but in going towards it, not in transforming the *objects* into thoughts and representations, but in making what was invisible to common eyes visible, i.e., in making it objective." (*S.W.*[1], Bd. 2, p. 331).

4. *Realism or Conventionalism*

Despite Feuerbach's humanistic approach some of the traditional problems of philosophy persist in arising out of his own formulations to plague him for an answer. Granted that on Feuerbach's approach it is impermissible to ask whether the thought of any individual agrees with the natural fact thought about, that the correspondence which establishes truth, and its absence which is the sign of falsity, must be made between the idea in the individual mind and the general idea of the species— between, say, the individual belief and the objective scientific judgment. Granted all this, what about the mind of the species ? What about the common sensations which check the truth of the private ones ? What about science, whose conclusions are based upon the possibility of universal agreement on the part of all competent observers ? What is the guarantee of their validity, the evidence of their truth ? Is the mind of the human species adequate to the things it professes to have knowledge about? In virtue of what? Or, in other words, what is the relation between the laws of thought—of human thought—and the laws of things?

No matter what its verbal form, we have here the most important problem of ontology. Ontologically, it is irrelevant whether the thought which presumes to render that which is not thought is personal or social.

The two generic types of answer which may be made are well known. The realistic theory holds that there is some pattern of identity between things and the true ideas concerning them, that the laws of logic and science are not the creations of mind—personal or social—but the independent characters of things discovered by mind. Nominalism, of which conventionalism is one variety, maintains that, strictly speaking, nothing corresponds in the external world to ideas, laws or principles. These are the products of the mind, elaborated for its own convenience. They represent the ways in which men organise their experience and in the last analysis have their source in the same social anthropology as other phases of human culture.

Now the whole spirit of Feuerbach's philosophy demands an answer in the nominalist vein. That is objective which is not imposed upon man by unmediated nature but what men agree upon as a norm of behaviour. The very laws of nature are conceived as norms because man understands by law—a must, a necessity, a command. There is no more need, then, to suppose that the *laws* of nature are independent of man, who, when he conceives them, must think in terms of his own nature, than the laws of society or psychology. In fact this implicit nominalism of Feuerbach was the fly in the ointment of Marx and Engels in their Feuerbachian period. Engels seems worried lest the laws by which bridges are built be transformed into convenient constructions of humanity.

None the less, on this most important metaphysical question, Feuerbach speaks in an uncertain voice. Where he touches upon the problem peripherally, throughout his *Essence of Christianity* and subsequent philosophical studies, he writes as a nominalist. But where he is explicit, his position turns out to be an emphatic Aristotelian realism. Laws, relations and universals generally, have the same objective status as things. "The *laws of reality* are also *laws of thought*" (*S.W.*[1], Bd. 2, p. 334). By the laws of reality, Feuerbach means, in the first place, space and time under whose sway he does not hesitate to put thought, rejecting both the idealist and the nominalist view that they are phenomenal forms (Ibid., p. 332). The laws of reality also include the laws of logic—not the so-called logical expressions of formal logic which Feuerbach calls " only abstract elementary forms of speech " but the metaphysical presuppositions of logic. He holds that the recognition that the true laws of logic are metaphysical, that " logical relations are metaphysical relations " is one of Hegel's profound insights (p. 199).

This also explains Feuerbach's recurrent reference to Spinoza's dictum about the identity of the order and connection of ideas and things. It serves to block off the approach to idealism suggested by that strain in his thought which asserts the reality of the immediately experienced. If that alone is real which is given to our senses, and if our senses, as he sometimes seems to say, only give us a report of discrete qualities, how can we ever establish the existence of *relations* between qualities, of the *laws* of their succession and organisation ? The answer of idealism is that the mind introduces order in experience, that the understanding legislates for the realm of experience by its own autonomous activity. The result is either a dualism, as in Kant, between the material presented to the mind and the categories of intelligibility by which the mind moulds the material, or a monism, as in post-Kantianism, in which matter itself disappears as a construction of mind. Feuerbach's realism, then, is an auxiliary principle introduced to save his naturalism from the dangers of his own extreme sensationalism.

" ' With our senses,' I once wrote, ' we read the book of nature: but we do not understand it through them.' Correct ! But the book of nature is not composed of a chaos of letters strewn helter skelter so that the understanding must first introduce order and connection into the chaos. The relations in which they are expressed in a meaningful proposition then become the subjective and arbitrary creations of the understanding. No, we distinguish and unify things through our understanding on the basis of certain characters [*Merk-male*] of unity and difference given to our senses. We separate what Nature has separated; we tie together what she has related; we classify natural phenomena in categories of ground and consequence, cause and effect because factually, sensibly, objectively things really stand in such a relation to each other " (*S.W.*[1], Bd. 2, pp. 322-3).

V

FEUERBACH'S " DEGENERATE " SENSATIONALISM

Feuerbach's portrait as a philosopher would be incomplete if we were to omit a phase of his thought which, it must be conceded at once, is more important for an understanding of the *reception* of his ideas than for their development. For this phase was a short-lived enthusiasm induced by the first experimental steps of organic chemistry. But it must be treated here, if only to present the context in which appears his famous sentence " Man is what he eats " (*Der Mensch ist was er isst*)—a sentence which the philosophical philistines have used as a pretext to condemn rather than to read Feuerbach's works.

Feuerbach sincerely believed that his critique of religion and philosophy marked the turning point in the history of Western thought. And if not all of his disciples made the same claims for his philosophy, even the critical among them, like Ruge, referred to it as " the third cock's crow of German spiritual freedom." Feuerbach's last word in the period of his thought we have just been considering was a call for philosophy to break its *mésalliance* with religion and enter into a living union with science. In his *Vorläufigen Thesen*, he maintained that " philosophy must ally itself once more with science and science with philosophy " (*S.W.*[1], Bd. 2, p. 267).

Carrying out his own programme, Feuerbach reached for the nearest science at hand which would justify his humanistic interest. And without stopping to answer the very difficulties which he had so cogently argued against Dorguth's absolute materialism, he proceeded to swallow bag and baggage the natural philosophy of Moleschott, compared to whom Dorguth and all the materialists of the eighteenth century were models of critical restraint. Feuerbach's philosophical extravagance was apparently an effect of his reading Moleschott's *Lehre der Nahrungsmittel*, a work now only of historical interest and even in its own day of dubious scientific importance. It appeared to Feuerbach as if the long-sought-for bond of unity between mind and body, spirit and nature, had at last been discovered through the revolutionary principles of food chemistry. Philosophers in their quest for truth have been overlooking what was, *literally* speaking, under their noses. Feuerbach runs lightly through all the major philosophic categories—Substance, Existence, Being, Essence, Thought—and no longer identifies them with sensibility, love and passion but with something more basic still. Only Feuerbach's own words can allay the suspicion that we are inventing them.

" How the concept of Substance has vexed philosophers ! What is it, Self or Not-Self, Spirit or Nature or the unity of both ? Yes, the unity of both. But what does that mean ? Sustenance [*Nahrung*] only is substance. Sustenance is the identity of spirit and nature. Where there is no fat, there is no flesh, no brain, no spirit. But fat comes only from Sustenance. Sustenance is the . . . essence of essence. Everything depends upon what we eat and drink. Difference in essence is but difference in food " (*S.W.*², Bd. 2, p. 82).

One would imagine that a thinker of Feuerbach's calibre would content himself with the negative observation that *without* food there can be no human activity; that certain types of food under certain conditions produce certain reaction, and pass on from these irrelevant commonplace truths to more significant statements. Instead he delivers himself of a piece of rhetoric which would lend itself admirably to philosophic caricature and which might serve as a number in some unwritten Gilbert and Sullivan light opera:

" Being is one with eating. Being means eating. Whatever is, eats and is eaten. Eating is the subjective, active form of being; being eaten, the objective, passive form. But both are inseparable. Only in eating does the empty concept of being acquire content, thereby revealing the absurdity of the question whether or not being and not-being are identical, i.e., whether eating and starving are the same.

" How the philosophers have tortured themselves with the question as to where and with what philosophy begins. . . . Oh, you fools, who open your mouth in sheer wonder over the enigmas of the beginning and yet fail to see that the open mouth is the entrance to the heart of nature: who fail to see that your teeth have long ago cracked the nut upon which you are still breaking your heads. We begin to think with that with which we begin to exist. The *principium essendi* is also the *principium cognoscendi*. But the beginning of existence is nourishment [*Ernahrung*]; therefore, food [*Nahrung*] is the beginning of wisdom. The first condition of putting any thing into your head and heart, is to put something into your stomach " (*S.W.*[2], Bd. 2, p. 83).

Feuerbach had a strong sense of humour. And one feels almost certain that he is indulging it; that this passage is directed against the popular scientific evangelists who were crying up as a new truth, a simple fact, known to everybody, but now clothed in a new technical robe, trailing clouds of chemical formulæ behind it. Indeed, it contains an even more delicious parody. Substitute " knowing " for " eating " and you have pure idealistic doctrine with typical argument and expression. Feuerbach *seems* to be making fun of the idealists, for whom knowing is like eating, the " object " being to " food " as the " subject " is to " eating." But alas ! Feuerbach is in deadly earnest. His motto is *Der Nahrungsstoff ist Gedankenstoff*—a doctrine which he makes the basis not only of a philosophy of personality but of a philosophy of history. What human beings eat affects their feelings and temperament; the activity of the group depends upon the temperament of its members. Consequently, concludes Feuerbach, the vicissitudes of the struggle between different groups in history reflect the character of their diets. Food-chemistry becomes the key to history. Feuerbach does not content himself with abstract generalities here. He goes into some detail. Potatoes, for example, are the staple diet of all the workers of European countries. But since potatoes have no great quantities of the phosphorescent fat and proteid necessary for healthy brain and muscle, the fate of the working-class is hopeless. " Sluggish potato blood " (*träges Kartoffelblut*) can never supply them with revoluti₄nary energy. The struggle between England and Ireland, Feuerbach cites as a case in point:

> " Poor Ireland," he laments, " you cannot conquer in the struggle with you stiff-necked neighbour whose luxuriant [*üppige*] flocks supply its hirelings with strength. You cannot conquer, for your sustenance can only arouse a paralysing despair not a fiery enthusiasm. And only enthusiasm will be able to fight off the giant in whose veins flow the rich, powerful, deed-producing blood [roast-beef] " (Ibid., p. 90).

If potatoes account for the defeat of the Irish in their struggles against the English, it is the use of salad which " did " for the Italians, and the exclusive vegetable diet of the Hindoos which bind them to the chariot wheel of the British Empire.

And then comes that classic passage one sentence of which, torn from the only context which could give it a particle of sense, has gone the rounds of the world:

> " We see of what important ethical significance the doctrine of food has for the people. What is eaten turns to blood, the blood to heart and brain, to the stuff of thought and temperament. Human fare is the foundation of human culture and disposition. Do you want to improve the people ? Then instead of preaching against sin, give them better food. Man is what he eats " (p. 90).

Despite its comic features there is one aspect of this doctrine which, if properly developed, would have had important implications for a re-orientation of Feuerbach's humanism towards the social problem. If man is what he eats, the immediate central problem of mankind is not political, ethical, cultural, but economic. To improve mankind means at least to improve its fare. And since it is the fare of the working class which is in greatest need of improvement, the workers can be organised as the conscious lever of social change. Feuerbach, however, brings the revolutionary moral home in a more literal fashion. If the worker's fare is bad, his social future cannot be made any better unless a dietary substitute is found for his present spiritless fare. The revolution of 1848, he contends, ended with the triumph of reaction because the majority of the population were martyrs to their potato diet. Potato blood can make no revolution ! The future of the poorer classes looks dark. It is broken by only one ray of light from Moleschott's chemical laboratory.

" Shall we therefore despair ? " he inquires. " Is there no other foodstuff which can replace potatoes among the poorer classes and at the same time nurture them to manly vigour and disposition. Yes, there is such a foodstuff, a foodstuff which is the pledge of a better future, which contains the seeds of a more thorough even if more gradual revolution. It is— beans ! "

Had this become the ideology of a mass movement, its fundamental revolutionary principles would have been drawn from the formulæ of food chemistry, its strategy and tactics directed to working out specific menus rich in deed-producing elements, and its central agitational slogan "beans instead of potatoes"! This phase of Feuerbach's thought, if we call it such, manifested itself in 1850, some years after the influence of Feuerbach upon Marx and Engels had waned. Marx had already committed to paper his criticism of Feuerbach's doctrine when Feuerbach made his fantastic somersault back to the most " vulgar " of " vulgar materialisms." It is a sign of the homage in which, despite their criticism, both Marx and Engels held Feuerbach that they never refer to it in their writings. What interested them much more was precisely the advance which Feuerbach made over traditional philosophy and the incomplete character of that advance. To the relationship between the thought of Feuerbach and Marx, we now turn.

CHAPTER VIII

KARL MARX AND FEUERBACH

THROUGHOUT the preceding studies the relationship between Marx and Feuerbach has received peripheral mention. In the following pages I wish to examine this relationship more closely, particularly the advance which Marx's work represented, according to his own conception, over Feuerbach. The foregoing has already made clear, I hope, that Marx, in the decisive years between 1841 and 1844, was a Feuerbachian—to be sure, with critical reservations. *Die heilige Familie* was written in behalf of the philosophy of " real humanism "—a phrase directly out of Feuerbach. In the unpublished papers of 1844, which appear under the title of "Philosophische-ökonomische Fragmenten" in the *Gesamtausgabe* (Abt. I, Bd. 3, pp. 33–172), the Feuerbachian influence is even more perceptible.[1] And in the very manuscript in which he definitely breaks with Feuerbach, *Die deutsche Ideologie* (1845–6), we find a warm defence of Feuerbach against the attacks made upon him by Bruno Bauer and Max Stirner. Feuerbachian elements, not to mention characteristic modes of expression, abound even in the maturest works of Marx. Like Feuerbach, Marx calls for a reconstruction of philosophy as a method of approaching the practical problems of man. Like Feuerbach, he regards human beings in their empirical social contexts as the carriers of the cultural process. Like Feuerbach, he explains the false traditional conceptions of the world in terms of fetishistic expressions of activities unconsciously engaged in at different times and periods.

What fundamentally separates Marx from Feuerbach is his *historical* approach and his *concrete* analysis of those factors of social life which appear in Feuerbach only as abstractions. Another way of putting this is to say that Marx differs from Feuerbach even where he adopts Feuerbachian principles in the

---

[1] Consider such a typical passage as: " A consistently carried out naturalism or humanism distinguishes itself from idealism as well as materialism and at the same time unifies what is true in both. We can also see that only naturalism is capable of grasping the acts of world history " (*Gesamtausgabe*, I, 3, 160).

stress he places upon the dialectical method and the concrete application he makes of it. On several occasions he specifically reproaches Feuerbach for his lack of dialectic and goes so far as to attribute to him a share of the responsibility for the neglect by contemporaries of the *rational* kernel of Hegel's method.[1] Feuerbach had simply repudiated Hegel's philosophy without attempting to disengage Hegel's methodological insights from his systematic errors. Marx himself died before he could write the materialistic dialectic in which he had planned to criticise, in immanent detail, the logic of Hegel. But the methodology of his work as well as his explicit criticisms of Feuerbach suffice to provide the main outlines of his philosophy. Since Marx's criticism of Feuerbach preceded his own constructive achievements, they are of great importance in tracing the development of Marx's thought.

The real significance of Marx's criticism of Feuerbach has not been adequately grasped by the overwhelming majority of his zealous and " orthodox " disciples. They have failed to understand Marx because to most of them the philosophy of Feuerbach has been a sealed book. Here as well as in other important works of Marx the very language used will mislead the reader unacquainted with the technical jargon of those whom Marx criticised. Because I believe that Marx's critical theses on Feuerbach represent *in nuce* a turning point in the history of philosophy, I propose to adopt a method of exposition which may strike the reader as pedantic but which will at least put him in a position where he can control my interpretations by the text of Marx's remarks. Instead of giving a discursive description of Marx's views, I shall state his eleven theses on Feuerbach, discussing each one in detail. On several points I shall draw upon relevant passages from *Die deutsche Ideologie.*

Thesis I

" The chief defect of all previous materialism—including Feuerbach's—is that the object, reality, sensibility, is conceived only in the form of the object or as conception, but not as human sensory activity, practice [*Praxis*], not

[1] Letter to Engels, Jan. 11, 1868 (*Gesamtausgabe*, Abt. III, Bd. 4, p. 10).

subjectively. That is why it happened that the *active* side [of the object], in opposition to materialism, was developed by idealism—but only abstractly, for idealism, naturally, does not know real, sensory activity as such. Feuerbach wants to recognise sensory objects which are really differentiated from objects of thought, but he does not conceive human activity itself as an objective activity. Consequently in the *Essence of Christianity*, he regards only the theoretical attitude as the truly human one, while practice is conceived and fixed only in its dirty-Jewish form. Hence he does not grasp the significance of ' revolutionary,' of practical, critical, activity."

There are two different points made by Marx here which must be noted and clarified. The first is Marx's criticism against *all* materialisms from Democritus to Feuerbach; the second is his criticism of the attempted Feuerbachian solution of the difficulty which Feuerbach in common with all other materialists faces. The first raises the question to what extent the mind— or since Marx, like Feuerbach, does not separate the mind from the body—to what extent *man*, is active in knowing. The second presents the distinctively Marxian conception of *Praxis*.

Marx was a close student of ancient and modern materialism. His dissertation concerned itself with the difference between the Epicurean and the Democritean philosophies of nature. He was at home, as his short excursion in *Die heilige Familie* into the history of materialism shows, with modern materialisms. He could trace down to its finest nuances the influence of Cartesian rationalism and Locke's empiricism upon French medical theory out of which the materialistic sensationalism of the Encyclopædists developed. He followed with keen interest the progress of the biological sciences in the nineteenth century. In all of these philosophies he finds one fundamental defect, an inability to explain the facts of perception and knowledge—in short, the facts of *meaningful* consciousness and action.

No matter what form traditional materialism took, it explained not only the composition of man's body but the contents of his mind as resultant effects of elements and energies streaming into him from without. The human mind was conceived as passive and plastic. Even where, as in Locke, the mind was endowed with certain powers by which it combined the original ideas derived from without, there was no adequate recognition of the part which human beings played in reacting upon, altering, and transforming their environment. Since materialism, operating with a simple cause-effect relationship, could not account for the redirective activity of man, it could not account for the actualities of human thinking and its practical fruits. At most it pictured thinking as a private, subcutaneous reflection upon what had already happened, an incandescent afterglow, beautiful, perhaps, in design and colour, but absolutely impotent to affect the course of things.

The corrective to this " scientific " way of explaining mind away came not from the materialists themselves but from the idealists. Despite the fantastic and, literally construed, unintelligible constructions of the German idealists from Kant to Hegel, their great contribution was their insight into the essential *activity* of mind. Here is no place to repeat the arguments of Marx against the vagaries of all idealistic schools but it must be remembered that when he broke with idealism, it was not in order to return to the simple materialism which made thinking appear to be either unnecessary or miraculous, but to provide a materialistic basis for the genuine discoveries the idealists made in their analysis of consciousness. That is why both Marx and Engels regarded themselves as the heirs of whatever was sound in the classic German philosophic tradition. Stripped of all distorting elements, the contribution of idealism consists in the illumination it sheds upon the relation between the acts of consciousness and the *contents* of consciousness. Not only the simplest thought but even the simplest perception cannot be plausibly explained as an effect of a mechanical impulse, for the very description of the mechanical impulse as an object of knowledge presupposes some active subject who approaches it with *this* category rather than *that*, with a whole set of values, assumptions, memories and anticipations which, whatever their origin, *now* contribute to what is seen and thought. The idealists saw correctly that in what-was-given-to-knowledge something was involved about the subject-to-which-it-was-given. Their errors arise out of attempts to deduce the very existence and character of the given from the activity of mind, and from the fatal step by which the relatively autonomous activity of mind became transformed into absolute independence of complex material conditions.

In mythological form, Hegel had described in his *Phänomenologie des Geistes* and *Logik*, the way in which objects and subjects were reconstituted in an interacting process whose constituent elements were *materials*, furnished by nature and previous history, and *activities*, resulting from the psycho-physical powers of man in some historical context. In mythological form, I repeat, because the whole process was supposed to have transpired in a timeless divine Subject. Feuerbach had riddled the conception of a divine Subject by showing that in so far as the predicates of the divine Subject were meaningful, they were nothing more than representations of the powers of the human mind, expressed in the language of metaphor and hyperbole. The secret of the growth of the divine Subject of self-consciousness was declared to be nothing more than the development of the mind of man. But Feuerbach's abstract conception of man and his disregard of the historical factors conditioning the emergence of the human mind led him to a blank confrontation of nature and man which generated the same insoluble problems that had plagued earlier materialists. They had wrestled with the antithesis between " things and consciousness," and ended in a blind alley because they could not get any process started between the two except by dissolving the latter into the former. Feuerbach, despite the overtones of natural piety in his writings, began by contraposing " man and nature," too. When he projected his solution of the opposition, he oscillated between an unbridged dualism of the natural and the human, and a reduction of the natural to a form of human sensibility.

Both materialists and idealists had taken as the presuppositions of their philosophy a relatively fixed element—matter in the one case, the subject in the other—to serve as a starting point for the development observable in nature, man and society. Marx's own starting point was not presuppositionless. But since he was attempting not to deduce history but to discover the rhythms of its flow, he avoided introducing as an explanatory principle abstractions which had no empirical function, and which could not be vindicated by observing the ways in which human beings actually behaved. " The presuppositions with which we begin," he writes in *Die deutsche Ideologie*, " are not arbitrary; they are not dogmas. They are real presuppositions from which we can abstract ourselves only in imagination. They are individuals as they actually are, their actions, and their material conditions of life—those which they find at hand as well as those which their own activity produces. These presuppositions are observable in purely empirical fashion " (*Gesamtausgabe*, Abt. I, Bd. 5, p. 10). Feuerbach, too, had said that man was the presupposition of his philosophy. But what kind of man ? " Essential man "—not men as they existed here and now, in city and country, in high estate or low—but man as such, *realiter*, a kind of man in which " a pack of scrofulous, work-worn, starving men " were equal to all other men, a type of man in the light of whose meaning all historical differences between individuals, groups, and classes were superficial accidents. Marx starts with human beings but with human beings understood " not in a fantastic fixity and completeness, but in their real, empirical, perceptual process of development. As soon as their active life process is described, history ceases to be a collection of dead facts, as it still is among abstract empiricists, or an imaginary activity of imaginary subjects as among the idealists " (Ibid., p. 16).

To say that human beings must be the starting point of any attempt to understand history, is to say that human *needs* must constitute the starting point of all inquiry. Again, not the abstract needs of Feuerbach but the primary needs of production, reproduction, communication. The gratification of these needs requires the discovery of instruments which are partly the cause and partly the result of an increasingly pervasive division of labour in social life. But the very processes of gratifying *old* needs gives rise to *new* needs—technological, psychological, and spiritual. The movement of history is not imposed from without by the creative fiat of an Absolute Mind nor is it the result of a dynamic urge within matter. It develops out of the redirective activity of human beings trying to meet their natural and social needs. Human history may be viewed as a process in which new needs are created as a result of material changes instituted to fulfil the old. According to Marx, the whole of theoretical culture, including science, arises either directly or indirectly as an answer to some social want or lack. The change in the character and quality of human needs, including the means of gratifying them, is the keynote not merely to historical change but to the changes of human nature.

The concrete needs of men are the true middle term for Marx between nature and history. The *possibility* of having needs and satisfying them, that which makes men *need-ful* creatures, has its explanation in the physical environment of man and the biological structure of his body. The specific forms through which these needs, both of the senses and the mind are gratified, as well as the development of these needs, are attributable to man's social organisation. The interaction between physical conditions and social organisation is history. Philosophies themselves are critical historical activities which arise to fill some social need,[1] prevail among those groups that recognise them as a justification of their way of life, and systematise the unconscious principles and prejudices by which men attempt to direct the course of daily affairs. Conditioned as they are by their environment, human beings can change that environment or preserve it because their activity, including thought, is an objective activity having objective effects.

Surely, the critical reader will protest, is not a great deal of this already contained in Feuerbach's philosophy ? Does not Marx's thought reduce itself to a filling in of details in a position whose chief outlines were laid down by Feuerbach ? This brings us to the more specific criticism which Marx makes of Feuerbach's theory of practice (*Praxis*).

The last two sentences of the first gloss on Feuerbach contrast Feuerbach's contemplative or purely theoretical attitude towards life with Marx's " critical, practical " standpoint. They also contrast Feuerbach's " dirty-Jewish "[2] conception of practice

---

[1] " The real content of all epoch-making systems is the needs of the time in which they arise. At the basis of each system there lies the whole previous development of a nation and the historical forms of class relationships with their political, moral, philosophical and other consequences " (*Gesamtausgabe*, I, 5, 445).

[2] Although Marx was free of anti-Semitic prejudice, he unfortunately was not over-sensitive to using the term " Jew," often with unsavoury adjectives, as an epithet of abuse. It is a vicious form of idolatry to defend his practice, as L. Rudas seems to do by indirection in his preface to the recent English translation of Engels' *Feuerbach* (Marxist Library, Vol. XV, International Publishers, 1935, p. 12). Nor do I see what purposes were served by the publication, *without critical*

with what Marx regards as a true one. For purposes of exposition these two contrasts may be discussed independently. The first very briefly, for it arises again in a subsequent thesis.

In rejecting Feuerbach's identification of the theoretical attitude with the human attitude, Marx is criticising him not so much for his inadequate materialism as for his vestigial idealism. It is one thing to overcome the idealistic hypostasis of different phases of temporal activity by demanding a return to the facts of experience. It is quite another to carry out the necessary reform and be faithful in the analysis to one's own programme. Feuerbach, because of his unhistorical and abstract conception of man, needs, object, community and communism, sins against his own programme and relapses into idealism. He holds up against the existing order an ideal of what man should be, of man as he could have been at any time and any place, of the essential man. Since this ideal is not related to the concrete needs of men in the concrete social situations in which they find themselves, it can provide no leverage with which to change the existing state of affairs. Unable to make a practice, a revolutionary and revolutionising practice, of his ideal— Feuerbach makes a religion of it. Indeed, for Marx, the religious attitude consists in the belief in, or worship of, unhistorical abstractions. All thought, all conceptions, arise as generalisations of concrete modes of response to specific historical situations. When they are taken as eternally valid, independently of the possibility of their application to fresh situations, men become victimised by the creations and discoveries of their own minds. Whether they are aware of it or not, they become Platonists, supernaturalists, behind whose backs the world continues in its accustomed way. In Marx's eyes, the whole theoretical tradition of western-European philosophy with its apotheosis of Reason, its conception that thought has an underived and independent history, its identification of theoretical activity with divine activity, and when divinity was no longer fashionable, with the

comment, of certain letters of Marx to Engels which possess no scientific value, but which are studded with references to "der jüdische Nigger Lassalle" (cf. especially Gesamtausgabe, Abt. III, Bd. 3, pp. 82, 84). Without going to the lengths of Bernstein and Mehring, whose edition of the letters shows signs in places of political editing, certain purely personal details in the correspondence of Marx and Engels, set down, in haste, only for their own eyes, could have been judiciously omitted, or at the very least, made the subject of critical editorial comment.

" highest " type of human activity—all this represented a religious pattern of behaviour. He found this tradition moulding the outlook even of those who imagined themselves extremely radical. It was the ground for his contention that the Young-Hegelians, despite their world-shattering phrases and militant atheism, were religious, and that the battles they fought were sectarian episodes in a common religious tradition which they shared with their opponents.

True, Feuerbach never lost sight of human Praxis and its influence upon the development of culture. But precisely because of his abstractions, he could not grasp, maintains Marx, the true Praxis. Feuerbach takes the general form of human Praxis to be the same as the kind of Praxis he examined in his *Wesen des Christenthums*. There he points out that religion, too, has a Praxis stemming from the needs of the heart. Its motives were practical; its instruments, prayer and miracle; its character, a cosmic egoism which assumed that the world could be compelled to gratify human desires. Feuerbach was openly disdainful of the narrow practicality concealed in the finery and tinsel of religious ritual. In his eyes, the ritual, imagery and belief of historic religions represented a gratification in fancy of what could not be secured in reality. It was a sublimated expression of the animal needs and animal fears of man. The positive religion of the worship of man through love of one another which Feuerbach put in the place of traditional religion was free —so he thought—from religious Praxis. It was enlightened by science and socialism, both very vaguely conceived. In place of the egoism animating the wish to make the world over to *our* heart's desire, he set up an unselfishness whose pleasant duty it is to love one's neighbours to the very death. In place of the miracle and prayer which are the common resort of fearful souls in distress, he defended the ennobling conception of the universality of law, of the eternity of scientific objects, of a cosmic democracy in which all things are equally important— or unimportant. At times Feuerbach seems to oppose to the degraded practicality of man a kind of Spinozistic intellectual love of God. But running through all of his descriptions of the highest form of theoretical knowledge is the belief that man is truly human only when, like God, he views things *sub specie æternitatis.* The very fact that man conceived God as an eternal knower was indirect testimony of the value he placed upon the thinking life—for the attributes of God are but the idealised attributes of man.

Marx opposed Feuerbach's conceptions both of theory and practice. A theory was a guide to action; practice, the specific activities which had to be carried out to test the theory. Practice (*Praxis*) was something much wider than *practicality*. It was selective behaviour. Its character was not given by personal interests which might or might not have been present but by the skills and techniques, the living traditions and modes of procedure, which man brings to whatever he sees and does. Praxis could not be contrasted with science, for science has a Praxis, too. The scientific objects which the scientist studies are essentially related to the practices of scientists. These in turn are related to the basic practices of the culture which supports science. Marx rarely discusses science without underscoring the influence of modern commerce and industry upon its development. Marx's theory of the Praxis could explain what all other philosophers recognised but which they could not begin to account for, without writing fairy-tales, viz., *how knowledge could give power.* For Marx knowledge gives power by virtue of the activities it sets up in transforming things in behalf of social needs. The meaning of any theory is ultimately to be found not in what men say but in what it leads them to do or leave undone. Actual or possible Praxis is not only the locus of meaning but also the test of truth. This point is expressed in Marx's second thesis.

Thesis II

" The question whether human thought can achieve objective truth is not a question of theory but a *practical* question. In practice [*Praxis*] man must prove the truth, i.e., the reality, power and this-sidedness of his thought. The dispute concerning the reality or unreality of thought—which is isolated from practice [*Praxis*]—is a purely *scholastic* question."

To the modern reader these sentences suggest pragmatism, but in view of the multiple ambiguity of this term it is advisable to avoid its use and to search more directly for Marx's meaning. Marx here equates the real and the true, the unreal with the false. Reality cannot therefore in this connection mean existence, since false ideas exist as well as true. Reality has the sense of the " actually " or " genuinely " true, that which is established to be " really " true in the face of critical inquiry and doubt. For idealism, the truth of any idea consists in its coherence with other ideas. Inasmuch as existence was essentially ideal it was possible to discover the truth, although not the whole truth (that was accessible only to Absolute Mind) by developing consistently the logical implications of any meaningful sentence. It is obvious that such a theory of truth could never submit to control by empirical fact, for in the first place, according to its assumptions, there were no " empirical " facts but only logical necessities. Secondly, granting the " appearance " of empirical fact there was no way of telling which of a number of equally consistent theories was true without going outside of the systems of coherent propositions. For example, on what grounds could the consistently developed propositions of a paranoic be rejected for a more plausible account ? Thirdly, since the idealists assumed with Hegel that truth can only be found in the whole, knowledge of everything *must* be relevant to knowledge of anything else. Numerous other paradoxical consequences flow from this theory which need not be developed here. They can all be deduced from the difficulties mentioned.

Materialism, strictly speaking, did not and could not develop a theory of truth. The very existence of ideas constituted a difficulty which it originally tried to answer by regarding ideas as a tenuous kind of matter, and later, as sense-impressions of varying degrees of complexity resulting from the bombardment of material particles on sensitive nerve endings. But how could ideas derived in such a way be characterised as true or false ? The standard formula which was invoked, viz., that a true idea was one which " agreed " or " corresponded " with its object, raised problems just as baffling. The proper meaning of correspondence presupposed a qualitative identity between the entities corresponding with each other, as e.g., the correspondence between a yard stick and some other standard measure, or a picture and an original. But what could this common

element be ? Material ? This would mean that ideas would have
to be of the same stuff as things. A palpable absurdity ! Ideal ?
The materiality of the world would disappear and we would be
back to Hegel and the coherence theory of truth.

Usually the materialist shifted the problem so that it became
a question of what *caused* ideas. But the difficulties could not
be evaded—in fact they were multiplied. False ideas have causes
as well as true ideas. What criterion, then, enabled us to distinguish between the two ? Further, if ideas are effects, then the
question suggests itself: what is it that is known, the non-ideal
causes of ideas or the non-material effects themselves ? Here, at
least, two answers were possible. The causes might be known or
the effects might be known. If the causes were known, then
truth could not consist in an " agreement " between the causes
and effects, for causes do not at all have to be like effects, any
more than unripe apples necessarily have to resemble the cramps
produced by eating them. Some other theory of truth would
have to account for the facts of knowledge. If only effects were
known, that is to say, if the ideas produced by the molecular
agitation of the nervous system were objects of knowledge, the
implications were even more startling. How could effects (ideas)
be compared with their causes (things), since according to the
supposition of the case, all that our knowledge of causes (things)
could consist in was the possession of their effects (ideas)? What
assurance have we, then, on this view, that there *are* causes of
our ideas ? To call ideas " effects " of things is question-begging.
We are aware of ideas as mental *events*. They may not be caused
at all, or if caused, they may be caused by other mental events,
and not at all by things. The indecisiveness of the materialist's
theory of truth leads either to the subjective idealism of Berkeley,
viz., only ideas are objects of knowledge, and what we call things
or matter is merely a complex of ideas, or to the scepticism of
Hume, viz., only ideas are objects of knowledge and there is no
telling whether they are caused by something which is not an
idea.

Marx's conception of truth cut under all of these theories.
We have seen in a previous study why he rejected subjective
idealism as represented by Bruno Bauer. It could not begin to
account for the compulsive features of experience. Its solipsism

was not only a theoretical *reductio ad absurdum*, and inconsistent at that, but a mockery by indirection of the efforts of the working class to liberate itself from poverty and degradation by asserting that these were nothing else than their private constructions. Traditional materialism, although congenial to Marx in its social intent, was muddled both in its theory and practice. By professing to see in all human history and activity nothing but a special case of universal physical categories, and in human thought a mere resultant of mechanical or chemical influences, it made unintelligible the *redirective* judgments of the revolutionist whose primary aim was to transform the world. Not that Marx was unaware that a great many materialists had been revolutionists and had urged their revolutionary proposals in the name of materialism. In *Die heilige Familie* he describes the almost obvious connections which exist between a philosophical theory that explains men's ignorance, criminality, etc., in terms of their conditions and the gospel of socialism which seeks to eliminate the social factors which make for inhumanity. But in *Die deutsche Ideologie* he raises two allied questions concerning the theoretical and practical adequacy of this socially enlightened materialism. They concern the possibility of justifying on the materialist view, judgments of value about conditions; and explaining how, if men are completely determined by their environment, they can change that environment. These problems are the subject of the next thesis. But it is clear that in the practical judgments Marx made as a revolutionist, e.g. certain actions must be performed, if certain desirable consequences are to follow, we have a conspicuous illustration of a type of judgment whose truth could never be established by the idealistic or traditional materialistic theories.

When Marx says that any dispute about the truth or falsity of a judgment which is isolated from Praxis is a scholastic question, he is saying that such questions cannot be answered in principle, that in short, they are no genuine questions at all. The truth of *any* theory depends upon whether or not the actual consequences which flow from the Praxis initiated to test the theory are such that they realise the predicted consequences. In other words, for Marx all genuine questions are scientifically determinable even though for a variety of reasons we may never know the answer to some of them. Since all judgments are hypotheses, the expectations which enter into the process of discovering the truth about them are not the personal and private expectations of the individual thinker but the public and verifiable expectations which logically flow from the hypotheses entertained. What a man wants to believe is relevant only to *what* he believes, but not to its truth. There is no will to believe in Marx but a will to action, in order to test belief and get additional grounds for further action if necessary. What takes place as a result of practice is not a relevant consequence of the theory unless the conditions involved in the meaning of the theory are met. The defeat of the Paris Commune, e.g., is not a refutation of Marx's theory of the way political power is to be conquered because the objective conditions presupposed by that theory were absent when the political Praxis occurred.

The continual admonitions of Marx and Engels (and of Lenin and Trotsky, too) that their theories were not to be taken as dogmas—admonitions more honoured in the breach than in the observance by most of their reputed followers—warn against accepting beliefs as if they were fixed truths, truths which *must* be realised independently of the results of Praxis. What *must* be, come what may, expresses a *resolution* of the pious believer, not a scientific prediction which depends upon many factors, *including what the predictor himself does.*

Marx did not live to develop the *implications* of his scientific theory of truth. That is not a ground for denying that he held it. Not only do his glosses on Feuerbach and other writings[1] declare its principal features but his cardinal doctrines of the class-struggle and historical materialism demand it. Part of the reason why Marx did not state it in more precise and detailed form is to be found in his belief that a theory of truth, like any method, is to be judged by the concrete applications made of it. And when it is recalled that Marx wrote not to achieve absolute theoretical clarity but to guide the action of the working class, and that in the light of contemporary standards of analytic rigour almost every field of nineteenth-century thought,

[1] Particularly his first draft of an introduction to his *Critique of Political Economy*, reprinted as an Appendix to the English translation. This manuscript is of the first importance for the consideration of Marx's methodology.

including many technical disciplines, fall short of *verbal* accuracy, only an unhistorical literary prudery will demand that he be judged by our own standards of expression and not by the intent, spirit and fundamental sense of his doctrines.

Thesis III

" The materialistic doctrine that men are the products of circumstances and education, and that changed men are therefore the products of other circumstances and a changed education, forgets that circumstances are changed by men, and that the educator must himself be educated. Consequently materialism necessarily leads to a division of society into two parts, of which one is elevated above society (e.g. in Robert Owen).

" The coincidence of the transformation of circumstances and of human activity can only be conceived and rationally understood as revolutionising practice [*Praxis*]."

This gloss is directed against some contemporary forms of Utopian Socialism which, despite their materialistic approach to natural phenomena, relapsed into idealism in their social and historical theory. The Utopian varieties which were not materialistic in their natural theory, i.e., which were consistently idealistic, are not under discussion. Marx raises the question about Utopian Socialism here because he considers Feuerbach to belong to this school. In *Die deutsche Ideologie* he specifically says of Feuerbach that "in so far as he is a materialist, history does not exist for him, and in so far as he treats of history, he is no materialist " (loc. cit., p. 34). In addition, it was crucial for Marx to differentiate clearly between his own realistic theories of social struggle and those of an influential group which professed to have the same ideal goals in view.

Every simple theory of the causal dependence of mind upon matter encounters difficulties just as soon as it hitches that theory to some programme of reform or revolution. For a programme presupposes a plan which is *not yet* realised and suggests methods of changing the social world, based upon the causal dependencies established by science, which have *not yet* been adopted. If every idea or programme is a reflection of the existing world, and is *only* that, how can human action be intelligently guided by some ideal which is yet to be, which outruns existence and lights up a possible path for its future development ? *After* history has run its course, by looking away from the multitude of occasions on which the consequences of human activity have had a redirecting influence on the stream of events, it is easy to argue that human ideals were nothing but passive, mirror-like reflections of antecedent realities—even though analysis discloses such a mode of speech to be metaphysical nonsense. But when human beings are faced by real alternatives of action—i.e., alternatives both of which cannot be realised although both may be attempted—it is impossible to hold that human ideals are " images." At those moments they are obviously plans of action !

The Utopian socialists could explain in part how the state of affairs which they deplored came about. They could also explain why such a state of affairs did not appear deprecatory to others. But they could not explain in the slightest their own ideals of social reform. They appeared to themselves as if they were outside of the social process—as if they were historical mutants whose fertilising ideas would revolutionise the existing order. The philosophy of other people was determined by circumstances and education but not their own philosophy. And, in fact, how could it be on their simple materialistic assumptions, since their circumstances and conditions were quite similar to those of " the others " who disagreed with them ? That is why Marx properly points out that this mixture of socialism and materialism leads to a belief in a division of society into two parts—one of common-run people whose ideas are simply determined by circumstances and education, the other of choice Utopian spirits who are elevated above society and social laws, the rare gifts of the gods to an errant humanity. The cult of leadership among the Utopian groups, their assumption that they could appeal to any social class, from paupers to princes, for support of their ideals, their belief in a cure-all for every evil including natural stupidity—all flowed from the view that the keys to salvation were in the possession of a handful of right-thinking men—call them saints or scientists or philosophers or social engineers, as you please.

Since it followed from their own doctrines that there was nothing which determined their social ideals, it seemed plausible to the materialistic Utopians that there was no reason why these ideals could not have been embodied in practice at any time, except for chance or ignorance. Some of the Utopians of the nineteenth century actually defended this view and sketched accounts of what history would have been if their ideas had prevailed at an earlier time. But most of them, refusing to surrender the rigorous determinism involved in their physical materialism, transferred the determinism to an ideal or conceptual plane. In Hegelian fashion, none the less vicious for being unconscious, they explained the succession of historical ideals as moments in an unending development of Mind. The life history of ideals became the life history of society. In *Die deutsche Ideologie* Marx calls attention to the process by which men like Stirner, for whom Feuerbach was not materialistic enough, ended up by embracing the philosophy of history of absolute idealism. The process, as described by Marx, consists of three steps:

(*a*) Dominant historical ideals are cut loose from the complex of social conditions and needs of the dominant classes. " Therewith the domination of these ideals or illusions in history is proclaimed."

(*b*) Since certain ideals are connected with others both organically and temporally, an *order* of development is introduced of which the different ideals are successive phases.

(*c*) To avoid the appearance of mysticism suggested by the notion of an immanent development of ideals, *certain individuals* are regarded as the carriers of these ideals. These are " the thinkers, ideologists and philosophers " who are conceived as " the makers of history." " Therewith all materialistic elements have been eliminated from history and one can give free rein to his speculative fancy " (Ibid., p. 39).

We have already seen how Marx conceived of the interacting processes between nature, society and man. The development of the forces of production gives rise to new needs. In the struggle to achieve these needs, ideals are forged to guide activity directed towards a transformation of society. These ideals "express " the needs of the groups or classes who rally around them as standards, " express " them in the sense that they are *outgrowths*, not reflections, of material conditions of need. The struggle to achieve institutional change produces changes in those who participate in the struggles. The Praxis of trying to bring about a new social order, not abstract doctrine, educates the workers. No Messiah can assure them of anything save of that which they can win for themselves. Marx's great insights that human beings cannot change the world without changing themselves, and that actual social struggles, under certain conditions, are the best school for acquiring an education in social realities are not isolated thoughts but organically connected with his materialistic theory of history—a theory which in his *Deutsche Ideologie* he develops in greater detail than he does in any other writing. In a chapter of the section on Feuerbach, entitled by Marx himself, " Concerning the Production of Consciousness," he writes of his theory of history:

" This philosophy of history rests upon the development of the real process of production, taking in fact its point of departure from the material production of immediate life, tracing the forms of social intercourse bound up and produced by this mode of production and conceiving civic society in its various stages as the foundation of the whole of history. It also describes civic society in its actions as state power and explains the origins and developing processes of the whole of its various theoretical creations and forms of consciousness, religion, philosophy, morality, etc. In this way it presents the situation in its totality (and therefore the reciprocal interactions between the various factors upon each other). In any given period this philosophy of history, as distinct from the idealist conception, does not seek for some category but remains continually upon real historical *ground* explaining not practice out of ideas but the formation of ideas out of material practice. In this way it reaches the conclusion that all existing forms and products of consciousness can be resolved not through mental criticism, or by being dissolved into ' self-consciousness ' or transformed into ' apparitions,' ' ghosts,' etc., but only through the practical overthrow of the real social relations out of which these idealistic fantasies [*Flausen*] have developed. It is not criticism but revolution which is the driving force of history—as well as of religion, philosophy and every other theory. This philosophy of history shows that history does not find its end by disappearing into ' self-consciousness ' or becoming ' spirit of our spirit ' but that at every stage it is confronted by a material result, a sum of productive forces, an historically created relation to nature and of individuals to each other, which every generation inherits from its predecessors. This mass of productive forces of forms of capital and of circumstances, on the one hand, is modified by the new generation, and, on the other hand, prescribes to the new generation its own conditions of life, accounting for its special character and determinate development—showing that circumstances make men as much as men make circumstances. This sum of productive forces, capitals and forms of social intercourse which every individual and every generation finds as something given, is the real source of what philosophers have represented as ' substance ' and ' the essence of man,' the real source of what they have hypostasised or struggled against, and whose effects and influences upon the development of men have not in the least been affected by the revolt of the philosophers of ' self-consciousness ' and ' the ego ' against it. These given conditions of life of the different generations also decide whether or not the periodically recurring revolutionary upheavals of history are strong enough to overthrow the basis of the existing order. Where these material elements of a total revolution, i.e., on the one hand, the existing productive forces, and, on the other, the creation of a revolutionary mass rebelling not merely against individual conditions of existing society but against the whole ' production of life ' itself, the ' total activity,' upon which society is based—where these are not present, then it is immaterial for practical development, as the history of communism proves, whether or not the *idea* of this revolution be proclaimed a hundred times over " (*Gesamtausgabe*, Abt. I, Bd. 5, pp. 27–8).

Thesis IV

" Feuerbach takes his point of departure from the fact of religious self-alienation, from the splitting up of the world into a religious, imaginary world and a real one. His achievement consists in dissolving the religious world and revealing its secular foundations. He overlooks the fact, however, that after completing this work the chief thing still remains to be accomplished. The fact that the secular foundation lifts itself above itself and fixates itself as an independent empire beyond the clouds can only be truly explained in terms of the internal division and contradictions of this secular foundation. The latter must first be understood in its contradictions and then through the elimination of the contradictions practically revolutionised. For example, once the earthly family is discovered to be the secret of the holy family it must be theoretically criticised and practically transformed."

This thesis, together with VI and VII, contains the main points of Marx's criticism of Feuerbach's psychology of religion. Feuerbach had found the essence of religion to be rooted in the human feelings of dependence upon the external forces of the natural and social world, and had declared the chief agencies of the processes of compensatory expression for emotional frustration to be ritual, mythology and theology. Grant, says Marx, that wherever religion is present, it has the characteristic features Feuerbach selects for emphasis. But as an explanation of religious thought and behaviour, Feuerbach's theory is inadequate because it is too abstract. It leaves totally unexplained the historical *diversity* in religious phenomena and contents itself with a mechanical table of needs which different kinds of religion fulfil. For example, if in any religion there prevails a belief in a God who created the world out of nothing, this expresses, according to Feuerbach, the irrational needs of man's nature. " He deifies nothing but his own irrationality " (*Essence of Christianity*, Eng. trans., p. 83). If, on the other hand, we find in any religion a belief in the eternity of the world, then the rational needs of man's nature are asserting themselves. But Feuerbach never descended from these vague generalities to explain why one, rather than the other, of these beliefs was accepted at any given time. Nor did he ask whether these needs are always invariant in man—and if not, what determines their appearance and disappearance. Supposing further that we grant a fixed need for, or tendency towards, irrational expression. Off-hand one can think of a thousand different irrational beliefs, aside from a belief in the creation of the world out of nothing, which would satisfy all the conditions of man's irrational nature. Why, then, *this* particular kind of irrational belief and not others?

It is here that Marx's own psychology of religion comes into view. Religion is not born of a natural, tragic split within the human breast. The real forces impelling men to find satisfaction in some dreamy empire where they enjoy the uncontested power denied them in this life are not merely psychological but social. The source of religion is to be sought in the antagonisms between the way men actually produce and the traditional, social, legal and moral forms under which that production is carried on— or between the new needs generated in the course of their social Praxis and the old needs which give rise to, and yet oppose, the new needs. From these antagonisms results the fragmentation of experience, the absence of unified control of the collective lot, the worship of the abstractions which express the needs of yesterday, the contrast between an everyday self and an ideal holiday self—all of which constitute the cultus and theology of religion. Religion, according to Marx, is to be construed from the real conditions of man's empirical life and not from his essence. And if these conditions are such that they generate certain kinds of emotional conflicts and theoretical illusions, then these illusions and conflicts must be removed by removing that which gives rise to them.

Here again it must be pointed out that Marx is making predictions and not establishing anything by definition. It remains to be seen whether the emotional conflicts and theoretical illusions associated with religion will disappear with the transformation of the economic order which, according to Marx's hypothesis, is responsible not only for the ways in which these conflicts and illusions are expressed but for their very existence. The same is true as far as the existence of the state in a class-less society is concerned. Only a religious attitude, and not a scientific philosophy, can assure us that the state is *destined* to

" wither away." So it may, in name ! But the real question is
whether any new social conflicts will arise, necessitating the
existence of separate bodies of armed men standing over against
the community as a whole to enforce special interests. This
cannot be settled by definition but by history—a history
determined in part by how Marxists interpret Marx.

If Feuerbach claimed to have discovered the secret of theology
in anthropology, Marx sought to transform anthropology into
realistic sociology. Feuerbach had shown the religious world to
be illusory; Marx asks, however: " How does it come about that
these illusions arise ? " (*Gesamtausgabe*, I, Bd. 5, p. 215). Neither
Marx nor any of his orthodox followers have worked out detailed
analyses of the great religions of the past from the standpoint
of historical materialism. Some interesting attempts to uncover
the social contradictions at the basis of religious constructions
have been made by men like E. Bernstein, Max Weber, E.
Troelsch and R. H. Tawney, but not along strictly Marxist lines.
In this field, as in so many others, a casual phrase of Marx's,
penned in 1843 when he was still a Feuerbachian, has been
substituted for his considered philosophy. Marx's sentence,
" Religion is the opium of the people," has itself acted like
opium upon the minds of his followers, who have repeated it as
if it constituted all that can be said on the subject. If religion
were the opium of the people, the necessary precondition of all
criticism would be the awakening of the people from their
drugged slumbers. This is precisely the position which Marx
criticised when he argued against B. Bauer, Stirner, Feuerbach
and others that the political and social movement of the working
class must not be explicitly or programmatically anti-religious.
The working-class movement, according to Marx, must in the
first instance be directed against the *milieu* whose social antagonisms are eased through the cultural opium dispersed by those
classes which control the means of production, education and
communication.

Thesis V

" Feuerbach, not satisfied with abstract thinking, appeals
to *sensory thinking* [*Anschauung*]; but he does not conceive
sensibility as a practical, human-sensory, activity."

This links up with the argument of Thesis I. That Marx regards it as important is indicated by the fact that he returns to it in several different ways in *Die deutsche Ideologie*, where Feuerbach is criticised for not grasping the sense object (*sinnlicher Gegenstand*) as a sensory activity (*sinnliche Tätigkeit*). Here again, Marx's historical sense asserts itself against formalism in a twofold way. To the idealistic identification of reality with thought, Feuerbach had countered with the identification of reality with sensibility or sensation. Feuerbach's description of the nature of sensation was no more empirical than the idealistic description of the nature of thought. The latter overlooked the historical materials which were the prior condition of effective thinking; the former overlooked the elements of selective activity determining the concrete character of sensation. For Marx sensations were not merely experienced effects of things acting upon the body, they were effects of an interaction between an *active* body and the things surrounding it. The sensations which appear to be passively experienced to a large degree depend for their frequency, their specific context, and even their relative intensity upon where the body looks and listens— in short, upon where the body *attends* as well as upon *what* it attends. In fact, this is the differential characteristic between living and non-living things, pre-eminently present in man because of his more highly developed nervous system and intelligence.

In *Die deutsche Ideologie* Marx goes even further and shows that sensation has not only a biologically selective dimension but a *social* dimension. Given the " same " environment, defined as the co-presence of a number of different things or actions in a fixed physical area, it is well known that subjects drawn from different cultures will " see " different things and interpret them differently. Tradition, education, language, and all the other aspects of culture intertwined with the basic mode of production influence what seem to be purely biological reactions. This, in fact, differentiates the biological reactions of man from those of other living beings. Man's hunger, for example, is a natural phenomenon, but the ways in which he gratifies his hunger and the character of what he regards as food are social facts. Through social organisation man is continually modifying his primary natural environment, reducing its rôle to that of a pure limiting condition. Through social organisation, particularly industry, Marx asserts, the *given* can sometimes be explained as well as the ways in which the given is *taken*. If you want certainty, Feuerbach had preached in one of the phases of his philosophy, open your eyes and grasp the given as an immediate, natural datum, e.g., that cherry tree over there. What met one's eyes, Marx retorted, was likely to be not a God-given eternal fact of nature but a socially mediated object.

" He [Feuerbach] does not see that the sensory world which surrounds him is not something immediately given from eternity, something always the same, but the product of industry and the social situation, in the sense that it is an historical product, the result of the activity of a whole series of generations, each one standing on the shoulders of those preceding it, developing previous industry and forms of social intercourse, and changing their social order in accordance with changed needs. Even the objects of the simplest ' sensory certainty ' are given through social development, industry and commercial relations. The cherry tree like almost all fruit trees was transplanted to our zone, as is well known, through *commerce*; it was only *by virtue of* this action of a determinate society at a determinate time that it was given to ' the sensory certainty ' of Feuerbach " (*Gesamtausgabe*, I, 5, 33).

Marx adds immediately that this historical approach converts every " profound " philosophical question into a simple question of empirical fact. The questions of the possibility of this or that piece of knowledge, of the reliability of our perceptions, of things as they are and as they appear to be, if they have any meaning at all, are to be answered in terms of biology, psychology or history. A valid implication of Marx's position would be that psychology is either the study of animal behaviour or social behaviour. In so far as human reactions are isolated from a social context and correlated with various external stimuli, we are analysing animal behaviour or are in the realm of physiological psychology. In so far as allowance is made for the social context of human behaviour, we are in the realm of social psychology.

Thesis VI

" Feuerbach resolves the religious essence into the human. But the essence of man is not an abstraction residing in each single individual. In its reality it is the whole of social relationships.

" Feuerbach, who does not enter upon the criticism of this real essence, is consequently compelled:

(1) To abstract from the historical process and to fixate the religious feeling as something self-contained, and to presuppose an abstract—*isolated*—human individual.

(2) To conceive the essence of man only as ' the species,' as an inner, inarticulate, *natural* tie, binding many individuals together."

Thesis VII

" Feuerbach does not therefore see that the ' religious feeling ' is itself a *social product*, and that the abstract individual whom he analyses belongs in reality to a specific form of society."

The above glosses develop the argument made in Thesis **IV**. They deny that religion and the religious experience are primary *natural* facts about man. Until recently this was the assumption made by most armchair theorists of the origin of religion. Religion, for one, is an expression of a direct natural fear, socially unmediated, of unseen powers and uncontrollable forces. For others, it is an attempt to placate spiritual beings whose presence is suggested by phenomena of dreams and psychic illusion. For Schleiermacher, it is the feeling of absolute dependence upon the cosmic ineffable whole. For Feuerbach, it is the projection of an experienced need. All of these theories imply that man is a religious creature in the same sense as he is a food-clothing-and-shelter-seeking creature. They all assert that at the very least a common denominator can be found in all religious theory and practice which expresses their essential characteristic, and which remains invariant throughout their varying historic forms. Now for purposes of identification, Marx would never dream of denying that religious behaviour must exhibit certain properties enabling investigation to differentiate it from other forms of behaviour. But he does not look for these properties in the characters of individual religious belief or action. Believing that religion arises as a set of doctrines and practices whenever society has reached a certain stage in the division of labour, he tries to locate its specific character in the social functions which it fulfils.[1] The defining trait of religion, as developed by Feuerbach and other philosophers of religion, was a generalisation of one historical expression of " religious feeling." It was true that many contemporaries of Feuerbach would recognise his psychological analysis as an accurate account of their religious experience. But from Marx's point of view, a more adequate explanation of their religious experience would be found by analysing the concrete social situation out of which this religious experience developed. It could hardly be claimed that the religious experience of a nineteenth-century citizen of France or Germany was the same as the religious experience of a Greek or Roman citizen. So great is the pervasive character of the totality of social relations which give " the tone " to a culture, that Marx felt justified in claiming that there is a greater difference between ancient religion and modern religion than there is between ancient religion and ancient politics, education, art, or any other aspect of ancient culture.

Strictly speaking, for Marx there is no history of religion as such but only a history of the cultures of which religions are fragmentary aspects. To erect a definition of religion on the basis of one of its historic expressions, is to assume that there is a religious sentiment as such with which man is naturally endowed and which can be studied in its pure form once its accidental social and historical expressions are sloughed off.

Thesis VI restates in a few terse sentences the criticism which Marx passed upon Stirner. The " individual," whose psyche Feuerbach probed so deeply, is a rather late and complex product of *society*. No social phenomenon, therefore, can be explained in terms of any of the traits imputed to individuals as creatures of *nature*. Feuerbach realised the impossibility of ever deriving consciousness of the existence of oneself from individual behaviour. There is no *Ich* which is not the necessary

---

[1] Cf. discussion of Thesis IV above.

complement of *Du*. But the social bond between the self and others was conceived on the plane of grammar and common emotion—both of which, according to Marx, already presupposed a common social world of production. Where Feuerbach strives to make the social bond between men concrete, he falls back upon the biological facts of interdependence and reproduction. For Marx the social bond between human beings—a bond which makes their differences as well as their agreements intelligible—is the totality of social relations. If one must speak of the " essence of man," one must find it in man's civilisation, material and ideal, and not in biology.

Thesis VIII

" Social life is essentially *practical*. All mysteries which mislead theory into mysticism find their rational solution in human practice and in the understanding of this practice."

Here we have a heuristic principle of the first importance. It guided Marx in all of his own work. It served as the acid test of the meaning of the theories he opposed. It denies both the existence of insoluble problems and of mystical solutions to problems.

The disparity between what human beings do and the explanations they offer to themselves and others of what they do, is a striking phenomenon in all social life. Verbal behaviour seems to limp after physical behaviour. Even the history of science appears, from one point of view, to be a continuous effort to substitute more exact descriptions of what man sees and does, for less exact descriptions. Several reasons may be offered for this lag in our understanding. First of all, the body acts in some decisive way long before thought can strike a trial-balance of all factors involved. Secondly, " new " discoveries are made and " new " techniques developed while the " old " principles still exercise their sway. And since for anything to be intelligible it must at least impart a sense of " the familiar," the traditional principles are retained for explanatory purposes, at the cost of slighting the distinctively novel features of experience. In due course, the novel becomes familiar and principles are reformulated, but by that time the situation demands still further clarification and refinement of expression. Thirdly, the social context of theories and practices is lost sight of, and ideas are treated as if they were independent entities, irrelevant to the needs and interests of their proponents. The problems of why ideas and theories arise when they do, why they prevail, and why they develop a life so different from that planned for them by their authors, become mysteries or, more accurately, give rise to mystical solutions.

Marx was primarily interested in the effect which the neglect of social context had upon obscuring the relation between theory and practice. This social context was understood in its broadest terms and included not only the immediate social needs which influenced the direction and development of scientific research but the social habits of thought and action involved in communication. According to Marx the basic criteria of intelligibility presupposed a common activity in a common world. Somewhere along the line in every theory, a determinate form of behaviour exemplified its meaning. The alleged independence of the so-called non-existential sciences is due to a failure to relate their fundamental concepts to the concrete situations and concrete activities out of which they grow and to which they must in some form or another be applied. Were Marx alive to-day he would trace the flights to mysticism induced by recent work in modern physics to the fundamental methodological error of directly comparing the refined hypothetical results of theory with the crude data of experience. In the light of his genial insight, he would urge scientists to examine their conclusions in terms of the operations and practices necessary to achieve them, and to set forth the meaning of their theories as prescriptive guides to specific action.

Thesis IX

" The highest point which can be reached by *contemplative* materialism, i.e. materialism which cannot grasp the fact that sensibility is a practical activity, is the point of view of single individuals in ' civic society.' "

Thesis X

" The standpoint of the old materialism is ' civic society ';
the standpoint of the new materialism is *human* society or
socialised humanity."

The key to the meaning of these theses lies in the phrase
" civic society " (*bürgerliche Gesellschaft*), the title of the second
section of the third part of Hegel's *Rechtsphilosophie*. The mis-
translation of the phrase as " bourgeois " or " capitalist "
society by some " Marxists " makes nonsense of the passage,
for materialism is older than capitalism and is not always the
official philosophy of bourgeois society. Some who have recognised the reference to Hegel have assumed that Hegel is being
charged with a kind of contemplative materialism, forgetting
that the culmination of the Hegelian social philosophy is the
doctrine of the state in which the abstract rights, the individualism, the conflicts and compromises of sovereignty between
different social groups, all flowing from the nature of civic
society, are transcended. It is the Hegelian philosophy and
not contemplative materialism which represents for Marx the
highest philosophical expression of capitalism. It is significant
that the last ideological defence of developed capitalism is
everywhere a variation of Hegel's social and political philosophy,
particularly his theory of *die Korporation* which serves as the
transition in the *Rechtsphilosophie* to the nature of the state.

It is clear, then, that the meaning of Marx in these theses does
not lie on the surface. We must ask what Hegel meant by
" civic society," why Marx associates the theory and practice
of civic society with contemplative materialism, and why the
new materialism is declared to be the philosophy of a truly
human society.

Civic society in Hegel is the complex of organised social ties
which knot individuals together by the cords of self-interest.
The individual in such a society is himself a system (*Ganzes*) of
needs or wants, some of which are an expression of natural
necessity, some a result of arbitrary choice. He regards himself,
or the fulfilment of his needs, as his sole end, and all other
individuals as necessary means to his self-expression. His social

and political philosophy is individualism, which assumes that everyone else is by nature self-seeking and free. Whatever social and governmental constraints exist are external to the minds and feelings of those who abide by them. They are compromises which are made necessary by the conflict of activities in the collective pursuit of individual gratifications.

According to Marx traditional materialism could only conceive of human consciousness as a passive form of sensation. Sensation was a property of human bodies arising whenever they were subjected to the impacts of other things and bodies. Mind, together with all intellectual processes like memory and generalisation, is sensation modified and organised in such a way as to increase or diminish the basic feelings of pleasure and pain. The natural tendency of all bodies despite their verbal behaviour is to preserve themselves, and more concretely, to pursue their own self-interest. According to some materialists, this was supposed to be a deduction justified by the laws of mechanics. The gratification of self-interest is the source of all duty to one's self and to one's fellow-man.

The completest expression of the materialistic " self-interest " theory of human activity seemed to Marx to be the philosophy of Bentham. In *Die deutsche Ideologie* Bentham's views are submitted to close analysis and the basic assumptions of utilitarianism are rejected. " Interest," as conceived by Bentham— " whose nose," says Marx, " must first have an interest before it makes up its mind to smell "[1]—is described as a needless third term introduced between human beings and the varying ways in which they live their life. The reason, however, why all natural impulses are first related to some imaginary interest is that a peculiar set of social relationships has made it impossible to gratify natural desires directly or to lose oneself in activities for their own sake. The existence of a social and economic order in which production is dependent upon a market, upon " free " labourers, upon the expectation of profit, affects every human relationship within it. Everything is vain in such a culture except the " useful." But to have utility means to be exploitable. The rule of " live and let live " makes way for the maxim " exploit or be exploited." " The objective expression

[1] *Gesamtausgabe*, Abt. I, Bd. 5, p. 192.

of this utility is money in which is represented the value of all things, human beings and social relations " (Ibid., p. 388).

Marx admits the progressive rôle which the theory of utilitarianism played in helping to clear the ground of feudal anachronisms. In stressing the importance of the *mutual* exploitation of one another through competitive effort, a common attack was made by the bourgeoisie on the *institutional* exploitations of feudalism—political, patriarchal and religious—which prevented free scope for the development of commercial and competitive talents. At no time, however, did the utilitarians apply their criteria of moral validity to the institutions of capitalism and their consequences. Criticism was directed only against those vestiges of an earlier social period which restricted the field of " personal exploitation." Whereas in France the theory of utilitarianism assumed " a moral form," in England its content rapidly became more and more economic. The special forms which the division of labour took were justified as the expressions of, and contributions to, social utility. Variations in market exchanges resulting from competition were equated to each other by the use of a least common denominator of relative utilities whose values established themselves only *post hoc*, i.e., after the exchanges were made. The result was, said Marx, that " its economic content gradually transformed the theory of utility into a pure apologia of the existing order, into a proof that under given conditions the present relations of human beings to each other represent the best and most useful relations possible. All subsequent modern economic theory carries the same character " (*Gesamtausgabe*, I, 5, 392).

The standpoint of the old materialism is the standpoint of civic society, because it is " atomic." It assumes that each individual organism is a God-given independent whole with private pains, pleasures and interests. Existing social arrangements are explained as contractual obligations to which each individual commits himself out of his own interest. The standpoint of the new materialism is the standpoint of the *human* society, because in emphasising the historical and cultural determinants of private experience it claims that what any man is must be explained, so to speak, in terms of what all men are. But what all men are must be inferred from what they do, from the institutional conditions under which they do it, and the historical forces which have moulded and are reshaping these conditions. This is another way of establishing the truth that the nature of man is not a biological fact but a social one. The organising relations and traditions of society are not something put on and off by individuals; they enter deeply into what appear at first glance as immediate reactions of the single organism. The theorists of an atomistic, civic society were aware that the consequences of the private pursuit of private interest rarely squared with the expectations of pain and pleasure entertained by the overwhelming mass of citizens. They either explained the discrepancy as the result in each case of false calculation or they sought refuge in a mystical conception of a pre-established harmony operating in invisible ways to bring about an undefined social welfare. Marx's conception of man pointed to the necessity of a direct collective control of all social institutions which influenced man. Such a control presupposes a theory of social interest which in a human society must give meaning and content to private interest. " Socialised humanity," in Marx's view, does not destroy individuality; it modifies its form, enriches its content and makes it a value accessible to all. In a similar way, Marx expected all values whose expressions are now frustrated by class interests in a class society to take on new forms and content after economic class divisions have disappeared.

Thesis XI

" Philosophers have only *interpreted* the world differently: the point is, however, to *change* it."

This oft-quoted remark evidently continues a line of criticism begun in *Die deutsche Ideologie.* Marx had pointed out that the Young-Hegelians, despite their " world shattering phrases," were doing nothing more than rebaptising the world as they found it with a new set of distinctions. Feuerbach, too, was not chary of using radical phraseology. But since he, like the others, sought the key to social change in the alteration of a personal attitude, in a generalisation of the feeling of love already implicit in much of common-day behaviour, Marx refused to take him at his revolutionary word. For all his talk about man, humanity, and communism, Feuerbach never investigated what the social conditions of men were, to what extent the qualities of humanity which he regarded as " essential to the species " were historical, and what programme of action his communism laid upon him. In Feuerbach's eyes, as we have already seen, the concrete differences between a group of healthy men and a mass of " scrofulous, overworked men faint with hunger " are less important than the common characteristics which they share as members of an ideally defined human species. Since his abstract materialism does not come to grips with the specific causes which produce differentiations in the human species, Marx argued that Feuerbach cannot do justice to the historical elements in culture. The latter are precisely the factors which must serve as points of leverage in social change. Where Feuerbach does pay fleeting attention to historical situations, particularly in religion, he tries to find the key to them in presumably invariant patterns of human feeling and behaviour.

In reading Feuerbach one cannot help sensing the illusionism which pervades his writings. He writes as if the demonstration of a truth were itself a proof that the truth would prevail, as if to have exposed an error were tantamount to passing a sentence of death upon it. Stressing feeling as he does, he nevertheless pays little attention to the *social* sources of feeling. Despite his criticism of the superficial rationalism which explains all conduct in terms of consciously entertained ideas, he himself relapses into that very position when he expects institutional changes to be affected by his analyses. At times he strikes a different note as when he reflects upon the outcome of the German revolution of 1848. But he always returns to his rationalistic faith. His pathetic trust that the future of atheism belongs to America where the absence of feudal traditions makes human beings more accessible to argument, is a case in point. His friend Kapp who had been in America and had some first-hand experience with American piety hastened to disillusion him but Feuerbach clung to his comforting belief to the end of his days.[1]

A more conspicuous illustration of Feuerbach's illusionism is

[1] Cf. L. Feuerbach, *Briefwechsel und Nachlass*, Bd. 2, p. 7.

his characterisation of himself as a communist. His grounds for such bold language, which later contributed to bringing down on him a visitation from the police and a thorough house searching, were philological rather than political. In a review of Max Stirner's book which makes merry over Feuerbach's religion of humanity and the inconsistencies between his method and conclusions, Feuerbach attempts to fix the character of his own philosophy in the following words:

> " Feuerbach is not a materialist, idealist or a believer in the philosophy of identity. Well, then, what is he? He is in thought as in deed, in spirit as in flesh, in essence as in feeling —*man*; or rather, since for him the essence of man is given only in society, communal man, Communist " (*S.W.*[1], Bd. 1, p. 342).

Marx seized upon this passage as epitomising the confusion and limitation of Feuerbach's thought. A term whose meaning *in use* refers to allegiance to a specific political organisation is converted into a purely abstract category. The abstract category expresses in an abstract way the commonplace that human beings find each other necessary for existence. Nothing is said about the variety of specific forms this necessary relation of one to the other can take and has taken, or about their relative justification at definite historical periods. Finally, the whole purport of Feuerbach's description is to bring to consciousness an existing fact whereas " the real communist aims at the revolutionising of the existing order " (*Gesamtausgabe*, I, 5, 31). The point of Marx's impatience with Feuerbach's failure to concretise his descriptions and to distinguish between the historical and natural elements in his analysis becomes clearer. If the existing facts about the relations of men to each other are natural, or in Feuerbach's language, are " essential " to the nature of man, then it is nonsense to talk about revolutionis'ng them.

Marx admits that Feuerbach has gone as far as a pure theoretician or philosopher, in the traditional sense, can go without ceasing to be a theoretician or philosopher. For practice, on every conception of philosophy except Marx's own, is a foreign element in philosophy. It involves decision, conflict, an element of partisanship in behalf of one among a number of possible alternatives. The kind of philosophy Marx called for and which his own activity illustrated, involved not merely risking an idea but risking one's whole person in carrying it out. Without an attempt at carrying out ideas, philosophy becomes a mere playing with possibilities unrelated both to the quest for truth and the furtherance of the good life—its professed objectives. In a dim way Feuerbach, too, had realised this. But his false conception of the nature of practice led him to confine the philosophical activity to thinking about ideas. Confronting the simple, and even on his own view, the artificial dichotomy between passionless thought and thoughtless passion or activity, he identifies philosophy with passionless thought, i.e., thought unrelated to practice. His whole way of phrasing the alternative reveals not only patent inconsistencies with his other doctrines but a failure of nerve in realising his own call for the reconstruction of philosophy. He writes of the relation between reason and passion in history as follows:

" Reason writes history but passion makes it. Everything new therefore is an injustice against the old. . . . One can think without doing an injustice to anyone, without inflicting pain upon anyone, for thoughts do not go further than one's own head. But one cannot act without setting one's whole body into motion, without running up against obstacles on all sides, without wounding even against one's will " (*S.W.*[1], Bd. 2, p. 408).

Marx rejects the disjunction as being neither exhaustive nor exclusive. It is true that there is no action without a violation of some right or interest. It is not true that such action need be blind, uninformed by theory or reason. It is true that one can think without acting directly but it is not true that no injustice is thereby done. For existing injustices are tolerated and remain unaltered. Philosophical activity may be conceived as action in behalf of values and interests which have been criticised by knowledge and reason. The very fact that philosophy is an activity in a world of space, time and incompatible interests, makes it clear that its goals cannot be absolute truth or absolute justice. But the fact that action is thoughtful makes it possible to achieve beliefs which are *truer*; the fact that thought leads to action makes it possible to achieve a world which is *more just*.

This, I believe, is the sense of Marx's final thesis on Feuerbach.

SOME PHILOSOPHICAL FRAGMENTS OF MARX
(Translated by Sidney Hook)

APPENDIX I

KANT AND POLITICAL LIBERALISM
by Karl Marx

THE KEY to Saint Max's[1] critique of liberalism as well as to that of his predecessors is the history of the German bourgeoisie. Let us examine several aspects of this history since the French Revolution.

The situation of Germany towards the end of the previous century is faithfully reflected in Kant's *Critique of Practical Reason*. While the French bourgeoisie through the most colossal revolution known to history was swinging itself into power and conquering the European continent, while the already politically emancipated English bourgeoisie revolutionised industry, subduing India politically and the rest of the world economically—while all this was going on, the powerless German burghers were only able to carry things as far as the " good will." Kant consoles himself with the purely " good will " even when it remains without result; he assumes the *realisation* of this good will, the harmony between it and the needs and desires of individuals as something achieved in the *hereafter*. This " good will " of Kant's corresponds completely to the powerlessness, degradation and misery of the German bourgeoisie whose petty interests were never capable of developing into common national interests and who as a result were continually exploited by the bourgeoisie of other countries. These petty local interests corresponded, on the one hand, to the genuinely local and provincial limitations of the German bourgeoisie, and on the other, to its cosmopolitan pretensions. Since the Reformation German development had taken on a definite petty-bourgeois character.

[1] This is a reference to Max Stirner, to whom fully three-quarters of the huge manuscript of Marx's *Die deutsche Ideologie* is devoted. Stirner is also referred to as Sancho.—S. H.

The old feudal state was for the most part destroyed in the peasant wars; what remained were either court princes who gradually acquired considerable independence and imitated the absolute monarchy on a petty and provincial scale or smaller landowners who ran through their petty fortunes in the petty courts of their region and then took petty positions in the petty armies and ministries, or bumpkin squires whose manner of living would have made the humblest English squire or French provincial *gentilhomme* feel ashamed of himself. Agriculture was conducted in a fashion which could not be characterised as either large-scale farming or parcelling, and despite the continuing feudalism and socage, failed to drive the peasants to emancipation. This was as much due to the fact that this kind of activity could not permit a revolutionary class to develop as it was to the fact that there was no corresponding revolutionary bourgeoisie which existed by its side. As for the bourgeoisie, we can only call attention to several characteristic details. For example, linen manufacture which depended upon the spinning-wheel and hand loom acquired importance in Germany just at the time when these simple instruments were being displaced by machines. Most characteristic of all was Germany's relation to Holland. Holland was the only member of the Hanseatic League which acquired commercial significance, tore itself free, cut Germany off from all world trade (with the exception of two ports, Hamburg and Bremen) and dominated the whole of German commerce. The German bourgeoisie was too powerless to prevent Dutch exploitation. The bourgeoisie of small Holland with its developed class interests was more powerful than the numerically far stronger bourgeoisie of Germany with its indifference and petty quarrelsome interests. The splitting up of its interests corresponded to the splitting up of its political organisation, of the small principalities and free cities. How could *political* concentration be established in a country where all the *economic* conditions for such concentration were missing? The weakness of every individual element in social life (one can speak neither of the estates nor of classes but at most of estates that had been and classes which were to be) did not allow anyone to conquer exclusive power. The necessary consequence of this was that during the epoch of absolute monarchy which appeared here in its most crippled, semi-patriarchal form, the special organs (*Sphäre*) which in accordance with the division of labour were assigned to the administration of public interest, developed an abnormal independence which soon developed into the modern bureaucracy. The state constituted itself into an apparently independent power and maintained this position whereas in countries other than Germany its independence was only temporary and transitional. The anomalous position of the state explains not only the honest and scrupulous conscientiousness of the officialdom, unparalleled elsewhere; but also the current illusions about the state which circulate throughout all Germany, the apparent independence which the theoreticians enjoy as over against the bourgeoisie—and the apparent contradiction between the form in which the theoreticians express the interest of the bourgeoisie and these interests themselves.

The characteristic form which French liberalism, based upon real class interest, took in Germany, we find in Kant. Neither he nor the German bourgeoisie whose ideological apologist [*beschönigender Wortführer*] he was, observed that at the root of these theoretical ideas of the bourgeoisie lay material interests and a class will conditioned and determined by the material relations of production. Kant consequently separates the theoretical expression of these interests from the interests themselves. He transforms the materially motivated will of the French bourgeoisie into a *pure* self-determination of the *free will*, of the will in-and-for itself, of the human will. In this way he converts it into a purely ideological determination and moral postulate. The German petty bourgeoisie in consequence, shudders at the practice of this energetic bourgeois liberalism just as soon as it asserts itself either in the reign of terror or in shameless bourgeois competition.

Under the domination of Napoleon, the German bourgeoisie developed still more widely its petty usury and its grand illusions. Concerning the usurious spirit which dominated Germany at that time, Saint Sancho [Stirner] can inform himself by reading Jean Paul, to mention only belletristic sources. The German bourgeoisie cursed Napoleon because he compelled them to drink chicory and because he destroyed their national peace by conscripting them and quartering his soldiers upon them. They consumed all their moral hate against him and lavished all their admiration upon England; even though Napoleon by cleansing the German Augean stables and establishing civilised communications with the outside world performed invaluable services while England waited only for the proper occasion to exploit them left and right. In the same petty-bourgeois manner the German princes imagined that they were struggling for the principle of legitimacy and against the revolution; whereas they were only the paid foot soldiers of the English bourgeoisie. These general illusions prevailing, it was only natural that the groups of professional illusionists, the ideologists, the school-teachers, the students, the *Tugendbundler*, should talk big and give an exaggerated and sentimental expression to the general fantasy and indifference.

Through the July revolution . . . the perfected political forms of the bourgeoisie were imposed on Germany from the outside. Since the German economic relations had not even begun to correspond to these political forms, the bourgeoisie accepted these forms only as abstract ideas, as principles valid only in and for themselves as pious wishes and phrases, as Kantian self-determinations of the will and of man as he ought to be. They consequently handled these principles in a much more moral and disinterested manner than other nations. That is to say, they made their highly peculiar stupidity absolutely valid and remained unsuccessful in all their efforts.

Finally, the ever stronger foreign competition and world commerce, from which Germany could not withdraw, compelled the German petty and isolated interests to come together after a fashion. Since 1840 the German bourgeoisie began to think about safeguarding these common interests; they became national and liberal and demanded tariffs and a constitution. They are now almost as far advanced as the French bourgeoisie of 1789.

When one judges liberalism and the state, as do the ideologists of Berlin, within the local German frame, or restricts himself to a criticism of German petty-bourgeois illusions about liberalism, instead of regarding it in relationship to the real interests out of which it has developed, and with which it can alone exist, one comes to the most absurd and insipid results. This

German liberalism in so far as it has expressed itself down to the most recent times, is, as we have seen, already in its popular form, *Schwärmerei*, an ideological disguise of the real liberalism. How easy it becomes to transform its whole content into philosophy, into pure determinations of reason, into " knowledge of reason " ! And if one is so unlucky as to be acquainted with the official liberalism only in the sublimated form which Hegel and his pedantic followers gave to it, one reaches conclusions which belong exclusively in the realm of the saints. Sancho will furnish a sad illustration of this.

Translated from *Die deutsche Ideologie,* " Kritik der neuesten deutschen Philosophie in ihren Repraesentanten, Feuerbach, B. Bauer und Stirner, und des deutschen Sozialismus in seinen verschiedenen Propheten" (Marx-Engels, *Gesamtausgabe,* Abt. I, Bd. 5, pp. 175–8).

APPENDIX II

ON HEGEL'S " CONCRETE UNIVERSAL "
BY KARL MARX

IF FROM REAL APPLES, pears, strawberries, almonds, I form the general notion fruit, and if I go further and *imagine* that my abtract notion, *the* fruit, which is won from the real fruit, exists as an independent essence of the pear, the apple, etc., I declare therewith—*speculatively* expressed—*the* fruit to be the " *substance* " of the pear, the apple, the almond, etc. I say, therefore, that it is unessential that the pear be a pear; and the apple an apple. What is essential in these things is not their real, sensibly perceived existence [*Dasein*] but the essence which I have abstracted from them and substituted in their stead, *the* fruit. I then pronounce the apple, pear and almond to be merely existing modes of the fruit. My finite understanding, supported by my senses, distinguishes well enough between an apple and a pear, and a pear and an almond, but my speculative reason declares these perceptual differences to be unessential and immaterial. My reason sees in the apple what it sees in the pear, and in the pear what it sees in the almond, namely *the* fruit. The particular, real fruits are taken now only for apparent fruits [*Scheinfrüchte*] whose true essence, *the* substance, *the* fruit is.

It is hardly likely that by this method one will store up any great wealth of knowledge. The mineralogist whose entire science is restricted to the knowledge that all minerals are in truth forms of *the* mineral, would be a mineralogist—in his *imagination*. At each mineral the speculative mineralogist would say " *the* mineral," and his science would be nothing more than the repetition of this word.

The speculation which out of different real fruits has produced as the fruit of its abstraction *the* fruit, must consequently in order to make a show of possessing some real content, attempt to get back again in some way from *the* fruit, *the* substance, to the actual *multiform*, profane fruit, the pear, apple, almond, etc. Now as easy as it is to produce the abstract notion, *the* fruit, from real fruit, it is just as difficult to produce real fruit from the abstract notion of *the* fruit. In fact it is impossible to get from an abstraction to its *opposite*, unless I abandon the abstraction.

The speculative philosopher does abandon the conception *the* fruit, but he abandons it in a speculative, mystical way, i.e., with the appearance of not having abandoned it. He therefore only apparently transcends his abstractions. He reasons somewhat as follows: If the apple, pear, almond and strawberry are in truth nothing but *the* substance, *the* fruit, then the question arises, how is it that the fruit appears to me now as apple, now as pear, now as almond; whence this appearance of *variety* which contradicts so strikingly my speculative conception of the *unity* of *the* substance, *the* fruit ?

It arises, answers the speculative philosopher, because the fruit is no dead, undifferentiated, static essence but a living, self-differentiating dynamic essence. The variety of the profane fruit exists and has significance not only for *my* sensible understanding but for *the* fruit itself, for speculative reason. The different profane fruits are different life-forms of *one* fruit; they are crystallisations which *the* fruit itself builds. For example, in the apple, *the* fruit gives itself an " appley," in the pear, a " peary " existence. One must no longer say, as was said from the standpoint of substance, the pear, the apple, the almond are *the* fruit; but rather *the* fruit posits itself as apple, posits itself as pear, and posits itself as almond. The differences which separate them are really self-differentiations of *the* fruit and convert the special varieties of fruit into different members in the life process of *the* fruit. *The* fruit is therefore no longer an empty, undifferentiated unity; it is the unity as the " whole " [*Allheit*] as the " totality " of fruit, forming an " organically organised series." In every member of this series, *the* fruit reveals itself as a more highly developed and definite existence until finally as " summary " all fruits constitute that living unity which every one of them implicitly contains in itself and produces out of itself; just as for example, all organs of the body are continually being dissolved by the blood stream and continually being built up again.

If Christian religion knows only of *one* incarnation of God, for speculative philosophy there are as many incarnations as there are things. . . . Its chief interest consists in producing the existence of real, profane fruit and to say in a mysterious way that there are such things as apples, pears, almonds and raisins. But the apples, pears, almonds and raisins which we find again in the speculative world are only *apparent* apples, *apparent* pears, etc., for they are the living expression of *the* fruit. Since this last is an abstract figment of the understanding, they are also abstract figments of the understanding. What pleases you in this speculation is to find once more the real fruits, but real fruits which have a higher mystical significance, which grow in the ethereal realms of your mind as incarnations of *the* fruit, of the *Absolute Subject,* and not out of the material soil of the earth. When you therefore return from the abstraction, the *supernatural* notion, *the* fruit, to the real *natural* fruits, you thereby give to the natural fruits, too, a supernatural significance and transform them into mere abstractions. Your chief interest consequently becomes to establish the *unity* of *the* fruit in all its living forms, as apple, pear and almond, to prove that a *mystic connection* exists between all these forms of fruit, and to show how *the* fruit *gradually* and *necessarily* realises itself, e.g. from its existence as raisin to its existence as almonds. The value of the profane fruits no longer consists in their *natural* characters but in their *speculative characters* which they acquire at a determinate point in the life-process of " *the* absolute fruit."

The ordinary man feels that he is saying nothing extraordinary when he says that apples and pears exist. But the philosopher, when he expresses this existence in speculative fashion, feels that he has said something *extraordinary*. He has accomplished a *miracle*, he has produced from the unreal *conceptual* notion, *the* fruit, real, *natural* entities, apples, pears, etc. That is to say, he has *created* these fruits out of his *own* abstract understanding, for he regards himself as an Absolute Subject which exists outside of himself, in this case, as *the* fruit. In recognising any existent thing, he imagines that he is completing a creative act.

It is quite clear that the speculative philosopher can believe in this process of continuous creation only by smuggling the well-known experienced characters of the apple and pear into the logical determinations which he pretends to have discovered. He does this by using the only thing the abstract understanding can create, i.e., abstract formulæ, to give things *names*; and also by mistaking his *own* activity by which *he* jumps from the representation of an apple to the representation of a pear, as the self-activity of the Absolute Subject, i.e., *the* fruit.

This operation is called in the jargon of speculation understanding Substance as Subject, as inner Process, as Absolute Person. And this understanding constitutes the essential character of the *Hegelian* method.

Translated from Marx's *Die heilige Familie*, 1845, " Das Geheimnis der spekulativen Konstruktion " (Marx-Engels, *Gesamtausgabe*, Abt. I, Bd. 3, pp. 228–31).

APPENDIX III

MARX ON BENTHAM AND UTILITARIANISM

THE PHILOSOPHY which preaches self-enjoyment is in Europe as old as the Cyrenaic school. Just as the *Greeks* in ancient times, so the *French* in modern times are the matadors of this philosophy, and indeed for the very same reasons—their temperament and their society give them above all others the capacity of enjoyment. The philosophy of pleasure was never anything else but the clever language of certain pleasure-privileged social classes. The form and content of their pleasures were continuously conditioned by the entire complex of the rest of society, and carried the marks of all its contradictions. But it was when this philosophy pretended to have a general validity and proclaimed itself as the philosophy of life of society as a whole that it degenerated into pure *phrases*. It sank to miserable moralising, to sophistical rationalisations of existing society—and even transformed itself into its opposite by declaring the involuntary asceticism [of the proletariat.—S. H.] to be a kind of pleasure.

The philosophy of pleasure emerged in modern times with the decline of feudalism and the transformation of the feudal landed nobility into the lusty pleasure-loving and extravagant court nobility of the absolute monarchy. Among the nobility it still took the form primarily of an immediate, naïve philosophy of life which had its expression in memoirs, poems and novels. It became a real philosophy only at the hands of several literary representatives of the bourgeoisie who, on the one hand, shared the education and mode of life of the court nobility and, on the other, subscribed to the more general outlook upon affairs of the bourgeoisie—an outlook rooted in the more general conditions of existence of the bourgeoisie. These writers were therefore accepted by both classes although from quite different points of view. Among the nobility, the language of pleasure was understood to be restricted to the confines of the first estate and its conditions of life; by the bourgeoisie it was generalised and applied to all individuals considered in abstraction from their actual conditions of life so that the theory of pleasure became transformed into a stale and hypocritical sermonising. As the further course of development overthrew the nobility and brought the bourgeoisie into open conflict with the proletariat, the nobility became devoutly *religieuse* and the bourgeoisie solemnly moral and strict in its theories . . . although the nobility in its practice did not in the least renounce pleasure while the bourgeoisie even made of pleasure an official economic category—*luxury*.

The connection between the pleasure-experiences of individuals at any time and the class relations of their time as well as the conditions of production and communication which produce the class relations within which individuals live, the limitation of all traditional pleasures which do not flow from real life activity of the individual, the connection between every philosophy of pleasure and the actual pleasures at hand, and the hypocrisy of every philosophy of pleasure which presumes to generalise for all individuals regardless of their differences—all of this naturally could not be discovered until the conditions of production and communication of the traditional world had been criticised, and the opposition between the bourgeois view of life and the proletarian socialist and communist point of view created. Therewith all morality—whether it be the morality of ascetism or that of the philosophy of pleasure—was proved to be bankrupt.

.   .   .   .

To what extent the theory of mutual exploitation which Bentham already at the beginning of this century developed to the point of boredom can be regarded as a phase of the previous century, has been demonstrated by Hegel in the *Phänomenologie*. Compare the chapter on " The Struggle of the Enlightenment with Superstition " in which the theory of utility is presented as the final result of the enlightenment. The apparent absurdity which dissolves all the manifold relations of human beings to each other into the *one* relation of utility—this apparent metaphysical abstraction proceeds from the fact that within modern bourgeois society all relations are subsumed under the one abstract money and business relation. This theory arose with Hobbes and Locke in the period of the first and second English revolutions, the first blows by which the bourgeoisie conquered political power; it received its true content among the physiocrats who were the first to systematise economics. Already in Helvetius and Holbach we find an idealisation of this doctrine which corresponded completely to the oppositional point of view of the French bourgeoisie before the revolution. In Holbach all individual activity based on reciprocal response, e.g., speaking, loving, etc., is represented as relationships of utility and use [*Nützlichkeits- und Benutzungs-verhältnisse*]. The real relations which are here presupposed are therefore speaking and loving, determinate behaviour forms of determinate properties of individuals. These relations are now not to have their own *characteristic* significance but are to be interpreted as expressions and manifestations of a third artificially introduced relation, the relation of *utility*. This circumlocutory distortion ceases to be senseless and arbitrary as soon as the individual relations mentioned no longer appear as valid expressions of self-activity but as disguises—by no means of the category of use—but of a third genuine end and relation which goes by the name of utility-relation. The linguistic masquerade has a meaning only when it is the unconscious or conscious expression of a real masquerade. In this case the utility relation has a quite definite meaning, i.e., I can only serve myself in so far as I deprive others of something (*exploitation de l'homme par l'homme*). Further, in this case, the utility which I derive out of a relationship is quite foreign to it. As we saw above in discussing the power or capacity to do anything, something is demanded of it which is a foreign product, a relation determined by social conditions—and this is the utility relation. And this is precisely the case for the bourgeois. Only *one* relation is intrinsically valid for him—the relation of exploitation; all other relations are valid only in so far as they can be subsumed under this relation. And even when relations appear which cannot be directly classified as one of exploitation, he at the very least does so in his illusions. The material expression of this utility is money, the measure of value of all things, human beings and social relations. Of course one can see at a glance that I cannot by reflection or will abstract the category of " usefulness " out of the real relationships to others in which I stand, and then presume to present these relationships as if they were the real expression of a self-evolving category which is itself derived from them. To proceed in this way is completely speculative. In the same fashion and with the same justification, Hegel presented all relations as relations of objective mind. Holbach's theory is the historically justified philosophical illusion of the rising French bourgeoisie whose lust for exploitation can still be interpreted as the desire to assure the full development of the individual in a social intercourse liberated from the old feudal bonds. Liberation from the point of the bourgeoisie—competition—was the only possible way during the eighteenth century to open up to the individual a new career for freer development. The theoretical proclamation of this consciousness which corresponded to bourgeois practice, the consciousness of mutual exploitation as the general relation of all individuals to one another, was a daring and outspoken sign of progress, a secular *enlightenment* in relation to the political, patriarchal, religious and sentimental embellishments of exploitation under feudalism; embellishments which were appropriate to the existing form of exploitation and were systematised by the literary representatives of absolute monarchy. . . .

The different phases in the progress of the theory of utility and exploitation hang intimately together with the different epochs of bourgeois development. Its real content in Helvetius and Holbach never amounted to much more than a transcription of the manner of life of the literary man in the time of absolute monarchy. They expressed not the facts but rather the wish to reduce all relations to the relation of exploitation and to explain social intercourse out of material needs and the methods of gratifying them. But the problem was set. Hobbes and Locke had before their eyes not only the early development of the Dutch bourgeoisie (both lived for a while in Holland) but the first political actions by which the English bourgeoisie burst their local and provincial fetters and achieved a relatively developed manufacture, shipping and colonisation: especially Locke who wrote in the period of English economy which witnessed the rise of the joint stock company, the Bank of England, and English naval supremacy. For both of them, particularly Locke, the theory of exploitation is filled with an immediate economic content. Helvetius and Holbach had before them in addition to English theory and the development of the Dutch and English bourgeoisie, the experiences of the French bourgeoisie still fighting for its right to free development. The universal commercial spirit of the eighteenth century had gripped all the classes in France in the form of speculation. The financial embarrassment of the government and the debates to which it gave rise over taxation concerned at that time the whole of France. To which must be added that Paris in the eighteenth century was the only world city, the only city in which personal intercourse between individuals of all nations took place. These premises, together with the universal character of the French, gave the theories of Helvetius and Holbach their characteristic, generalised colour but deprived them at the same time of that which was still present among the English—its positive economic content. A theory which among the English was a simple observation of fact became among the French a philosophical system. As found in Helvetius and Holbach, the theory is universal but robbed of positive content, and essentially lacking the rich fullness of meaning discovered only in Bentham and Mill. The former epitomise the fighting, the still undeveloped bourgeoisie; the latter, the ruling and developed bourgeoisie. The positive content of the theory of exploitation, neglected by Helvetius and Holbach, was developed and systematised by the physiocrats. But since they took as their point of departure the undeveloped economic relations of France in which feudal landed property still had great importance, they remained limited by their feudal conception and declared landed property and agricultural labour to be the productive forces which conditioned the whole organisation of society. Further development of the theory of exploitation took place through Godwin, but more especially through Bentham who more and more assimilated into his system the economic content which the French neglected. Godwin's *Political Justice* was written during the time of the French terror, the chief works of Bentham during and since the French Revolution and the development of large industry in England. The complete unification of the theory of utility with political economy is to be found finally in Mill.

Political economy which earlier had been cultivated either by men of finance, bankers, and merchants, that is to say, by people who had some immediate contact with economic relations or by men with general culture like Hobbes, Locke and Hume for whom it had significance as a branch of encyclopædic knowledge —political economy was first elevated to a special science by the physiocrats. Since their time it has been treated like one. As a special technical science it absorbed into itself other relations, political, juristic, etc., in so far as it reduced these relations to political ones. It regarded, however, this subsumption of all relations to itself as valid for only one aspect of these relations and acknowledged that they possessed some significance independently of economics. The complete subsumption of all existing relations under the utility relation, the unconditioned elevation of this utility relation to the sole content of all the rest, is to be found in Bentham, [for whom] after the French Revolution and the development of large industry, the bourgeoisie steps on the scene no longer as a mere class among others but as a class whose conditions of existence are the conditions of existence for the whole of society.

After the sentimental and moralistic paraphrases which among the French constituted the entire content of the utility theory had been exhausted, the only thing that remained for the development of this theory was the question: How were individuals and relationships to be used or exploited? The answer to this question in the meantime had been given by political economy. The only possible progress therefore lay in assimilating the content of political economy. It had already been proclaimed in economic theory that independently of the will of the individual the primary relationships of exploitation were determined through production as a whole and were found ready to hand by individuals. There remained therefore for the theory of utility no other field save speculation concerning the position of the individual to the fundamental relations, the private-exploitation of the given world by the particular individual. And on this point Bentham and his school delivered themselves of lengthy moral disquisitions. The whole criticism of the existing world by the utility theory was therewith restricted to a narrow field of vision. Limited by the presuppositions of the bourgeoisie, there remained for criticism only those relations which had been inherited from an earlier period and which stood in the way of the development of the bourgeoisie. To be sure the theory of utility developed the conception that the whole complex of existing relations was bound up with economics but it did so in a partial and narrow way. From the very outset the utility theory had the character of a theory of general or public utility [utilitarianism]. This character only became significant with the assimilation of economic relations into the theory, particularly the division of labour and exchange. In the division of labour the private activity of the individual becomes a common utility; the common utility of Bentham reduces itself to the same common utility observable in general in competition. Through the introduction of economic relations like ground-rent, profit and wage-labour, the definite relations of exploitation of the different classes were introduced, for the kind of exploitation is dependent upon the position in life of the exploiters. Up to this point, the utility theory could tie up with definite social facts; its further divagations into the kinds and arts of exploitation peter out into copy-book maxims. Its economic content gradually transformed the utility theory into a pure apologia for existing affairs, into the proof that under existing conditions the present relations of men to each other are the most advantageous and commonly useful. All modern political economy has this character.

Translated from *Die deutsche Ideologie* (Marx-Engels, *Gesamtausgabe*, Abt. I, Bd. 5, pp. 396–7, 387–92).

INDEX

ANN ARBOR PAPERBACKS FOR THE STUDY OF COMMUNISM AND MARXISM

For a complete list of Ann Arbor Paperback titles write:

THE UNIVERSITY OF MICHIGAN PRESS ANN ARBOR